THE SCIENCE OF SIN

Also available in the Bloomsbury Sigma series:

THE SCIENCE OF SIN

WHY WE DO THE THINGS WE KNOW WE SHOULDN'T

Jack Lewis

BLOOMSBURY SIGMA
LONDON • OXFORD • NEW YORK • NEW DELHI • SYDNEY

BLOOMSBURY SIGMA
Bloomsbury Publishing Plc
50 Bedford Square, London, WC1B 3DP, UK

BLOOMSBURY, BLOOMSBURY SIGMA and the Bloomsbury Sigma logo
are trademarks of Bloomsbury Publishing Plc

First published in 2018

A catalogue record for this book is available from the British Library

Library of Congress Cataloguing-in-Publication data has been applied for

ISBN: HB: 978-1-4729-3614-1; TPB: 978-1-4729-3616-5;
eBook: 978-1-4729-3617-2

2 4 6 8 10 9 7 5 3 1

Illustrations by Julian Baker

Typeset by Deanta Global Publishing Services, Chennai, India
Printed and bound in Great Britain by CPI Group (UK) Ltd, Croydon CR0 4YY

Bloomsbury Sigma, Book Thirty-eight

To find out more about our authors and books visit www.bloomsbury.com
and sign up for our newsletters

Contents

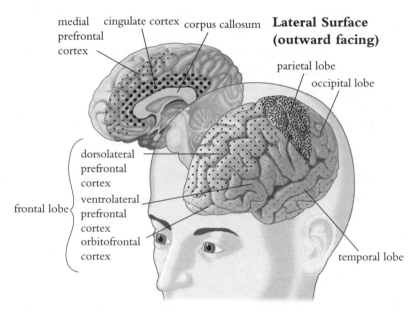

**Medial Surface
(inward facing)**

medial prefrontal cortex · cingulate cortex · corpus callosum · **Lateral Surface (outward facing)**

parietal lobe

occipital lobe

dorsolateral prefrontal cortex

frontal lobe

ventrolateral prefrontal cortex

orbitofrontal cortex

temporal lobe

An illustration of the medial (inward facing) and lateral (outward facing) surfaces of the human brain, in case the reader wishes to refer back to this page to clarify which surface of the brain later illustrations refer to.

CHAPTER ONE

In the Beginning

In the centuries before the Enlightenment brought us the scientific method and evidence-based answers to humanity's questions, the opinion leaders were invariably men of either a religious or philosophical persuasion. They shared a fondness for careful observation of human behaviour and did the best job they could, given limited available resources, of finding answers to difficult questions about how we should live our lives, the nature of the universe, the purpose of life, where we go after we die and so on. They pondered long and hard over the problem of what constitutes a 'good' versus a 'bad' life and, all things considered, did a pretty good job of identifying the aspects of human nature that cause social problems and those that promote a good quality of life.

Philosophers looked for their inspiration from within, establishing absolute truths through repeated iterations of deduction and then stress-testing their conclusions through debate with like-minded folk. Meanwhile, religious types sought inspiration from the outside world, looking up to the heavens in search of divine guidance.

The philosophers had a dual-labelling system: good behaviours were dubbed virtues and those that led to bad outcomes were labelled vices. However, the most successful global religions tended to focus on behaviours that were forbidden – those considered to distract from a full appreciation of God – flagging them as sins. And the list of sins tended to grow and grow and grow.

Saint Gregory the Great – pope from 590 to 604 AD – brought us not only the delights of Gregorian chanting, but was also kind enough to take the time to assemble the seven deadly sins. His particular list of the capital vices* was chosen

---

* The seven 'deadly sins' and 'capital vices' are used interchangeably throughout this book.

as the basis for this book's exploration of what science might have to say on the matter of sin, for three main reasons.

First, Christianity is the belief system with which I happen to be most familiar – an accident of growing up in west London in the eighties and nineties. Despite being born into an atheistic/agnostic family, I still ended up singing a *lot* of hymns over the course of my childhood. The daily morning assemblies of my Church of England primary and secondary schools required it, and as a young kid I even chose to sing in my local church choir of my own free will. I never bought into the stories* I heard during the many hours I spent in that perpetually chilly, incense-infused chamber of worship, but I was grateful to be accepted into the fold and for the opportunity to sing on a regular basis. In fact, some of the most transcendent moments of my entire life occurred while singing religious songs I didn't believe in as one voice among many, during my introduction into the Christian belief system. It gave me genuine first-hand insight into how effective religion can be in making people feel part of a community.

Second, the sinful septet has the advantage of being broadly familiar to people from many walks of life, thanks in no small part to the 1995 serial killer thriller *Se7en*† starring Brad Pitt, Morgan Freeman, Gwyneth Paltrow and Kevin Spacey. The seven deadly sins are generally recognisable to most people, even those born into cultures where Christianity is not the religion of choice, although most struggle to name them all. Go on. Give it a go. No peeking.

Third, the number seven is scientifically auspicious. When it comes to the limitations of human working memory, seven is something of a 'magic number'. Indeed, a psychology paper published in 1956, written by George A. Miller of Princeton University, was entitled 'The Magic Number Seven, Plus Or

---

* I did, however, buy into the messages contained within a poem that my mum hung on the back of the toilet door in my childhood home that I must have read thousands of times. To me every single word rings true. See Appendix 1.
† If you haven't seen it, I'd highly recommend it – it's a classic!

Minus Two'. It presented evidence to suggest that, on average, the human brain struggles to simultaneously hold more than seven pieces of information in mind. This suggested that there was little chance for the average person to have a hope of retaining 10 separate instructions in their head at any given time, like the Ten Commandments for instance. Pope Gregory the Great may have pre-empted this discovery by well over a millennium when he distilled the various sinful human temptations down to a much more manageable number.

We will consider the possible neurological causes for behaviours that more or less fit the mould of each capital vice in turn. Over and over again we'll see that, in moderation, each of the seven commonly encountered human temptations is a perfectly acceptable, if not entirely necessary, part of our repertoire of behaviours. If they were to be abolished completely then it is quite possible that our species would never have survived.

Pride, for example, can have healthy or unhealthy consequences depending on how it manifests in an individual. Being too self-centred rubs other people up the wrong way, but not taking pride in what you do can also lead to problems. A touch of lust is clearly vital for the perpetuation of the species, but when libido is allowed to dominate all decisions it can cause great suffering. Gluttony enabled our hunter-gatherer ancestors to survive periods of food scarcity, but is now killing us off in droves *and* damaging quality of life through the scourge of obesity. Sloth is a force of evil when it encourages people to shirk their duties, but at other times it is vital, allowing us to recuperate from illness, or indeed preventing it from developing in the first place. Even envy, greed and wrath have both benign and malicious components.

The descent of the species
Since the eras of the various prophets whose words spawned the world's most popular and influential religions, mankind's knowledge has expanded exponentially. One of the key milestones was understanding the true, evidence-based origins of life. No Adam and Eve-type original humans ever

landed, fully formed, on Earth by the hand of an all-powerful, all-knowing God. Humanity came to be through a far more gradual process. The main breakthrough in our understanding consisted of the realisation that the blueprint for biological organisms – DNA – is passed from parent to offspring, and when this genetic material is copied, combined and passed from one generation to the next, tiny errors are inevitably made. Usually these mistakes make no difference to the organism's survival prospects, but occasionally they do. When one of these unavoidable, accidental changes happens to give the offspring an advantage over its competitors, the re-written package of DNA has a better chance of being passed down through successive generations. As a consequence of many such fortuitous genetic cock-ups accumulating over unimaginably long periods of time, giraffes ended up with vastly extended necks, enabling them to reach the high branches that were inaccessible to other animals; Darwin's finches got their specialised beaks, allowing access to foods other birds on the Galapagos Islands couldn't get at; and humans ended up walking on two legs rather than down on all fours, a tweak to the primate genetic code that turned out to be invaluable for long-distance running and freeing up our hands for using tools. This vastly improved our hunting capabilities and in turn our prospects of surviving long enough to pass on those bipedal genes. This is the process by which, over the course of millions of years, evolution gradually forged humans from ancient sea creatures. We *Homo sapiens* are just a serendipitous tangle of poorly copied DNA that went on to confer exceptional brain-building capacities.

Walking upright on two legs was only the beginning. Between 350,000 and 200,000 years ago the surface area of our ancestors' brains began to expand, from generation to generation, at a faster rate than ever before. The enlargement of the prefrontal cortex in particular, right at the front of the brain behind our bulging foreheads, began to support a wider repertoire of behaviours than other animals of our size. It supported various new cognitive capacities enabling us to think more creatively, communicate and cooperate with each other in more sophisticated ways, predict the future with greater accuracy and ultimately figure out how to bend the environment to our will. But a bigger brain meant a bigger head, which presented a major problem.

The only big-brained babies to make it out alive into the outside world were those that happened to exit the womb earlier than usual (for a primate of our size and complexity). A human infant's brain doubles in size during the first year of life alone. Can you imagine if that happened while still inside its mother? Making an early exit might have saved the lives of both mother and child, but it left our newborns incredibly helpless relative to our non-human primate cousins. It takes many more years for our young to develop the basic skills necessary for survival compared to them. The longer offspring are dependent on others for survival, the greater the pressure to develop social skills to help them get on with others over long periods of time. Many animal species cooperate in groups, but the unique ability that enabled our species to ultimately dominate the entire planet was the capacity for flexible collaboration with very large numbers of people, including strangers as well as blood relatives.

The emergence of various brain specialisations that facilitate effective long-term collaboration with others can be explained by a positive feedback loop. Our larger brain made us *need* the cooperation of others in order to survive the many years of vulnerability until sexual maturity was finally reached and the genes could be passed on to the next generation, but the larger brain also provided the *means* – in terms of the additional brain real estate – to support the sophisticated social skills that enabled us to get on with many different individuals over such long periods of time.* Round and round this cycle went, through many hundreds of generations, until our brains ended up three times larger than our chimpanzee and bonobo

---

* Another way of looking at it is that the *extra time* our species requires to develop a full mastery of our oversized brains made us both reliant on long-term group collaboration and facilitated the development of the relatively sophisticated social skills that make it possible.

cousins, despite sharing around 98.5 per cent of our DNA with both.

Benefits of a Bigger Brain

This extra brain capacity provided our ancestors with the computational power to support all sorts of unique capabilities never before seen on Earth. Language, for example, improved our ancestors' capacity to form relatively large and stable groups that could cooperate with each other over long timescales, and it also greatly facilitated the accumulation and exchange of knowledge. Not only did speech enable social bonds to be cemented through gossip, rather than the physical grooming that takes up most of our chimp and bonobo cousins' spare time, but it also vastly accelerated the development and acquisition of all sorts of new skills and knowhow.

In a world without language chimps can still learn how to use tools – like nut crackers and moss sponges – purely by observing the example set by others. But the ability to use words to guide an apprentice offers a greater degree of flexibility and nuance, allowing more sophisticated skills to be passed from one human to another.

After many thousands of years of hunting and gathering, our ancestors exchanged the spears, slings, bows and arrows they had previously relied on for acquiring meat for spades, scythes and ploughs. The switch to agriculture and animal husbandry provided a more consistent supply of food, eliminating the need to keep moving on periodically in search of fresh resources. This move to a more static lifestyle changed everything. Once humans found themselves staying in the same place for generation after generation, they started putting their oversized brains to use figuring out ways to manage their resources. For example, why use animals to provide just meat and clothing when they could pull the plough for you? With the use of beasts of burden, irrigation systems and other innovations increasing productivity of an ever-expanding range of crops came surplus. With the accumulation of surplus (which their nomadic forebears would never have been able to haul around with them) came the need for systems of storage, accounting, distribution and all sorts of other inventions. This set the scene for the emergence of cities and civilisations. To hit the fast-forward button yet again: horsepower was then followed by steam-power, gas and liquid fuels by electricity and eventually nuclear. Before we knew it, in an historic blink of the eye, we found ourselves downing our tools to squint instead into the screens of our ubiquitous personal computers and smartphones.

The most incredible feature of the human brain is arguably its phenomenal capacity to adapt to the pressures of whatever environment it finds itself in, whether natural or constructed. Neuroplasticity (see the glossary for more, p. 283) describes the process by which more or less anything we do regularly and intensively, and sustain over long periods of time, induces physical changes in the very fabric of our brain. These changes enable us to perform whatever skills we have been practising more efficiently next time round. This is the process by which we sharpen our skills through trial and error, and produce brains that are able to shape the local environment in increasingly sophisticated ways. We can build all sorts of useful structures on land, underwater, up in space; we can redirect rivers, blast holes in mountains and much more. In turn, the environments we spend time in shape our brains, and those brains acquire skills that enable us to re-shape the environment, and these new environments shape brains further, and so on.

The point to bear in mind is that none of the logistical, engineering, scientific, financial and architectural innovations that enabled us, collectively, to shape the very surface of our planet to suit our needs would have been possible without first developing the human brain specialisations that support social interaction on a grand scale. To achieve this our brains had to become specialised to read between the lines when it came to understanding other people, giving us the ability to perceive their moods, intentions and ulterior motives. Our emotional repertoire expanded to help us modulate our behaviour in a way that sought balance between our own selfish needs and those of the other people around us. Where this was successful it enabled us to secure long-term membership of large cooperative groups (referred to throughout as the 'InGroup') that went beyond just blood relatives. At first this primarily served the purpose of providing safety in numbers to protect against various threats. The dangers posed by starvation, predation and attack by human competitors (referred to throughout as the 'OutGroup') were much more easily circumvented by working together.

The bigger the group, the greater the benefits – up to a point. Communities of humans tend to be relatively stable up to around 150 people. This appears to be the optimal size for a cooperative group of humans both across the world and throughout history. It is thought to reflect limitations in how much social information a human brain can keep track of, not just regarding their own relationships, but other people's too. Our capacity to sustain larger cooperative groups than any other primate probably stems from our ability to learn not just from our own personal experience, but also from other people's experiences. Even *with* the benefit of gossip to circulate information about other people's reputations, to boost our social capacities, if a group of humans has more than 150 members, we end up losing track of who's who. That makes the maintenance of social harmony within the group much more challenging. For human cooperatives to remain stable across populations larger than 150 people, we needed to invent God (or gods).

Faces in the Clouds
The deadly sins can be thought of as the extremes of seven very common categories of human behaviour that tend to cause people to fall out with each other. If everybody resisted those seven particular temptations, then there would be less social friction, more cooperation, and so everybody would win. The trouble is, human nature is such that someone will always try to bend the rules in their favour. There is always somebody in any suitably large group of humans who will try to cheat the system. If, however, the group shares the belief

that rule-breaking will always eventually be uncovered and that the punishments for transgressions are suitably severe, then the numbers of people who act on these temptations might at least be kept to an absolute minimum. Gods come in very handy when it comes to enforcing codes of conduct on a grand scale. It has even been convincingly argued* that the belief in a God or gods is inevitable for any creature with a brain like ours. Considering some of the fundamental mechanisms in the human brain that enable us to sense, comprehend and even anticipate events in the world around us, belief in the supernatural is entirely predictable. Hindsight is a wonderful thing.

The first mechanism to consider is the brain's tremendous capacity for noticing patterns in the world around us from the sensory information received. The brain then uses these patterns to make predictions and then updates the internal model according to whether the expectations were matched or not. When it doesn't work out as expected, the brain buzzes away, correcting the mechanism that makes the predictions so that it functions better next time round. On the other hand, if what happens actually matches what the brain's internal model predicted, then that particular model is reinforced. These pattern-spotting and predicting mechanisms help us to predict the future – not in a supernatural clairvoyant sense, just in the sense that by getting good at detecting patterns we improve our ability to anticipate what is likely to happen next.

Let's consider a couple of examples. These patterns can operate across different timescales, from seconds to days. For example, imagine you are trying to find a safe place to cross a river and you see in the distance a section of the water where ripples on the surface indicate that it might be shallow enough to cross. If you go all the way there, only to realise that the pattern you saw on the water's surface from a

---

* By Michael Shermer in his excellent book *The Believing Brain*.

distance did *not* predict a good place to cross (it wasn't shallow at all, just an eddy current) you may choose to ignore such ripples in the future. On the other hand, if you found a nice path of stepping stones just under the water's surface, you'd know that your prediction that a distinctive pattern of surface ripples indicates the location of a shallow crossing seemed to work and so might come in useful again in the future.

An example across a longer timescale would be a chain of successive events. If event A is almost always followed by events B and then C, all we need is for event A to happen and we can be forewarned to prepare ourselves for C. For example, let's say that event A is the heavens opening with a torrential downpour, event B is getting soaked to the skin, and event C is becoming ill over the next few days. When our internal model of how the world works registers the approach of event A – dark clouds looming overhead – we can see into the future, drop what we're doing and take steps to avoid event B (getting soaked) to reduce the chances of event C happening (being ill).

Our capacity to make sense of the world involves many thousands of predictions about what we might see, hear, touch, smell and taste next, in whichever environments we spend our time in and have extensive experience of. These internal models of how the world works are all gradually refined and integrated through experience. For children, the world is full of surprises. By adulthood we've largely seen it all before and it feels this way because our brains have accumulated considerable experience, whereas during childhood, all these internal models were a work in progress. Our brains are essentially cunningly evolved biological machines that work very hard to minimise surprise.* Eventually they get good at

---

* Professor Karl Friston of the Wellcome Department of Cognitive Neuroimaging in Queen's Square, London was instrumental in developing this influential theory.

anticipating what happens next, but it is not a perfect system and false alarms are commonplace.

We have an inbuilt tendency to find patterns wherever we are. For instance, specific areas of our brains are dedicated to processing faces. This gives us extraordinarily powerful skills, which enable us to instantly recognise a person's face, for example, even though we haven't laid eyes on them for decades. Yet this also leaves us prone to seeing faces when they are not there. Perceiving human faces and other shapes in the completely random shapes of clouds passing overhead is a good example. As the perception of meaningful patterns in meaningless sensory information usually causes us no harm, our tendency to detect patterns that aren't really there persists. If such experiences had for some reason led to the demise of our ancestors, this tendency would soon have been eliminated from the repertoire of human behaviours. The point is that unless a sensory misunderstanding is deadly, or at least severely limits prospects for passing on genes to the next generation for some reason, there's no reason for our tendency to misperceive the world in harmless ways to change. Nobody ever died from seeing a dragon in the clouds.

The second mechanism that contributes to belief in the supernatural involves our highly social brain making us prone to assigning agency to non-human things. We have a powerful inclination to relate to non-human animals, and even inanimate objects, as if they are humanlike agents. Many people talk to their pets, even though goldfish, cat and horse brains lack the uniquely human specialisations that support language, thus precluding their understanding of the meaning of our words. During adolescence, many of my friends and I nicknamed our cars. We would talk to these machines, speaking their names aloud when urging the old bangers to start up on a cold day, or to struggle up a steep incline. These cases of anthropomorphism are harmless. If anything, these playful, one-way conversations with our vehicles brought a measure of comfort. It created the illusion that we could exert some kind of influence over a situation in which we were wasting our breath. In the absence of any obvious penalty, car and pet owners continue to gain emotional benefit from these 'illusions of control'. A harmless brain hiccup.

This tendency to attribute agency wherever possible even seems to work for geometric objects, so long as they move in a purposeful way. A classic study from the 1940s involved showing people a cartoon of a large triangle that starts moving towards a much smaller triangle and a circle. The smaller pair then move away from the larger shape at great speed. Observers interpreted the scene as if the geometric objects had thoughts, feelings and intentions, assigning agency to them, and typically offering explanations along the lines of: 'The big triangle is a bully that is picking on the small triangle and circle, who are running scared, but then figure out how to trick the big triangle and escape.'

Disney and Pixar would have been dead in the water without the twin human tendencies of identifying meaningful patterns and assigning agency wherever possible. We have a whole host of brain areas dedicated to understanding and interpreting human interactions, and we often misapply these interpretations to non-human phenomena.

Comforting Ideas

Our innate capacity for detecting meaningful patterns where none actually exist, together with the tendency to use neural machinery that evolved to support an understanding of human interactions when dealing with inanimate entities, can be consoling even when it's wrong. Every time a lightning bolt strikes (event A) and I brace myself for the potentially deafening boom of thunder overhead (event B), it occurs to me how utterly reasonable it was for any ancient human, with no access to the meteorological facts pertaining to what really causes this assault on the senses, to conclude that some omnipotent deity might be expressing its discontent. The same goes for earthquakes, volcanic eruptions, floods, plagues and tsunamis – they seem angry to us. Humans are prone to relating events in the natural world to how events involving our fellow man make us feel. Indeed, there is even evidence to suggest a direct relationship between religiosity and how often natural catastrophes occur in a given part of the world. The concept of *religious coping* suggests that finding an acceptable (albeit completely fictitious) explanation for the cause of natural disasters enables people to deal with the stress of impending doom much better. Furthermore, it's so much easier to put memories of the traumatic event out of your mind if you're convinced that your god was expressing anger with the conduct of your group of human beings, and now that the warning has been delivered and heeded, life can return to normal. If we are told by a suitable authority figure that by taking certain steps we can avoid displeasing the deity in the future, the performance of these actions will bring a sense of peace. The belief that it might be possible to exert some measure of control over the likelihood of future acts of God is extremely comforting, even when it has no bearing on reality.

Until the true scientific basis for these phenomena was established by empirical research, the only authoritative explanations to account for the causes of such events were provided by the fertile imaginations of whoever was believed to curry favour with the gods, whether soothsayer, shaman, wizard or priest. If the prevailing religious belief system provided a convincing explanation, ideally even a specific course of action to follow (sin less, pray more) to foster the illusion of control over the uncontrollable, people would be consoled and acceptance of the religion in question would increase. Even if following the prescribed rituals to the letter was completely ineffective, so long as the lack of efficacy was never explicitly revealed it was still entirely possible to find bliss in this kind of ignorance. The impossibility of definitively disproving this kind of phenomenon plays a vital role in a variety of superstitions. In the absence of tangible evidence to the contrary, we continue to touch wood, salute magpies and wish on falling stars, just to be on the safe side. After all, you never know…

Gods are ideas: ideas that help to organise very large groups of interacting humans under a shared belief system. If everybody believes that an all-powerful God is keeping an ever-vigilant watchful eye over the whole community and the penalties for misbehaviour are suitably severe, then each person should be motivated to regulate their own behaviour accordingly. It's not perfect, but so long as the *majority* believe that, regardless of whether or not they get caught out misbehaving by other people, their all-powerful God will know what they've done and step in to punish them – people will *tend* to choose behaviours that stay within the agreed rules.

The genius of this system is that, as it's impossible to establish whether you will be rewarded or punished in the afterlife until after you are dead, whether or not the God or gods in question actually exist is irrelevant. The *shared belief* that punishments and rewards will ultimately be dished out by an all-seeing, supernatural force should be enough to get people to at least try to regulate their own behaviour. Given the choice between heaven or hell, the only logical thing to do is to try to stick to the rules, whatever they may be.

As long as everyone sings from the same supernatural hymn sheet, a greater degree of trust can potentially be achieved among *all* fellow believers during their short time on earth. Shared belief enables us to do what was previously impossible: to cooperate not just with other members of the InGroup – the 150 or so people whose reputations for honesty or dishonesty our brains *can* keep track of – but with strangers too. Without a shared belief system we had no idea whether members of the OutGroup could be trusted to cooperate as agreed, or would simply take advantage of us at the first opportunity. You don't even need to share the *same* belief system. So long as everyone understands the others' God or gods, and the constraints that religion places them under, then even members of other religions might be trusted to stick to an agreed code of conduct, if only to save their own souls.

Once a system of belief catches on, no matter how misguided the details might turn out to be, there are huge benefits to be had from buying into the big idea. Especially given that big brains capable of contemplating their own existence inevitably start to consider frightening existential questions like 'Why am I here?' 'How do we know the sun will come up again tomorrow?' 'What happens after I die?' Any belief system professing to be able to explain all the inexplicable and terrifying turns of fate that people experience in their lifetimes, and beyond, has the potential to bring great comfort. People will happily turn a blind eye to a few contradictions and factual inaccuracies here and there if the net benefit of peace of mind is on offer. The believer will often sleep better at night* than the non-believer who, in the absence of any reassuring explanations to create the illusion of control, might spend much of their existence hobbled by fear of the unknown.

Spreading the Word

Humans have no doubt been letting the natural impulses described by the seven deadly sins get out of hand, thus causing chaos within the InGroup, for many tens of thousands of years. Over the millennia of undocumented pre-history village, clan or tribal elders no doubt found effective solutions to the problem of how to keep anti-social members of the InGroup in check. But the strategies employed probably differed somewhat between groups, making cooperation between InGroup and OutGroup problematic.

Even when different InGroups lived by similar rules, the capacity to transmit knowledge accumulated over a lifetime was held back by the limited capacity of human memory and the shortcomings of word of mouth as a means of communication. As anyone who's played Chinese Whispers as a child (or Telephone in the USA) will know, tales have a tendency to become warped over the course of successive tellings.

As a consequence of inadequacies in the passage of verbal wisdom from one generation to the next, although ancient humans may not have always ended up reinventing the wheel, they probably did end up making the same mistakes over and over again. Once the art of writing developed into a method for accurately preserving and duplicating the

---

*Worrying unnecessarily about the fate of one's soul notwithstanding.

wisdom of previous eras, accumulating across multiple
generations, there were still problems with availability and
distribution. Either there weren't enough books to go
around or, where they were accessible, literacy was a privilege
of the educated few. When education did become available
to the majority and the invention of the internet enabled
mankind's collective knowledge to be spread far and wide,
we soon found ourselves overwhelmed by the deluge. The
challenge now is to separate the informational wheat from
the chaff.

The point is that humankind has no doubt been studying
our own behaviour in one way or another ever since we
started roaming the planet. The wisdom distilled from
centuries' worth of observations eventually found its way into
books. Although science books tend to be the most factually
accurate, the religious ones have the best stories and so tend
spread the furthest. It is through stories that information is
most readily exchanged and retained.

Stories engage people emotionally, in a way that lists of
facts and instructions simply don't, and emotions tend to
make memories less likely to be forgotten. Furthermore, a
well-structured narrative can be understood by everyone and
in this regard the books of religion have a much better track
record than the books of science. Stories are the information-
containing format our brains became especially adapted to, so
much so that even our sense of 'self' is essentially based on the
narratives we tell ourselves when we think back to the most
poignant memories from our life experience. This is mostly
thanks, once again, to that inherent need to maintain social
bonds through exchanges of gossip, and a long heritage of
story-telling through the ages. After all, it's the primary
method by which humans have shared ideas ever since we first
managed to tame fire. Sitting around the hearth, huddled
together in an effort to keep out the cold, the dark and our
fears, the primaeval desire for verbal interaction fostered a
fondness for the exchange of information in the form of
stories.

So let me tell you a story.

A Story

Over the past 20 years or so, whenever the sun comes out and I've got free time on my hands, one of my favourite things to do is go roller-skating in London's Hyde Park. There's a long, wide strip of perfectly smooth tarmac that runs alongside the north bank of the Serpentine Lake. I always make time during these trips to skate over to Marble Arch and stop by at Speaker's Corner. I enjoy listening to the people who gather there to exercise their right to free speech. Over the years I've heard Christians debating with Jews, Muslims deliberating with Hindus and Buddhists, Marxists arguing with Conservatives and every imaginable combination thereof. Rather than focusing on the orator up on their soapbox or stepladder, I often find myself watching the faces of the bewildered tourists who, blundering into the mêlée, stop to see what all the fuss is about, usually finding themselves spellbound by the passionate rhetoric. Their bemused expressions often betray a sense of shock: perhaps they are surprised that debates on such inflammatory topics as religion and politics are permitted by the authorities. That Londoners of all creeds, colours and intellectual capacities, from all sorts of different walks of life, have a place to gather and express their views is, in my view, a wonderful thing to behold. I love listening to people having a good old rant, but I rarely participate, unless suitably baited.

The last time I stopped by, I found myself listening to a heated conversation between a Christian and a Muslim. Both parties were good-looking, charismatic, well-groomed young men. One was trying to convince the other that Islam does not sanction the murder of Christians. He rattled off a long passage in Arabic from memory – which took over a minute to recite in full – then he went on to recite the translation in English, again from memory. At the end he said words to the effect of, 'Does it say anywhere in this passage that Muslims should kill Christians?' Everyone in the 50-strong crowd remained silent. When he repeated the question and no one answered, I felt sorry for him because it seemed that nobody had really been listening properly. Feeling moved to spare him the embarrassment of the continued silence, and as I had been following the logic of his argument, I answered on behalf of the crowd: 'No'.

His face lit up, delighted eyes darted across in my direction and before I knew it he'd reached through the crowd, grabbed me by the sleeve and was pulling me towards him. All it took was a gentle tug on my arm and I simply rolled into the centre of the crowd.* It was at this point I realised he had a camera set up on a tripod to capture his performance and it seemed, whether I liked it or not, I was now part of the show.

'You're an atheist, right?' he said. Is it really that easy to tell, I thought to myself.

'Errr… I'm a neuroscientist,' I replied, hoping that the implication would be obvious without the need to be explicit.

'But you don't believe in God?' Ambiguity, it seemed, was not the order of the day.

'That is correct,' I confirmed hesitantly.

'OK then, so you are unbiased!' came the reply.

He went on to quote the whole passage again, in both Arabic and English, as before. Suddenly recalling a vague memory of hearing that it can sometimes get violent at Speaker's Corner, I felt my heart thudding in my chest and my mouth getting dry. When he reached the end of his translation he repeated his original question and looked at me expectantly. I dutifully repeated my reply, 'No!'

'You see, my friend!' he yelled triumphantly to the Christian guy, 'jihad is all about killing the unbeliever, not Christians!'

Can you see my predicament? Having already confirmed that I am an atheist, it seemed that I might have unwittingly put myself in the firing line. Feeling increasingly worried, I glanced around the crowd looking for signs of malevolent

---

* For those of you who haven't been roller-skating recently, I should remind you that the brakes on a pair of roller skates are on the front under your toes. The only way to apply them is to spin around, lean forwards and bend at the knees and ankles. I had no time to do that so all it took was a quick tug on the wrist and I just rolled, helplessly, into the centre of the crowd.

intent, trying to figure out whether anyone was going to make a move to see his argument through to its logical conclusion.

Had this conversation taken place elsewhere in the world, or even elsewhere in the UK, I could well have found myself in a spot of bother. Fortunately for me it seemed that this particular orator was trying to make an argument for peace – a laudable effort to find common ground between Christians and Muslims – and atheist-bashing was not, luckily for me, the order of the day.

With the performance concluded and the onlookers not yet baying for my blood, I flashed an appeasing smile to the crowd and bid them all farewell with a cheery: 'Right, that's my cue to leave then!' and skated off at top speed, back to the relative safety of the lake on the far side of the park. Roller skates may offer little in the way of resistance when you're yanked by the arm into the middle of a crowd, but there isn't a sprinter on Earth that can catch me at full speed on tarmac when I've got my skates on with a good dose of adrenaline surging through my veins.

My motives for sharing this story with you are three-fold. Firstly, this was the experience that ultimately inspired me to write this book. It ended up fanning the glowing embers of a passing interest in how ancient religious teachings might be reconciled with modern scientific knowledge into a fully-fledged passion. Secondly, it made me question a deep conviction I'd held for many years: that people should be allowed to believe whatever they like, no matter what those beliefs might be. As I mulled over those events at Speaker's Corner, it soon occurred to me that, had exactly the same dialogue taken place in the presence of a less liberal and open-minded crowd, I could easily have had my head kicked in. Since that fateful day, my tolerance of other people's beliefs has become more nuanced: when a belief system places constraint on what other people should and shouldn't think, it goes too far, particularly when used to sanction violence. If all religions were to be outlawed one day, I believe it could well have a negative impact on humanity's overall wellbeing but, at the same time, literal interpretation of any religious text (to this day I still have no idea what source that man was quoting) is extremely dangerous and must be discouraged to protect freedom of thought. Thirdly, it demonstrates how effective a personal anecdote can be in engaging the reader/listener on an emotional level. Whether you loved or hated my story, I should have aroused one emotion or the other, making the take home message easier to recall.

Healthier together

My primary motive for not supporting the abolition of religion is that shared faith is unrivalled in terms of its capacity to promote a meaningful sense of community, and there is strong evidence to support the idea that feeling connected to others is vital to our health. Despite the factual inaccuracies and tendency towards literal interpretation, there still is much wisdom to be found in the world's religious books. The use of storytelling is one area in which religion enjoys superiority over science. It can also be a limitless source of hope, helping people to stay positive in desperate circumstances where the scientific reality may offer little reassurance. To acquire a working understanding of a religious belief system, all anyone has to do is turn up at church, temple, mosque or synagogue once a week and listen in. If a stranger regularly turns up at a place of worship on a weekly basis, they will soon find themselves accepted by others as part of the InGroup, which can very quickly provide a sense of community membership. Science may hold many important answers to some of life's questions, but when a stranger walks into a public science lecture they will invariably leave the building feeling just as alone as when they arrived.

The fact is that people who manage to successfully forge enduring, cooperative, intimate relationships gain psychological and physical health benefits as a direct result. They even live longer. Those who find themselves estranged from family, friends and co-workers, on the other hand, often end up feeling extremely isolated. This isn't just a sad state of affairs; it actually makes them more vulnerable to a variety of health problems, including heart disease and cancer.

It is important to remember that it's the quality of the relationships that count here, not the quantity. A person with one or two trustworthy confidantes will often feel sufficiently connected. Another with a large number of flimsy, superficial friendships can find themselves feeling extremely lonely. In a world where online social connectivity is no longer merely a supplement to face-to-face social interaction, but for many people a wholesale replacement, this may be a point worth pondering.

We didn't evolve a brain that produces powerful urges to seek out and maintain relationships with other humans purely to gain better access to valued resources. Food, shelter, warmth and protection are indeed more easily accessed via a group effort, but that's not the whole story. We have proven ourselves able to achieve much more together and with much greater ease than any one person going solo. Yet the need for group membership runs much deeper than building cities and political institutions, inventing new art forms and taming the elements. For an intensely social species like the human being, it is a vital prerequisite for our peace of mind, contentment and good health. No (hu)man is an island.

In an increasingly post-religious world, many of the strategies that fostered docile obedience to the rules of social engagement in the past have been rendered obsolete. With disbelief in God spreading across much of the Western world, dousing the flames of hell and shattering the illusion of a paradise in heaven, where is the incentive to stay on the right side of the seven deadly sins? Is science sufficient to inspire us to do the things that keep us happy and healthy? Or, in the absence of God keeping a watchful eye over us, might the devil within start to run riot?

Brain science to the rescue?

The best part of science, in my humble view, is neuroscience. I'm biased, of course. Unlike many neuroscientists, who seem to delight in telling anyone who'll listen that we know next to nothing about the human brain, I happen to think there is a great story-so-far to be told. The collective endeavours of many hundreds of scientists who dedicated their lives to exploring the mysteries of the human brain have unearthed some real treasures: insights that could ultimately be just the ticket for helping us to achieve a better understanding of ourselves and each other. This body of knowledge has expanded to the point where it is starting to provide clues about what makes us do the things we know we shouldn't, pointing to specific brain structures that seem to be involved in driving our anti-social behaviours – those labelled sins by religions and vice by philosophers. There is much more to learn about the brain than we've discovered so far, but the same could be said of many things.

To say that brain science has come on in leaps and bounds in the last century or so would be an understatement. Believe it or not, the rapid progress that took place over the course of the twentieth century, in terms of understanding how human brains do what they do, owes a huge debt of gratitude to the First and Second World Wars. Had they somehow been miraculously avoided we might well still be waiting for several revolutionary new ideas that were direct spin-offs from the wars.* The theoretical insights and technological discoveries that resulted went on to inspire new tools that are used every day all over the world to plumb the depths of the human brain without having to cut open the skull. In one century, we've progressed from a state of almost complete ignorance to the point where augmenting human brains with man-made components that enable the blind to see, the deaf to hear and

---

* The two World Wars delivered countless soldiers into field hospitals, many of whom ended up with bullets and shrapnel lodged in various parts of their brains. Some very bright and meticulously organised field doctors, on both sides of the war effort, started paying close attention to which mental functions were consistently lost and which were preserved, according to the particular chunk of brain that had been damaged in each soldier. This provided some fascinating clues regarding the division of labour in the human brain.

Parkinson's patients to regain control of their movement is becoming almost routine.

Towards the end of the twentieth century the process of acquiring brain data using Magnetic Resonance Imaging (MRI) sped up sufficiently to take snapshots of whole brains in a matter of seconds rather than hours.[*] This facilitated the process of building up a more detailed picture of how the human brain's distinct functional units contribute to the production of our various sensory, emotional and cognitive capabilities. This picture is admittedly far from complete. For one thing, what is actually measured provides only a crude approximation of what individual brain cells might really be up to.[†] That said, our grasp has tightened sufficiently for a compelling story-so-far to be told.

Exploring the root causes of sin

The troublesome behaviours described by the seven deadly sins all tend to lead to social isolation, which has a deeply negative impact on an individual's wellbeing. The primary goal of this book is to use the latest discoveries from the world of neuroscientific research to better understand the root cause of what religions refer to as sin. My hope is that by better

---

[*] Professor Sir Peter Mansfield (1933–2017) led this amazing development.

[†] Neuroscientist colleagues whose experiments involve taking measurements from individual brain cells call researchers who use MRI 'blobologists' or 'blob hunters'. This is a term of disparagement. Many electrophysiologists feel that measuring changes in blood oxygenation resulting from the combined metabolic activity of millions of brain cells in any given chunk of brain – which is essentially what fMRI does – is utterly pointless given how little we currently understand about the function of basic networks of neurons. They may have a point. But as most of them work with rats and primates due to the legal and ethical impediments preventing them from introducing electrodes into human brains when there's no pressing medical need to do so, MRI is the best we've got for humans for now.

understanding what happens in the brain when such temptations arise, we might find better ways to inspire people to rein in their antisocial urges, improve community cohesion and thereby improve health and quality of life.

The process involves looking at what the ancients had to say regarding what exactly makes each capital vice such a socially destructive force and trying to establish how much trouble each causes in society today. We'll then sift through the highlights of the relevant neuroscientific, psychological, psychiatric and medical research approximating most closely to the behaviours described by each deadly sin – pride, lust, gluttony, sloth, greed, envy and wrath – in search of root causes to help explain why we do the things we know we shouldn't. The ultimate hope is to find better strategies for promoting InGroup harmony and avoiding inter-Group conflict, whether the reader believes in a god, gods, or no god at all.

CHAPTER TWO

Pride

You sign your place and calling, in full seeming,
With meekness and humility; but your heart
Is cramm'd with arrogancy, spleen, and pride.

William Shakespeare, *Henry VIII*

Pride is not all bad. The great philosopher Aristotle even considered it a virtue. Not just any virtue, but the very 'crown of the virtues', no less. His reasoning went along these lines: a proud person feels worthy of great things and so finds themselves motivated to achieve them. This particular concept of pride implies having sufficient self-confidence and determination to feel unintimidated by the challenges faced when grappling with ambitious goals. It can make us determined to reach our target, even in the face of adversity. Aristotle may have had a point. From the perspective of developmental psychology, conquering fear may well be one of the main reasons we feel pride in the first place.

The basic emotions of joy, sadness, anger, fear, disgust, interest and surprise emerge in the first six to twelve months after birth. The self-conscious emotions, pride among them, don't kick in until further down the neuro-developmental line. Somewhere around the age of two, infants develop the capacity to understand whether their own behaviour has been *good* or *bad*. When infants of this age receive feedback indicating that they've been good, they show signs of pride. When they realise that they've been naughty, on the other hand, they show the characteristic hallmarks of shame.

Pride is a positive, reinforcing feeling. It helps toddlers to find the balance between an intrinsic fear of the unknown and the natural urge to explore. Caregiver feedback to the child provides guidance by encouraging them to take on challenges *when it is safe to do so.* The pride children feel is an emotional reward for conquering their fears and achieving their goals, and such experiences make them more likely to persevere when confronted with obstacles in the future. Pride also incentivises children to explore their surroundings, which helps them to develop their capabilities.

Pride is a particularly devilish phenomenon to navigate because, while moderate levels are essential, problems arise at both extremes. Think back to childhood. One minute our parents would tell us: 'The whole world doesn't revolve around you, you know.' Next thing you know, your teacher is urging you to 'take more pride in your work'. We're told that if we do, then we might get better grades, perhaps even a prize or some other recognition of our achievements. If we followed the advice and managed to achieve that goal, we're then told: 'You should be proud of yourself!' So surely it's safe to conclude that pride is a good thing? The minute an adult overhears us bragging about our victory – in other words, we dare to express our feelings of pride – we suddenly find ourselves being scolded for arrogance. You just can't win.

Eventually most people realise that there is a big difference between feeling proud and letting it show to the outside world. Taking pride in something is acceptable when used as a tool to help us up our game and overcome obstacles, but being boastful about any accomplishments resulting from this strategy most certainly is not. Observing how sportspeople, musicians and actors conduct themselves in interviews and at awards ceremonies certainly suggests this is the case. To remain in people's good books, praise should be received with apparent humility – even if your heart is really 'cramm'd with arrogancy, spleen, and pride'.

Pride, then, is only a virtue when maintained as a well-kept secret. If we ever find ourselves on the receiving end of praise and want to avoid falling out of favour with others, the best thing to do, it seems, is to politely deny or deflect it. It's all very confusing. No wonder so many people get it wrong. But surely celebrities aren't the best source of moral guidance? It's hardly their realm of expertise. Perhaps the ancients can help?

A historical perspective

Pope Gregory the Great wasn't the first to warn of the dangers posed by the sin of pride when he wrote: 'For when pride, the queen of sins, has fully possessed a conquered heart, she surrenders it immediately to seven principal sins.' Around 139 BC the Testament of Reuben appeared, describing 10 malevolent behaviours that should be avoided at all costs. Pride was fourth on that particular list, while vanity (or *vainglory* as it was known back then) was just behind in fifth place. A few hundred years later, in AD 375, Evagrius the Solitary, a monk who spent much of the latter part of his life contemplating God in the deserts of Lower Egypt, formulated a slightly more concentrated list of eight key categories of evil thought. This particular list was compiled to guide his fellow desert monks, sweating it out in the wilderness, to help them guard against the various temptations they would need to resist if they wanted to go to heaven. Pride was relegated to eighth place and vainglory to seventh.

By the time Pope Gregory the Great completed his own reflections on the matter, compiled in a book published in the late sixth century called *Moralia in Job*, vainglory and pride had been merged into the sin of pride. This double-whammy of a capital vice was promptly elevated to the very top of the list. He proclaimed that pride was not just the most vicious of the seven deadly sins, but the very root of all evil; the 'queen' of sins, ruling over them all.

Christianity is not alone in encouraging humility in opposition to the diabolical influence of pride. Pride is one of the five 'mind poisons' in the Mahayana tradition of Buddhism that present obstacles to enlightenment; the Islamic hadith says that 'even an atom of pride' in the heart of a Muslim is sufficient to prevent them from gaining access to paradise; and the Hindu holy book – the *Bhagavad Gita* – contains several passages warning the faithful that pride is an ungodly

characteristic. The ancient Greeks had been warning against
the dangers of hubris for many centuries before Christianity
came onto the scene, since at least the sixth century BC.
Aristotle warned that 'Young men and the rich are hubristic
because they think they are better than other people.'

Rather than describing a ridiculously over-inflated sense of
self-importance and extreme arrogance as it is used in this day
and age, in ancient Greece 'hubris' was actually a law forbidding
acts of malicious shaming. The specific behaviours in question
were acts of physical and sexual violence committed with the
aim of inflicting shame on rivals. Theirs was a culture obsessed
with seeking honour and avoiding shame, so hubris started
out as the crime of robbing people of their honour. Now it
describes the overconfidence of those who believe themselves
to be superior to others.

In one of the most famous of all the ancient Greek
myths, Narcissus was the strikingly attractive male offspring
that resulted from the union of a nymph and a river god.
He had nothing but contempt for anybody who expressed
love for him. Much is made of his vanity and after he
rejects the love of the nymph Echo he is punished by being
shown his own reflection and falling in love with it.
The main take away point in terms of understanding why
the sin of pride can be so very damaging, is that this
self-obsession prevented him from forming meaningful
relationships with others.

The German bishop Peter Binsfeld, spent much of the late
sixteenth century thinking about demons. In 1589, he
published an influential list that assigned Lucifer to the sin of
pride. As the story goes, Lucifer fell from grace in the first
place because, convinced he was more important than all the
other angels in heaven, he tried to get them to worship him.
God, understandably, was displeased, finding this behaviour to
be completely unacceptable, so Lucifer and his cronies were
swiftly banished to the pits of hell. Unswayed, Lucifer felt that
it was 'Better to reign in hell than to serve in heaven.' We
might conclude that the threshold beyond which common-
or-garden pride spills over into the sin of pride is when a

person forms a deep conviction that they are superior to all others.

According to Dante, come Judgment Day, those who spend their lives heeding the whisper of Lucifer and acting as if they are more attractive, clever and important than everyone else end up lugging heavy stone slabs around hell for all eternity as a punishment for their hubris. The implication seems to be that, if the prideful sinner felt themselves far too important to do their own heavy lifting in life, then the most appropriate punishment for them in death is to do nothing *but* hard labour.

As science appears to be slowly but surely killing off the concept of an eternity of punishment in hell, and removing a potentially useful deterrent for discouraging people from being too proud in the process, the least it can do is try to explain why such behaviours arise in the first place. Happily, what religions describe as the sin of pride bears a striking resemblance to what science, psychology and psychiatry label 'narcissism'.

The term 'narcissism' was first coined by the late, great Sigmund Freud at a meeting of the Vienna Psychoanalytic Society over 100 years ago. Back then its meaning was very different to how we use it today, specifically referring to loving and caressing one's own body in a manner usually reserved for a romantic partner. If that were still the case it might have ended up in the lust chapter. These days the definition excludes such sexual connotations, focusing instead on a more general obsession with the self. Broadly speaking, narcissism involves an over-inflated sense of self-importance and grandiosity, often accompanied by severe difficulties with empathy that lead to problems in connecting meaningfully with others.

Recalling that Narcissus himself had real problems forming intimate relationships, for an intensely sociable animal like us humans this is the aspect of narcissism or pride that is most corrosive. To reiterate a key point from the introduction, feeling connected to others and being accepted as a member of an InGroup is a strong predictor of wellbeing. People who are isolated in the sense of being disconnected from any group that might be relied upon to provide support in times of trouble – whether family, friends or people from the local community – are those whose physical and mental health suffers the most. As the narcissist is unable to forge healthy relationships, this may be the key to understanding both their own suffering and that which they bring into the lives of others.

Narcissism comes in sub-clinical (not quite bad enough to get a formal psychiatric diagnosis) and clinical forms (sufficiently disruptive to qualify as a psychiatric problem). Both have been studied intensively over the past few decades, providing plenty of material to work with in pursuit of a better understanding of the sin of pride. There are seven different categories of narcissistic characteristics: grandiose self-importance and extreme vanity are those that usually spring to mind most readily, but there are five others that are less well known. Narcissists have a distinct tendency to exploit others. They feel that they are an authority on all matters. Their sense of entitlement tends to be sky high. They feel utterly self-sufficient, convinced that they don't really need other people. And, as we will see in the next section, they are often exhibitionists. Before we dig into the science, we'll take a quick look at how prevalent such narcissistic traits have become in our modern technologically enhanced world of texting, twerking and tweets.

You're so vain, I bet you think this book is about you

Gossip magazines and celebrity blogs often tot up the total number of selfies each star has posted on their various social media accounts. While Kylie Jenner tops the 2013 list on Instagram, sisters Kendall and Kim Kardashian were not far behind in fourth and fifth places.* The sheer volume of

---

*   mashable.com/2013/10/20/celebrity-selfies/?europe=true#CT WcRbpdwsqN

selfies cannot be used to reliably judge how vain someone is, but this type of self-promotional media machine is very influential. On Twitter, the three Kardashian sisters and two Jenner sisters boast a combined following of over 150 million people, and millions tune into their TV series *Keeping Up with the Kardashians* every week to catch up with the latest developments in a succession of photo shoots, shopping trips and family bust-ups. The popularity of this type of media could be spreading the acceptance of the extremes to which people will go to maximise their aesthetic appeal. While high vanity does not lead directly to narcissism (see p. 41), it is one of seven contributing factors, so it could exacerbate narcissism by encouraging acceptance of vanity as a social norm.

There was a time, not so long ago, when it was considered unmasculine for a man to fuss too much over his appearance. They would brush up for special occasions, of course, but in general men made a concerted effort to keep their grooming to an absolute minimum. This is no longer the case. Similarly, if a woman went under the knife for cosmetic surgery a couple of decades ago, it would usually be kept a closely guarded secret, perhaps shared with a few of her most trusted confidantes. If asked publicly whether or not she'd 'had some work done' most women would deny it. These days women are more relaxed about admitting to having a boob job, and may even offer a friend to 'have a feel if you want' when paid a compliment. Excessive vanity no longer seems anything to be ashamed of. From tooth whitening upwards, cosmetic procedures are now so commonplace that they are no longer particularly noteworthy.

If someone came up to you on the street offering to jab you in the face with a hypodermic needle, you'd probably call the police. Yet the number of men and women submitting themselves to botulinum toxin (Botox) injections, to hide the visible signs of ageing by smoothing out their wrinkles, rises every year. The British Association of Aesthetic Plastic Surgeons has published data indicating that, over the 10-year period from 2003 to 2013, there was a five-fold increase in the number of cosmetic surgical procedures that took place in the UK. Nose jobs, facelifts and breast augmentation were once the preserve of the rich and famous. Now they are routinely offered as birthday gifts to 16-year-old girls.

Hunting for signs of vanity among the stars of social media is child's play. Take self-proclaimed Instagram superstar Kurt Coleman, a man who describes himself as Australia's answer to Paris Hilton. When asked why he takes so many photos of himself, his documented replies include such comments as 'Because I love what I see in the camera'; 'I'm hot and I love myself'; 'People are really jealous of me, I can understand why, and I'll never change for anyone because I love myself'. While most people would think twice before admitting to having such a high opinion of themselves, the lack of humility suggests that vanity, grandiosity and inflated sense of self-importance are entirely acceptable online.

Let us also consider the antics of Dan Bilzerian. This gun-toting, tank-driving son of a millionaire has over 20 million followers on Instagram. In interviews he has talked of having survived not one, but two cocaine-induced heart attacks, he regularly keeps his fans updated with an endless stream of photographs documenting the fast cars he drives, the lethal weapons he shoots and the big cats he cavorts with. When video footage emerged on the internet showing him throwing a naked teenage porn star off the roof of a house into the swimming pool in the garden below, rather than the utter disregard he showed for the girl's welfare (she narrowly missed the edge of the pool) triggering widespread revulsion, his popularity surged. The world is becoming not just increasingly tolerant of, but seemingly hungry for, self-obsessed exhibitionism.

Usual suspects

To say that vanity is rife among celebrities is to risk stating the obvious, but who are the worst offenders? What type of celebrity would you guess is the most narcissistic? Music stars like Madonna, Justin Timberlake and Miley Cyrus? Diva-like actors, from Marilyn Monroe and James Dean through to Meryl Streep and Chevy Chase? Millionaire sportsmen like Usain Bolt, Michael Jordan and Cristiano Ronaldo, perhaps? Here we needn't rely on conjecture. In *The Mirror Effect*, Dr Drew Pinsky and Dr S. Mark Young administered the NPI (Narcissistic Personality Inventory) test to a large number of rich and famous celebrities to establish how different types of celebrity rank against each other in the narcissism stakes. Surprisingly, the dubious accolade of 'world's most narcissistic' goes to neither musicians, nor film stars, nor athletes. In fact, the type of celebrity that ultimately took the biscuit didn't even exist until recent times.

With an average score of 16.6 on the NPI test, musicians seemed to be the least narcissistic of all those tested. To put this into perspective, this is only slightly higher than the mean score of 15.3 established in an unrelated study that administered the test to over 2,500 everyday Americans. Actors registered as more narcissistic than musicians with an average score of 18.5. Comedians were a touch more narcissistic still with a mean score of 18.8. The crown for the big-headed kings and queens of celebrity narcissism, with a whopping average score of 19.4, went to reality TV stars.

If you ponder this result for a moment, it soon makes perfect sense. Reality TV naturally favours the narcissist. Even when they don't win whatever contest they may be involved in on screen, they are often the characters that play up to the cameras the most. So the narcissists are the ones that both audience and producers are most likely to focus on and remember. This creates a ratings-driven selection bias that makes them more likely to be selected to appear in subsequent series. If the most recently invented reality TV genre is anything to go by – the so-called 'constructed reality' shows – the casting process now seems to recruit exclusively from the ranks of the narcissists. In constructed reality TV shows, such as *Made In Chelsea*, *Geordie Shore* and *The Only Way Is Essex*, the stars are given only a minimum of direction, so there's even more of an incentive to create drama out of nothing – the narcissist's speciality.

The rise of the self-obsessed reality TV and social media star doesn't necessarily mean that the moral fabric of society is coming apart at the seams. We might be starting to develop psychological calluses that make their hubristic antics seem increasingly normal, but surely it can't do any real harm? The trouble is that reality TV sells the idea that anyone sufficiently self-obsessed can make it on TV, providing an incentive to nurture rather than suppress egocentric behaviour. A recent UK poll revealed that 'becoming famous' was the number one career aspiration for 16-year-olds. Worrying as this might potentially be, we all know that children are particularly impressionable during adolescence and perspectives usually change and mature over time. But what kind of impact, if any, might these narcissistic media idols be having on fully-grown adults like you and I?

Narcissism: you and I

For as long as I can remember, I've always been a show-off. This may be because, throughout my childhood, my parents always encouraged me to throw myself into new situations and to stretch myself at every opportunity. As a consequence, I experienced plenty of successes and failures as the years went by. Failing never really bothered me, because it came against a background of plenty of successes too. It turns out that many of those victories turned out to be nothing more than an illusion. Years later I found out that my dad often let me win to give me a taste of triumph against a bigger, stronger, wiser opponent. Illusion or not, I quickly accumulated enough positive experiences of trying out new hobbies, sports and activities that I soon found myself able to pick up new skills fairly quickly.

As a result of all these experiences, I've always had sky-high self-confidence. Inevitably, over the course of childhood this eventually led to the occasional accusation of cockiness, sometimes even arrogance. During the self-conscious years of my adolescence and on into adulthood, in quiet moments of reflection I've often wondered whether my parents might have accidentally created a monster, despite their best intentions. Am I a narcissist? I've worried about this on many occasions.

The Narcissistic Personality Inventory (NPI) was originally invented by Raskin and Hall in 1979 in the journal *Psychological Reports* and is a survey that measures all seven narcissistic traits on the basis of the answers to 40 simple questions. This cunning and surprisingly straightforward tool requires people to choose which of a pair of statements describes them best to quantify their levels of superiority, authority, vanity, entitlement, self-sufficiency, exploitativeness and exhibitionism.

When I finally summoned up the courage to take the NPI test, I discovered that – with 16 out of a possible 40 points – I'm not such a terrible narcissist after all. At least by US standards this score is close to the average (15.3) found in the control study against which the celebrity NPI scores were compared. My scores on the 'authority' and 'vanity' facets were, admittedly, higher than the others, but the other narcissism facet scores were lower, which seems to have balanced it out overall.

These scores made intuitive sense, to me at least. Given that I make a living partly as a TV presenter and partly through speaking engagements, a high vanity score might reasonably be explained by the fact that I'm required to look presentable when in front of camera or a live audience. When I'm not on show I tend to be quite scruffy and unshaven, so I feel safe claiming that any vanity is born of duty rather than vice. The inflated sense of authority could stem from 20 years spent studying the brain; a PhD is a universally accepted qualification of expertise, after all. That said, there is always the inevitable question of chicken or egg? Was I attracted to a professional calling that involved sharing what I have learned about the brain with large audiences because I'm a vain know-it-all? Or did the 20 years I spent acquiring brain knowledge and learning what is expected of a presenter gradually change me? Both explanations are plausible. Either way, I found the experience of taking the NPI illuminating. I'd recommend it. Go on, I dare you!

If you *do* fancy taking the test, you'll be happy to hear that some kind soul has taken the time to make an interactive version of the NPI test freely available online.* If you do decide to take the test then please do it now, before you read on. Otherwise there's a small chance that what you're about to read might bias your score. Also if you give it a go and get a high score, please don't worry about it too much. The NPI is *not* a clinically diagnostic tool. It's used to measure relative levels of narcissism among the general public. There's no threshold beyond which anyone could say, beyond all reasonable doubt, that your narcissism is necessarily problematic. Other tools do exist to serve this purpose, the test for Narcissistic Personality Disorder for example, but that requires a qualified professional to score it correctly. Right then. If you're going to do it, now's the time…

The NPI score provides a sense of where on the continuum a person is in terms of the spread of narcissistic tendencies typically found across a large population. Since its creation in the late 1970s it has been used extensively in psychological research. It really is ingeniously designed. It involves choosing between pairs of statements. If either of the pair were presented on its own, people might feel disinclined to admit that it described them well. When presented as a pair, however, each option seems perfectly reasonable in the light of the alternative. It's clever because it can be difficult to get people to admit to behaviours that are generally disapproved of in society and this test achieves that goal very well. The NPI has been proven to accurately measure narcissistic tendencies and give reliable,

---

* openpsychometrics.org/tests/NPI/

reproducible results. It's also a powerful predictor of other behaviours that a narcissistic person is likely to exhibit, beyond those explicitly covered by the NPI test. You've got to love a test that can tell you more about a person than they're prepared to reveal themselves.

High scores on the NPI test predict:

- the tendency to seek high-status partners, yet very little interest in forming intimate emotional bonds with them
- a propensity to claim other people's successes for themselves
- the desire to seize any opportunity to receive public admiration.

In combination with low self-esteem, high narcissism can even predict belief in conspiracy theories.

Narcissism, or the sin of pride if you prefer, has numerous antisocial consequences. When a narcissist persistently brags of achievements to others, or tries to claim other people's successes as their own, this can damage that other person's feelings or even their reputation. When a narcissist perpetually demands that the topic of conversation be brought back to the most important of all subjects, namely themselves, it can cause serious disruption to the normal social dynamic. If others dare to resist the constant demand for attention and admiration, they'll quickly find themselves on the receiving end of a torrent of abuse. Narcissists also typically have an inflated sense of their own intelligence and competence, which serves only to bolster their delusions of grandeur. Yet objective measurement of their intelligence and/or competence rarely supports this self-perception.* As their superiority seems utterly self-evident, they have no trouble dismissing any such objective evidence.

---

* Actually, most people are deluded in a similar fashion, but narcissists are worse than average.

A true narcissist is never wrong, so they miss out on opportunities to learn from their mistakes. They are self-absorbed, belligerently indifferent to other people's opinions or best interests, and fully prepared to manipulate others to get what they want. Their amorous dalliances lack commitment, are usually unsatisfying and often short-lived. The moment the positive reinforcement dries up, hostility erupts. Any and all opportunities to bolster their positive self-image are seized upon. One of the most interesting contradictions regarding your average narcissist is that they totally lack the capacity to feel empathy for others, yet at the same time they are incredibly sensitive to social feedback themselves, expecting consistent, positive treatment.

The most alarming thing about all the research conducted on this topic over the past few decades is that narcissism appears to be rocketing. Average NPI scores have steadily increased ever since the test was first invented. Admittedly, most of the relevant data comes from studies conducted in the USA, so it *could* just be a problem restricted to certain parts of North America. On the other hand, like the canary in the coal mine, this data might serve to give us advanced warning of what the future has in store for the rest of the world. Given how many past trends have been established on that side of the pond, only to spread to every corner of the planet a few short years later, you can bet your bottom dollar that it will soon be a global problem, even if it is not yet the case. As the indications suggest that this trend is set to continue, it seems likely that the various anti-social perils associated with pride are only going to get worse. There is a clear need to understand narcissism better if we are ever to have a hope of getting it under control. One important question is: what exactly is going on in the brains of these ever-increasing legions of narcissists?

The science of narcissism
One consistent observation to emerge from scientific investigations into the differences between narcissists and non-narcissists is in how they respond to social pressure. A recent

study required participants to perform one of two tasks while being observed by two silent strangers. They either took a maths test, or were given three minutes to prepare a six-minute talk about themselves to be delivered in a public forum, and judged by an expert. Such circumstances would be stressful for anyone, but narcissists – despite often seeming fairly thick-skinned – actually released significantly more of the stress hormone cortisol than their non-narcissistic counterparts. They also reported a greater degree of emotional turmoil than the non-narcissistic participants.

One of the most remarkable recent findings to emerge from the world of neuroimaging research is that the same brain areas that light up when we feel *physical* pain also become activated when we feel *social* pain. Whether that social pain arises from romantic rejection, being snubbed by peers or other similar situations, the unpleasant feelings associated with social pain appear to be generated by the same mosaic of brain areas that produce the physical sensations of pain arising from a stubbed toe or a banging headache. With this in mind, we now turn to a brilliant study conducted by Christopher Cascio and colleagues from the universities of Pennsylvania and Michigan. They used functional Magnetic Resonance Imaging (fMRI – see the glossary, p. 283) to compare brain activations of narcissists and non-narcissists as they experienced social rejection in a game called Cyberball.

Cyberball involves three different players passing a virtual ball from person to person. The person in the MRI scanner can see what is going on in the game on a projector screen that they can view through a mirror positioned just in front of their eyes. The other two players in the game are controlling their moves from an adjacent room (or at least that's what the person in the scanner is led to believe). Occasionally, the player in the scanner finds themselves being left out of the game, while the other two players pass the ball between themselves. When people were socially shunned in this way, three different brain areas were activated more powerfully in the brains of the narcissists than the non-narcissists. The strength of the activation reflected the degree of social pain each person felt. Not only that, but the higher each person's individual narcissism score, the greater the magnitude of the activations associated with social rejection. In other words, they found a positive correlation between the size of the activation – thought to reflect the severity of the social pain they were experiencing at the time – and how narcissistic each person was. The main implication here is that narcissists seem to feel the social pain of rejection more powerfully than other people. Could this be the root cause of their various anti-social tendencies?

The three areas in question were the anterior insula (AI) and two different parts of the cingulate cortex: the subgenual anterior cingulate cortex (sgACC) and the dorsal anterior cingulate cortex (dACC). We'll take a look at where exactly in the brain these regions reside (see figures 1 and 2) and briefly ˝discuss the specific roles that each are currently thought to play on the basis of many other brain imaging studies.

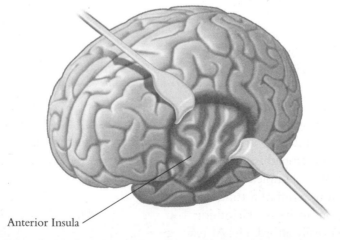

Anterior Insula

Figure 1 Using retractors to pull apart the overhanging frontal lobe and the underhanging temporal lobe reveals the insular cortex. The anterior insula is the portion of insula cortex towards the front of the brain.

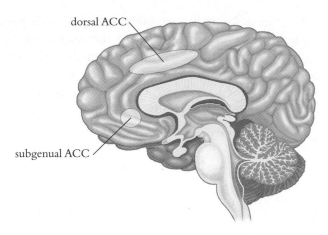

dorsal ACC

subgenual ACC

Figure 2 The cingulate cortex resides on the medial surface of each hemisphere. It hugs the dense bundle of white matter – the corpus callosum – that connects left and right brain hemispheres, wrapping around it like a belt or girdle (see illustration on p. 6). The anterior cingulate cortex (ACC) is the front-most part of this structure. The dorsal ACC describes the upper portion of the ACC and the subgenual ACC describes the lower portion residing beneath the knee-like section of the corpus callosum known as the 'genu'.

The AI is a brain area that sits at the bottom of the valley formed where the frontal and temporal lobes meet at the sides of the brain near each temple. The AI is involved in processing and creating the perception of many different types of sensory and emotional experiences, not just pain. It typically lights up in brain imaging studies whenever a person feels disgusted, anxious or in some way uneasy. It is also known to play an important role in empathising with other people's pain and responds reliably to unpleasant sights like a gory-looking wound, the noxious whiff of rotting food and even the over-expensive price tag on an item of clothing you were considering buying but can't really afford. The AI reacts to many things, but these things tend to share the common characteristic of being unpleasant.

The sgACC is part of the anterior cingulate cortex that is tucked just underneath the front of the corpus callosum. The corpus callosum is a handy landmark when looking at the inner surface of the brain because it's a huge bundle of neurons (brain wires) that connects the left and right hemispheres of the brain. Activations in this sgACC region are very well characterised. On the basis of many brain imaging studies investigating the perception of pain, this area seems to be involved in generating the feelings of distress associated with pain, whether it is physical pain or social pain. In other words, it seems to produce the negative emotional component of pain, the aspect of pain that 'hurts'. Incidentally, this particular brain structure has also been implicated in a wide variety of mood disorders.

The dACC is the upper (dorsal – like the dorsal fin on a dolphin's back) region of the front-most (anterior) third of the cingulate cortex. It is activated in many different circumstances, but most consistently when what happens in the outside world is somehow in conflict with your expectations. For example, if you flicked a light switch on and instead of the bulb lighting up, the sound of a crowing cockerel was triggered instead, the difference between your usual experience of cause and effect versus what actually happens would register as an activation in the dACC.

Considering what this dACC region is up to across a wide variety of brain imaging studies, it appears, broadly speaking, to be sensitive to conflicts – conflict between what a person expects to happen and what actually happens.* These expectations might be set by a lifelong exposure to the usual behaviour of light switches or, for that matter, how strangers usually conduct themselves in a game. Finding yourself left out and feeling neglected on the side-lines of a silly game for no good reason would likely make anyone feel upset, but in the brain of a narcissist it seems that such unpleasant feelings manifest themselves with greater intensity.

---

* Remember those internal brain models looking for predictable patterns in the outside world from Chapter 1?

To complete the circle, the initial finding we discussed regarding the narcissist's tendency to release more cortisol in socially stressful conditions is complemented by other studies suggesting that dACC activation is positively correlated with circulating cortisol. In other words, the greater the activation of the dACC, the higher the concentration of the stress hormone cortisol found in the person's bloodstream. It's impossible to be sure whether the increased dACC activation actually *causes* the increase in release of stress hormone purely on the basis of a correlation, but the possibility is worth bearing in mind

Narcissistic people, for one reason or another, seem to have an exaggerated stress response whenever they find themselves under social scrutiny. The above brain imaging data supports the idea that their experience of social pain is more acute than in non-narcissistic individuals. This could explain the common observation that when a narcissistic person's delusions of grandeur are not matched by other people's behaviour, they are prone to aggressive outbursts. It has been suggested that this may even be an attempt to externalise their social pain. It might also explain why narcissists are generally motivated to seek relationships that provide admiration over and above intimacy. Presumably the constant reassurance is just the balm they need to help soothe their excessive feelings of social pain.

Building a narcissist

One influential theory relating to what plants the seeds of narcissism describes two different parenting styles that, one way or the other, end up preventing a child from successfully differentiating between 'self' and 'other'. This process is powerfully influenced by the daily interactions between infant and parent or carer, or whoever else the infant spends most of their time with and with whom they build the closest bonds.

Broadly speaking, *neglectful* parents or carers don't put sufficient time into their interactions with the child to enable the establishment of where their 'self' ends and 'others' in the outside world begin. Problems can also arise at the other end of the spectrum with over-attentive, so-called *helicopter* parenting. By constantly jumping in to answer for their children and forever telling them what they should be doing, feeling and thinking, the child is prevented from developing the capacity to work anything out for themselves. Either parenting approach can interfere with the development of a healthy, independent sense of self, which can result in a life spent constantly seeking positive feedback from others for reassurance. The 'Goldilocks' zone between these two extremes of neglectful parenting style and helicopter parenting style is much more conducive to a healthy and well-developed sense of self. Under these circumstances a child is able to learn to judge the appropriateness of their own behaviour and their self-worth, with greater independence from others.

Aside from the influence of parenting styles that give too much and too little attention, the devil really is in the details when it comes to how feedback can steer pride towards virtue or vice. When parents and carers give feedback on whether a child's current conduct is good or bad, i.e. a transient judgement, they are on safe ground. The trouble starts when feedback is framed in absolute terms that sound much more permanent: 'You are such a naughty child' or 'There's my perfect little princess'. Such comments may seem perfectly harmless, but when used consistently, they could be inadvertently planting the seeds of narcissism.

Problems arise when parents or carers give feedback on behaviour using language that sounds like an evaluation of the child's overall value. If, rather than hearing comments along the lines of 'That was a very naughty thing to do' or 'Why are you being so difficult today?', the child consistently hears words to the effect of 'You are a bad child' or 'Why must you always be so naughty?', they will gradually internalise the message and may ultimately accept the idea that there is something wrong with them. This can lead to the belief, accepted deep down in the core of their being, that they are fundamentally bad, which may ultimately lead to the conclusion that they are undeserving of love. Sadly, it can all end up becoming a self-fulfilling prophecy, whereby the child behaves in accordance with whatever negative label they have been consistently given. At the heart of the most troublesome narcissists' external pursuit of admiration and positive affirmation is often a profound sense of worthlessness. This is the 'vulnerable' form of narcissism.

The alternative form of narcissism is 'grandiose'. This can also stem from inappropriate parental or carer feedback, but this time the problem is persistent positive feedback about how wonderful the child is, regardless of whether their recent behaviour has been good or bad. Over-indulgent parents, in trying to be perpetually supportive, can also create narcissists. When a child is placed on a pedestal, constantly on the receiving end of praise (regardless of their actual conduct) by parents desperate to avoid criticism for fear of hurting their child's feelings, the child can end up internalising the message that they can do no wrong. This leads to the development of an inflated sense of entitlement and 'grandiose' narcissism.

To nurture the positive aspects of pride in children, without accidentally inducing the diabolical consequences of narcissism, the rule of thumb is: give love unconditionally – establishing that the child *is* worthy of love – and keep feedback on whether their current or recent behaviour has been good or bad as a completely separate issue.

To complete our exploration of the possible neurological drivers behind the aspects of pride that have been interpreted as sinful over recent centuries we'll take a brief dip into a particularly destructive form of narcissism: Narcissistic Personality Disorder.

A worst case scenario

Although one in four US college students these days gets a high narcissism score on the Narcissistic Personality Inventory, with an incidence of around 1 in 100 Narcissistic Personality Disorder (NPD) is, mercifully, much less common. That said, rates of NPD also appear to be steadily rising, in the USA at least.

The diagnostic criteria for NPD were drawn up in 1980 and etched into the third edition of the bible of psychological ailments that is the *Diagnostic Statistical Manual of Mental Disorders* (known as the *DSM*). NPD is extremely unpleasant, both for the sufferer and for those around them. They rely excessively on others to regulate their self-esteem, and struggle with a whole host of severe psychosocial difficulties often involving emotional and drug problems. Their ability to regulate their own emotions fluctuates wildly according to how others treat them. If they don't get the admiration they need to support their grossly inflated sense of self-importance then their emotional state is immediately broadcast to the outside world – they just can't keep a lid on it, no matter how inappropriate the outburst might be. Core symptoms of NPD include: 1) a profound need for admiration, 2) a vastly over-inflated sense of self-importance and 3) a chronic lack of emotional empathy.

With regard to the lack of empathy, it is important to distinguish between two different forms. Emotional empathy describes the ability to actually *feel* what another person is feeling just by looking at and listening to them. It is triggered by picking up on subtle voice and body language cues. Cognitive empathy, on the other hand, is a different phenomenon. It is the ability to make a judgement about how a person is feeling and use that information to guide your interactions, but without actually *feeling* what they're feeling. The latest research suggests that NPD sufferers can make accurate *judgements* about other people's emotions, they just can't *feel* them, so the powerful role that empathy plays in most people's lives is dramatically reduced. Examining the brains of people with a formal diagnosis of NPD can help us to understand what happens at the pathological end of narcissism.

The study we are going to consider here used MRI in a different way to the previous experiment with non-clinical narcissists. Rather than looking for functional differences, identifying areas that are more or less activated under different circumstances, this study was in search of structural differences.

They wanted to find out if any parts of the NPD patients' brains were physically different, on average, to a comparison (control) group of people without a diagnosis of NPD. Lars Schulze and colleagues at the Free University of Berlin in Germany found a number of interesting differences.

First, the left AI (anterior insula) of people with NPD is smaller than that of the non-NPD people.* You'll recall that the functional imaging study of everyday narcissists (those without a psychiatric diagnosis of NPD) revealed that the higher they scored on the Narcissistic Personality Inventory test, the greater the activation was in this brain area when they were made to feel socially excluded. The smaller the volume of a brain area, relative to that found in healthy brains, often reflects disruption in the development of neuronal circuitry that is involved in regulating the brain structure in question. When this is the case, it reflects a reduced capacity to modulate that structure's activity levels under the influence of feedback from other brain areas. So the smaller left AI in these NPD patients may reflect difficulties in suppressing unpleasant feelings that result from not getting the admiration they crave. Equally, it could have more to do with the AI's role in empathy; its smaller size may contribute to their profound difficulties in feeling what others feel. Individual brain imaging studies rarely provide all the answers, but they do often start interesting discussions.

This study also observed that NPD brains have significantly less grey matter than non-clinical control patients in two parts of the cingulate cortex: the rostral ACC and the median cingulate cortex (see Figure 3). These areas are well known to play an important role in figuring out what is going on in other people's minds, a capacity known as Theory of Mind – a topic we will return to in later chapters, so this may help to account for the empathic deficits exhibited by NPD patients. The reduced volume of space occupied by all these areas in people with NPD compared to non-NPD people might help to

---

* Physically smaller in terms of the volume of space it occupies.

explain their need for a constant supply of admiration. If they are unable to feel what other people are thinking on the basis of instincts that the rest of us take for granted, it might explain their need to constantly seek out positive feedback from others.

Finally, a smaller volume of grey matter was also observed in part of the medial prefrontal cortex (mPFC) known to be an important part of the brain system collectively referred to as the Default Mode Network (DMN). The DMN is thought to be causally involved in the brain's capacity to generate our sense of self. We'll return to the topic of the DMN in a later chapter (Chapter 9, p. 219), but for the time being it is sufficient to note that one part of the DMN network appears to be shrunken in the brains of those with the most severe and disruptive form of narcissism known to medicine. Bearing in mind the parenting styles we met in the previous section that

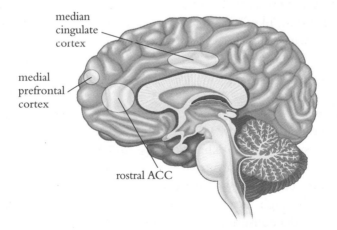

Figure 3 The rostral ACC is the segment of the ACC just in front of the corpus callosum. The median cingulate cortex refers to the section of cingulate cortex that lies midway between the anterior cingulate cortex (towards the front) and the posterior cingulate cortex (towards the back). The specific part of the medial prefrontal cortex region implicated in Narcissistic Personality Disorder has also been highlighted.

interfere with brain development in regions involved in understanding the boundary separating the self from others, it is interesting to note that in NPD, brain areas implicated in generating our sense of self and those that support our capacity to read other people's minds *both* seem to be compromised.

Echo chamber

If Facebook was a religion, with upwards of a billion users it would be the world's third most popular behind Christianity (around 2.1 billion) and Islam (around 1.5 billion). But while the world's major religions try to place the focus on fostering community over and above individual self-interest, Facebook is an ideal breeding ground for narcissism. Those who engage with it the most intensively tend to be the most narcissistic members of society. People with a greater number of Facebook friends tend to exhibit more narcissistic qualities than those with fewer. Social networking doesn't create narcissists from scratch, but as a medium designed around a mechanism of posting pictures, articles, videos and personal updates to seek affirmation ('likes') from others, it provides narcissists with exactly what they crave.

The same goes for reality TV. Narcissistic people are attracted to appearing on reality TV for similar reasons and the most narcissistic among them are the ones that tend to succeed. TV producers and editors of tabloid newspapers, magazines and websites actively favour those whose sense of grandiosity, vanity, exhibitionism and tendency towards aggressive confrontation creates the most spectacular and therefore tabloid-newsworthy drama. This provides a diet of extremely high levels of narcissism for the TV-watching, social-media consuming public, on a daily basis. Eventually, all this excessively narcissistic behaviour starts to seem normal, leading to an increased acceptance of narcissism, not just in terms of what we come to expect from the media, but also from those we interact with on a daily basis in real life. As a consequence, social sanctions that used to be implemented to punish excessive levels of arrogance and vanity are no longer being applied.

The normalisation of narcissism together with the absence of, or at least vastly reduced levels of media coverage for more appropriate role models appear to be pushing the rates of global narcissism ever upwards. As we've seen, this is currently being manifested in the steadily rising Narcissistic Personality Inventory scores in the population at large and may also contribute to the elevated rates of Narcissism Personality Disorder. Perhaps the most alarming aspect of all this is the impact this will have on the children of narcissists. Narcissistic parents are tremendously damaging for the entire family, but the children are particularly vulnerable.

Vices of pride

If St Gregory was right and pride really is the queen of all sin, we might anticipate that the epidemic of narcissism we currently find ourselves embroiled in could make all of the seven deadly sins more troublesome. Conversely, if we could only find a way to extinguish narcissism then we might just be able to nip all the other capital vices in the bud.

When a person truly believes in their feelings of grandiosity and self-importance, their exaggerated sense of entitlement will inevitably leave them convinced that they're more deserving than everyone else. They will feel perfectly within their rights to take more than their fair share of any commodity. Whether it is acting on feelings of sexual desire towards other people's partners (lust), screwing business partners over in financial transactions (greed), or leaving everyone else to do all the hard graft (sloth), how pride might fan the flames of the other deadly sins is abundantly clear. When a narcissist encounters someone with greater wealth, power or popularity it will often make them angry (wrath), or at the very least make them wish it was all theirs (envy). And, of course, those who feel more entitled than everyone else around the dinner table wouldn't think twice about taking the lion's share...

CHAPTER THREE

Gluttony

In general, mankind, since the improvement of cookery, eats about twice as much as nature requires.

Benjamin Franklin

S t Gregory's suspicion that pride is the root cause of all the deadly sins is bolstered by the curious observation that the steady increase in Narcissistic Personality Inventory scores in the US has been mirrored by the gradual expansion of waistlines. With the World Health Organization officially classing nearly a third of the world's population as overweight or obese, the sin of gluttony now poses a serious challenge for healthcare systems across the entire globe. It's got so bad that the term 'obesity epidemic' just won't do any more. Recent articles published in serious medical journals now declare it to have reached 'pandemic' proportions. In this chapter we will be exploring how this came to be and dig around in the human brain looking for clues as to why we are so bad at resisting those naughty but nice culinary temptations.

Aperitif
Body Mass Index, or BMI, is a scale that determines a person's weight in regard to their height. As taller people tend to be heavier, with shorter people generally tipping the scales to a lesser degree, BMI classifies people as underweight, normal weight, overweight or obese by taking both of these measures into account. Could this be just the scientific tool to define some threshold beyond which a person might be considered guilty of the sin of gluttony? There are many factors that contribute to a person's propensity to put on weight. But, just

for fun, let's briefly consider this idea to stimulate our appetite for the latest scientific insights into the recent escalation of this particular capital vice.

Good health outcomes are associated with a 'normal' BMI of between 18.5 and 24.9. Scores of 25 and over are considered 'overweight', crossing the 30 mark makes a person officially 'obese' and 40+ is considered 'morbidly obese'. The higher you ascend the scale, the greater likelihood of health complications such as diabetes and cardiovascular disease. That's not just bad for the individual's own health and quality of life, but also for those with the responsibility of improving health in the population at large and others tasked with the job of providing the necessary additional care.

I currently have a BMI of 25.4, which just about tips me over the threshold into the realms of being 'overweight'. Am I, therefore, a sinner? Is a BMI score in excess of 25 a reasonable benchmark for deciding who ends up in the third circle of Dante's hell, thrown into a pit of suffering along with rest of humanity's gluttons? Or should an eternity spent huddled together for warmth, shivering against the perpetual rain, hail and snow, be reserved for those with a score of 30+? Or 40+?

Given that I exercise more or less every other day (when injuries permit) I'd feel pretty hard done by if I found myself being sent to hell for committing the sin of gluttony. Surely slightly overweight people like myself, or those who only just tip the scales into one of the obese categories for that matter, should be sent into limbo first instead of being banished straight down to the fires of hell, no questions asked? The borderline cases might be permitted a few weeks in purgatory's fat camp to get in better shape so that we might ultimately be judged eligible to pass through the pearly gates.

Alternatively, perhaps we could subject ourselves to the rack just prior to Judgment Day? Such a machine, popular in mediaeval times as a torture device, could come to our rescue by counteracting a lifetime of spinal compression imposed by the force of gravity. Adding a precious extra centimetre or two

to our height could help us drop into a lower BMI category*
as effectively and probably more quickly than any efforts to
lose weight. At 186cm rather than 184cm tall, with exactly the
same body weight, my BMI would creep back into the
'normal' zone. Similar effects could also be achieved by
spending a few weeks orbiting Earth in the International
Space Station; zero gravity routinely adds an inch or two to an
astronaut's height.

Is this a cunning approach to getting back on the right side
of the sinner/saint divide? Or does it miss the point entirely?
Ridiculous as these proposals might be, it clarifies how slippery
the matter of determining who is and isn't a glutton can be.
It's not easy to find concrete boundaries that might help us
define where moderation ends and gluttony begins. As we
will discover, it's not as easy as merely observing people's
weight or body shape. To be guilty of sin the over-consumption
must be freely chosen. And the latest brain imaging of
clinically obese people suggests that their ability to exert free
will in this regard may have become permanently compromised.

Starter

Christianity's original beef with gluttony mainly seemed to
revolve around people's propensity to worship their bellies
over and above their God. St Paul railed against those who
'serve not Lord Jesus Christ, but their own belly', and went on
to point the finger at '…the enemies of the cross of Christ.
Whose end is destruction, whose God is their belly…'
Considering that gluttony was originally used to describe not
just overindulgence in food but also bingeing on alcoholic
beverages, it's easy to understand the theological opposition.
Drunken gluttons are particularly prone to letting their guard
down, and to allowing their moral defences be overcome.

---

* The formula for BMI is height/mass², reflecting the expectation
that taller people are generally expected to be heavier than shorter
people – which means that a BMI score can be reduced either by
losing weight, or by growing taller.

St Thomas Aquinas's[*] commentary on the dangers of gluttony read like a description of your average common-or-garden drunk: 'Excessive and unseemly joy, loutishness, uncleanness, talkativeness and an uncomprehending dullness of mind'.

In his day, St Thomas had a powerful and influential voice. He was instrumental in driving home the importance of factoring in the seven capital vices when making decisions about appropriate conduct. That said, he is alleged to have had a voracious appetite of his own. Rumour has it that a crescent-shaped piece of wood had to be cut out of the table at which he dined, in order to accommodate his huge belly. Some might say that this smacks of hypocrisy. Those of a more forgiving disposition would point out that gluttony was labelled a deadly sin in the first place *because* a hefty appetite is something that even the most devout struggle to curb.

Pope Gregory the Great detailed the various aspects of gluttony he felt distracted from the spiritual purity demanded of the pious, warranting its inclusion as one of the seven deadly sins[†]. St Thomas paraphrased this quite beautifully: 'Sometimes it forestalls the hour of need; sometimes it seeks costly meats; sometimes it requires that food be daintily cooked; sometimes it exceeds the measure of refreshment by taking too much; sometimes we sin by the very heat of an immoderate appetite.'

By modern standards, it's difficult to imagine how anyone could be considered anything other than gluttonous. We've all fallen foul of the urge to eat just for the sake of it, or found ourselves choosing the most expensive item on the menu. Many people are a bit fussy about how they like their eggs cooked, give in to the temptation to take more than their fair share, or eat way beyond the point of being full. Given the numerous influences in modern society that normalise such

---

[*] St Thomas Aquinas was a thirteenth-century Dominican friar, a prolific writer of theology who wrote a very influential book called the *Summa Theologiae*.
[†] Book XXX of Moralia in Job, verse 60

eating habits, no wonder the sin of gluttony is more evident now than ever.

Amuse-bouche

Anyone who, like me, spent much of their childhood staring at the gogglebox was probably first exposed to the concept of over-consumption while watching the children's programme *Sesame Street*. Remember Cookie Monster? The shaggy, blue, incoherently babbling, fluffy embodiment of the archetypal glutton. His entire existence revolves around finding 'Cookies!' – shoving them into his mouth, crumbs flying, until every last one has been wolfed down. Then, after the briefest of pauses, he bounds off in search of more. He simply can't get enough.

British woman Georgia Davis may have been inspired by such childhood influences. Once dubbed by the tabloid newspapers 'Britain's Fattest Teenager', at her peak weight she was reportedly eating up to 20 kebabs per week, and gorging herself on chocolate, crisps and Coca-Cola throughout the day. In April 2015, she found herself in the rather unpleasant predicament of having to be removed from her home by means of a crane, with the assistance of a dozen emergency vehicles, in a seven-hour operation to get her to hospital for treatment after a fall. At her most massive, she was alleged to have passed the 60 stone (840lb or 381kg) mark.

Common psychological motivations for overeating are varied but usually reflect a set-piece response to negative emotions, often generated by body image problems in the first place. What begins as an impulse to eat as a method of emotional self-management can soon develop into a compulsive, automatic response to feelings of sadness and anxiety. A recent study investigated four different eating styles that often lead to pathological increases in weight gain. In order from least severe to most severe, these are: gorging (which entails eating a large amount of food three times per day), snacking (perpetually munching between meals), grazing (repeatedly consuming small amounts of food throughout the entire day) and, worst of all, bingeing (complete loss of control over food intake). The further along this list of eating styles your own eating habits lie, the faster you are likely to find yourself gaining weight.

The *Guinness Book of World Records* bestows the dubious honour of the world's heaviest man ever upon Jon Brower Minnoch of Bainbridge Island, Washington, USA. Mr Minnoch died in 1983. At his heaviest he weighed in at a whopping 635kg, which equates to a nice round 100 stone or 1,400 lbs. At 1.85m, or 6ft 1in, this gave him a Body Mass Index (BMI) of 185.5. Bearing in mind that the morbidly obese category starts at 40+, Minnoch's BMI was astounding. However, Saudi Arabia's Khalid bin Mohsen Shaari pipped Mr Minnoch to the BMI post with a score of 204. Despite being lighter (610kg) Mr Shaari is also considerably shorter (1.73m). As the index is calculated as mass in kilograms divided by height in metres squared (kg/m^2) Mr Shaari ultimately came out victorious in the BMI stakes. The past tense is used here not because he's dead (at the time of writing he is very much alive) but because a few years ago, the King of Saudi Arabia ordered Mr Shaari to go into hospital for medical intervention to help him shed some of his excess pounds.

Everything discussed so far betrays an assumption that gluttony and obesity go hand-in-hand, but is this really the case? As 'gluttony' takes its roots from the Latin word 'gluttire' which means 'to gulp down', while obesity is a *likely* outcome of this habit the glutton is not *necessarily* going to become grossly overweight. It is more an attitude regarding when enough is enough. The origins of this word also help us to grasp the fundamental difference between gluttony and the seemingly very similar concept of greed. While greed is probably best thought of as the desire to take more than your fair share of any given commodity, gluttony refers specifically to gulping down food and/or drink in extremely large quantities.

Gorging in this manner, far from being considered worthy of contempt, is now a talent deemed worthy of praise, where only the most gluttonous get the adulation. Nathan's Famous hot dog eating contest on Coney Island, Brooklyn, New York City has taken place during every Fourth of July celebration since the 1970s. By the 1990s, the aim of the game was to ingest as many hot dogs (frankfurter sausages *and* buns) as possible within a 12-minute time limit. In 2000, the record stood at a whopping 25 complete hot dogs – a mean gobble rate of just over 2 per minute. Then, in 2001, a young gentleman from Japan entered the contest and promptly blew the competition away. Can you guess by what margin the record was beaten? Five hot dogs? Ten, perhaps? Surely no more than that, right? Takeru Kobayashi – or the Tsunami, as pundits liked to call him – demolished a whopping 50 hot dogs. You might imagine that for a man to not just beat but *double* a speed-eating record that was 30 years in the making, Mr Kobayashi must have been pretty huge. You may have men of gargantuan proportions like Jon Brower Minnoch and Khalid Bin Mohsen Shaari in your mind's eye? Well, Kobayashi is certainly no sumo. On the contrary. At 73kg and 1.73m he comes in with a very healthy BMI of 19. The exception to the rule? Not so.

The 2015 winner was a man known as Megatoad. He's the same height as Kobayashi, yet he weighs a meagre 54kg and so his BMI (18) makes him officially 'underweight'. He managed a whole 62 hotdogs in just 10 minutes – a gobble rate of just over 6 per minute. The moral of this story? Well, if there is one, it's that body weight and stomach capacity are surprisingly unrelated. And, perhaps more importantly, when not participating in eating contests both the Tsunami and Megatoad consume a healthy diet, which is how they both maintain a healthy BMI.

Another regular competitor, Joey 'Jaws' Chestnut, managed to consume 73.5 frankfurter sausages plus buns during a qualifying round in 2013 in just 10 minutes. That's over 20,000 calories – more than eight times the recommended daily intake for an average-sized man. Might such competitive gluttons also be heading directly to the purging fires of hell come Judgment Day, despite their perfectly healthy BMIs?

Eating competitions started springing up in the twentieth century. The ultimate goal may have been to glorify those whose digestive apparatus could survive the ordeal of stuffing huge quantities of food into over-stretched stomachs. More likely it was a clever marketing ploy. Public relations companies are fond of such stunts. The gradual normalisation of over-eating has been extremely effective in generating huge growth in the profits of multinational producers of high-energy, low-nutritional value, long-lasting, processed foods. These can be found conveniently packaged and ever-ready for immediate purchase in your local supermarket, petrol station or fast food outlet. The easy availability of delicious, affordable, highly calorific food has led directly to the expansion of waistlines across the globe.

Eating to excess like this is not a recent invention. The temptation for humans to overindulge in culinary delights has probably been around since the beginning of time. The main difference is that, while in developed countries the scourge of gluttony seems to be most prevalent among those of lower socioeconomic status, for most of human history such excess was usually reserved exclusively for the wealthy.

Tacitus described excessive consumption of both food and drink in his account of Emperor Nero's 'Ultimate Orgy' in AD 64. Another Roman author, Petronius, describes a debauched and ridiculously ostentatious banquet in what many consider to be the world's first novel – the *Satyricon*. It featured countless courses, including one for each of the signs of the zodiac, and a masterpiece consisting of live birds that burst out of the belly of a roasted pig! The wedding of Marie Medici and King Henri IV of France, famously had 50 courses. King George IV was known for his taste for bacchanalian banquets that would have had Bacchus himself running for the vomitorium.*

Main course
Large feasts have long been an annual tradition for people living in many temperate regions of world, particularly when

---

* Many believe that the vomitorium is an urban legend, but I can state with absolute authority that there is one in a fraternity house by the castle in Tuebingen – because I have had the dubious honour of using it!

celebrating the harvest or the end of the long, cold, hungry months of winter. However, these days such feasting is available to everyone all year round, at your local eat-as-much-as-you-want buffet restaurant. As we've seen, gluttony is also celebrated in the *Guinness Book of World Records* and is even made aspirational by the existence of eating competitions with big cash prizes. People now spend hours of their free time watching others eat on the internet. This particular fetish is so popular in South Korea that some are even making a living from eating vast quantities of food in the comfort of their own homes.

Gluttony is different from the other deadly sins in that the toll it takes on the body, when practised daily, is usually impossible to conceal from the outside world. Whether it's the beer belly hanging over the belt line, or burst blood vessels in the swollen nose of those who overindulge in alcohol, the signs are all too easy to spot. The long-term impact of gluttony is plain for all to see on UK high streets, rammed with fast-food restaurants, up and down the country. On the other side of the pond, US food outlets sell soft drinks by the gallon and even their regular-sized meals seem enormous to the average European eye. The waddling gait of morbid obesity is now encountered as readily as the ubiquitous burger joints in the average suburban shopping mall across the entire world.

Where does this human tendency to eat and drink to excess, whenever the opportunity arises, actually come from? Why would our species have evolved a brain that makes opportunities to gorge ourselves on high-fat and high-carbohydrate foods so difficult to resist? For the vast majority of human history, one of the primary threats to our ancestors' continued survival was insufficient availability of food. Under the prevailing circumstances of food scarcity it made sense to consume more calories than were actually needed whenever the opportunity presented itself, so the human brain's appetite regulation networks evolved accordingly. By over-eating, excess calories could be packed away into fatty storage under the skin and around the internal organs to see our ancestors safely through the lean times. Back in the Stone Age, eating until you were stuffed on high-calorie foods was an investment for the future and a sensible survival strategy in times of famine. Now that most people in the developed world live in an environment characterised by food overabundance rather than food scarcity, for the first time in human history we're actually more likely to die from obesity-related diseases than starvation. Ignorance is no excuse; it's been known that over-eating is as much a threat to our wellbeing as under-eating since the times of Aristotle: 'Drink or food that is above or below a certain amount destroys the health, while that which is proportionate both produces and increases and preserves it.'

That said, it could be reasonably argued that our whole neurochemistry actually evolved to encourage binge eating. Feelings of hunger aren't replaced by the sensation of satiety until a good 20 to 30 minutes after food hits the stomach. This gives us plenty of time to 'exceed the measure of refreshment by eating too much'. When our stomachs rumble they secrete a chemical messenger into the bloodstream, by the name of ghrelin. This travels up to the hypothalamus – the brain's hormonal HQ – to shift the brain into food-finding mode. Unless a more pressing matter comes along requiring urgent attention, triggering the release of appetite-suppressing adrenaline and cortisol, food will be the priority until it has been sourced. Once we've eaten our fill, however, the hormones that produce the feelings of satiety that we associate with a full stomach are much more sluggish. The gut releases a chemical called cholecystokinin (CCK) and fat cells release a substance called leptin, both of which suppress hunger. This introduces the time lag between being full and feeling full, because it takes a few minutes for sufficient quantities of these chemicals to be released in the body, travel up to the brain and finally exert their influence on the feeding regulation centres of the hypothalamus. These appetite-suppressing hormones, in combination with electrical messages sent up the spinal cord from stretch receptors in the stomach, eventually switch us *out* of hunger mode, but not before we've managed to stuff dessert into our jam-packed bellies.

One consequence of this is that the faster we eat, the more we usually manage to force into our stomachs before the brain actually registers that we're no longer hungry. The energy-sapping dip we experience after eating too much involves shifting blood into the gut to deal with all that food. This is because blood is diverted away from the brain as it surges into the vast tangle of dilated blood vessels that supply the gut to absorb all the chemical molecules released from the meal by digestion. We feel lethargic after a large meal partly because our stomachs are hogging all the blood and partly because hormones are released into the bloodstream to put us into a sedentary state, discouraging any unnecessary movement that would otherwise cause blood to be re-directed away from the stomach (giving you a stitch), back into muscle and/or brain tissue. The time lag between *being* full and *feeling* full also explains why eating competitions usually take place over a relatively short period of time: from 10 to 15 minutes.

Throughout human prehistory, a paunch of fat could make the critical difference between life and death, should food suddenly become unavailable for weeks on end. That Michelin-man tyre of fat around the belly, bum and thighs is where all those excess dietary calories are stored once the limited carbohydrate stores of glycogen reach capacity. Whether you overeat foods rich in fat or those with plentiful carbohydrates, *all* excess is ultimately converted into sub-cutaneous blubber. In lean times our body quite literally cannibalises these stores to prevent an untimely death through starvation: an evolutionary masterstroke. Anyone who finds themselves cursing their insatiable appetite and the resulting unsightly stores of fat hanging from their bodies should bear in mind that, had their ancestors lacked this capacity for excess calorie storage, the human race may well have fizzled out.

Survival favoured the greediest gobblers because those who ate to excess accumulated fat deposits that saved their skins when there was nothing left in Old Mother Hubbard's famous cupboard. Those with a more modest appetite would have perished in the lean times, often before they managed to pass on the very genes that enable restraint at the dinner table.

The Stone Age glutton's increased likelihood of out-surviving those with a less voracious appetite left us with another brain legacy that is far from ideal in the modern age: a hardwired preference for fatty and sugary foods. Several MRI studies have demonstrated much stronger responses to images of high-fat/high-sugar foods like cakes, pastries and pizza than healthier low-calorie options in the nucleus accumbens, a vital hub of the reward pathway that resides within the ventral striatum (see Figure 4).

The reward pathway comprises the ventral tegmental area, nucleus accumbens and medial Prefrontal Cortex, all of which use the neurotransmitter dopamine as a primary means of relaying information across the synapses that connect one neuron to another.

When we consider what we might want to eat for breakfast, for example, the ventral striatum is activated more strongly for options that are, based on past experience, likely to satisfy our hunger best compared to others we tend to find less satisfying. Whichever of the available foods triggers the most powerful response in the ventral striatum

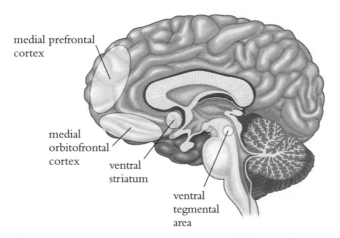

medial prefrontal cortex

medial orbitofrontal cortex

ventral striatum

ventral tegmental area

Figure 4 The ventral tegmental area is part of the midbrain from which dopaminergic neurons emanate, forming connections with other parts of the reward pathway. These include the nucleus accumbens in the ventral part of the striatum and the medial prefrontal cortex, particularly the part that sits over the eye orbits known as the medial orbitofrontal cortex.

is the one, all other things being equal, we will opt for. A more powerful response to the prospect of a high-carbohydrate/high-fat Danish pastry, in comparison to an egg-white omelette or a plain bowl of cereal, will *tend* to result in the choice of a pastry. This system evolved to help us to make all sorts of decisions: not just selecting the best available food options to eat when hungry, but also the best source of fluid to drink when thirsty and the best available partners with whom to have sex – all of which ultimately served the vital role of keeping us alive for long enough to pass on our genes.

The reason the temptation to eat naughty-but-nice foods is such a powerful force in most people's lives is that the high-fat/high-carbohydrate foods are hardwired to trigger stronger activations than low-fat/low-carbohydrate options in the brain's decision-making apparatus. This was a cunning design feature back in the days when the next opportunity to eat was a matter of perpetual uncertainty. Now, in a modern world where people's local environments have many shops and restaurants packed with affordable calorie-rich foods, it is a potentially lethal design flaw.

Second helpings

The stock thickens. As other ingredients are added to the neural pot we'll start to get a fuller flavour of the processes that influence what, when and how long we eat for.

First, our capacity to make healthy and disciplined eating decisions erodes over the course of the day. While some of us might be able to resist the high-fat/high-sugar breakfast options at the start of the day, opting instead for a healthy bowl of porridge oats with fresh fruit, later on our resolve will typically crumble as we allow ourselves to indulge in one form of sweet and fatty indulgence or another. Low blood sugar actually incapacitates the very neural circuitry of the prefrontal cortex that helps us to rein in the temptation to eat foods we know we shouldn't. Ironically it is at the very moment we need our willpower the most, when our low blood sugar compels us to seek food, that the brain areas that help us to make disciplined decisions desert us. In fact, low blood sugar leaves us vulnerable to a wide variety of hasty, impulsively made decisions, not just limited to giving in to the temptation to stray into a fast-food outlet. We also tend to get snappy or even, in the case of one study that looked at judges deliberating over whether or not to grant prisoners parole, deny people their freedom with greater frequency when it's been a few hours since we last ate something. This fascinating study showed that although the cases were considered in no particular order, inmates were much more likely to be granted parole directly after the judges had had a refreshment break. If blood sugar levels are running low, we are considerably less likely to make good, considered decisions, whether the choice concerns food or more important matters.

The frenetically busy lives of many modern city-dwellers lead to a high incidence of 'stress eating'. Dashing around like a pig on skates,* desperately trying to get a few items crossed off a lengthy 'to do' list, beset on all sides by unanticipated delays, obstacles and other impediments to making progress, we tend to make hasty decisions. Realising too late that we've allowed ourselves to become absolutely ravenous, ready to eat the proverbial horse, we consider our options for topping up those dwindling blood sugar levels. Glancing briefly at the healthy options, we soon start making plausible-sounding excuses to ourselves to account for the inevitably weak-willed decision: if ever there was a time we deserved some naughty but nice, surely it's after a day like this.

Science has finally established why our resolve seems to evaporate under stress, with or without low blood sugar. It turns out that the stress hormone cortisol does two things to our brain to facilitate the total demolition of self-control.

- Number 1: it ramps up sensitivity of the reward pathway to the delicious-looking and appetising aroma of high-calorie foods.

---

* I borrowed this turn of phrase from the wonderful Adrian Webster, co-author of my first book, *Sort Your Brain Out*.

- Number 2: it weakens lines of communication between the reward pathway and brain areas responsible for reining in the urge to consume those scrumptious temptations.

Given their propensity to over-release cortisol under socially stressful circumstances, this could have implications for the narcissist, perhaps even suggesting a neurobiological mechanism through which the sin of pride might impact on gluttony.

The quality of the previous night's sleep also has a powerful impact on appetite regulation. People invariably consume more food when they've slept badly the previous night. To complete the vicious cycle, what you really don't want to do in the critical hour before bedtime is eat a big meal. If you do, your stomach will generate excess heat as the enzymes break the chemical bonds between molecules in your food. This extra heat must be eliminated before you'll be able to get off to sleep, because brains need to cool ever so slightly before they can get into sleep mode. To aid this process the blood vessels in our hands and feet dilate as we try to get off to sleep in an effort to radiate excess heat away more effectively. Incidentally, if you're one of those who like to sleep with their feet poking out the end of the covers, you're instinctively aiding this process.

The concept of 'comfort eating' has gained support from recent studies showing that the neuropeptide oxytocin plays a role in regulating appetite. Oxytocin is best known for its role in generating feelings of comfort and safety when we experience positive social interactions like a hug (it is often nicknamed the 'cuddle drug') or being paid a compliment, but it also plays a role in generating feelings of satiety. A diet high in sugar results in reduced levels of oxytocin in the hypothalamus, leading people to seek more food.

The upshot of all this is a hypersensitivity to the temptation of culinary forbidden fruits and a deeply compromised capacity to resist them. Low blood sugar, high stress, a sleepy head and even being prone to boredom all seem to impede the areas of the brain responsible for impulse control that would otherwise help to steer us away from foods that bring us pleasure but make us fat.

This omnishambles of indiscipline effectively silences our conscience, allowing the circuits of confabulation to fizz into action. Our heads become filled with semi-rational-sounding excuses and weak justifications for our actions. Add alcohol into the mix, further eroding all remaining impulse control and, the next thing you know, you find yourself in the nearest kebab shop quicker than you can say taramasalata. Consequently, anyone who wants to exert more control over their ever-expanding waistline would be well advised to focus their mind on finding effective and convenient ways to manage stress and improve sleep quality (see Chapter 9, p. 219).

The bill

Obesity has come to be viewed by scientists and medical physicians alike more along the lines of food addiction than moral weakness. Why so many of us are succumbing to the primal urge to eat so much more than we actually need, and so often, is not straightforward. It's partly due to changing attitudes at home, and in society as a whole, regarding what constitutes normal portion sizes. Marketing plays a significant role in shaping these attitudes. Evidence is accumulating to back the idea that once people are in the habit of eating over-sized portions of high-calorie food, but not taking the regular, intensive, physical exercise that burn off those extra calories, fundamental changes occur within the brain that perpetuate these habits after just a few years.

Fat doesn't just accumulate under the skin – it also gets tucked in around the vital organs. This is known as visceral fat, and it poses the greatest threat to life and limb. Encouragingly for overweight people who decide to pro-actively shed some pounds, but are discouraged by the lack of aesthetic impact, this deadly visceral fat is the first to go. Serial MRI body scans reveal that, despite the more visible fatty deposits under the skin being notoriously slow to shift, the lethal stuff deeper down – that which quite literally throttles vital organs including the heart, lungs, kidneys and liver – is whittled away much more quickly.

All the excess fat molecules that end up swimming around in the bloodstream of those who routinely eat high-fat or high-carbohydrate diets end up causing metabolic chaos. One aspect of this is that obesity greatly increases the likelihood of both stroke and heart disease. This is, in part, due to the accumulation of a sticky, fatty substance called atherosclerotic plaques on the inner surface of blood vessels that supply the brain and heart, respectively. When the many arteries providing the heart with the raw materials it requires to pump continuously 24/7 become gradually narrower, beyond a certain threshold, the muscles will start to malfunction. They may end up unable to contract with the appropriate timing (cardiac arrhythmia), or sections of the heart's muscular wall may completely give up the ghost, preventing the pumping action from occurring at all (heart failure).

Strokes are the end result of a very similar process, but the blood vessels affected are those that supply the brain, rather than those that supply the heart. There is a huge amount of piping that could potentially be affected when it comes to keeping a greedy organ like the brain perpetually stuffed full of fresh blood. Laid end to end, the brain's blood vessels would stretch for over 400 miles – that's over three laps of the M25 motorway around London! Despite only weighing 2 per cent of our overall body mass, the brain consumes 20 per cent of the oxygen and glucose available in the blood (at rest, much more when concentrating hard on something) and it requires a constant supply of energy because there's no room for storage.

As with the heart, before brain blood vessels get completely blocked, they become narrower than usual, which can be sufficient to prevent the brain areas they supply from functioning at full capacity. There's clear evidence of mild cognitive impairment in those classified as severely obese. In other words, various thinking processes are rendered sluggish by obesity. Part of the explanation may boil down to the fact that brain blood vessels can get completely blocked without causing obvious impairment. If the blood vessel is small enough, supplying a tiny piece of brain tissue, the so-called 'silent cerebral infarcts' can go more or less unnoticed. Yet they can still cause mental dysfunctions characterised as mild cognitive impairment. They slip under the medical radar by avoiding major disruption to the brain's business-as-usual.

If one of the brain's larger blood vessels gets clogged up with gunk, however (the most common site for this is the Middle Cerebral Artery), it can mean curtains for a much larger chunk of brain. These are the full-blown strokes that often cause paralysis down one side of the body and permanent loss of whatever other cognitive functions are served by the brain areas that have lost their blood supply. Once a brain area dies completely, it will never recover. Other surviving brain areas can sometimes be retrained to compensate for the loss of function, but no matter how seriously people take their rehabilitation, it is rare (though not impossible) for people to get completely back to normal. Given that obesity is a well-known risk factor for stroke, you'd think people might start to seriously reconsider their diet when they notice their clothes getting tighter.

If you're merely overweight these revelations will hopefully increase your resolve to stop the slide into obesity now. If you are chronically obese it may help you better reconcile yourself with the true extent of the challenges you face. Either way, brace yourself, because the following might make for uncomfortable reading.

It has been revealed recently that the brains of the chronically obese are different from those of people with healthier BMIs. It has been known for a long time that obesity is associated with low-grade inflammation across the entire body. This accounts for the increased risk of diabetes, cancer and cardiovascular disease. The inflammation results largely from an increase in the production of proinflammatory cytokines, manufactured in the body's fatty tissues. The increase of these agents, and the inflammatory processes that they encourage, are now increasingly being linked to cognitive decline. What's more, these same substances appear to accumulate in brain areas undergoing age-related neurodegeneration, which means that it may be no exaggeration to say that obesity accelerates the rate at which the brain ages.

A recent study comparing the brains of several thousand people across a wide range of age groups and BMI values finally managed to quantify the damage that obesity causes to brains in an understandable and memorable way. Being overweight in middle age leads to a loss of white matter, the wire-like connections that neurons use to ferry electrical messages between distant brain areas. The degradation observed was equivalent to that seen in people 10 years older, but with a leaner body. This is the true cognitive price that obese people are paying for allowing the temptations of gluttony to take over their eating habits on a daily basis. Obesity can now be seen, from an unflinching scientific perspective, as a health condition that damages the brain in a way that leads to a plethora of changes that together increase susceptibility to normal ageing mechanisms. This may explain why several studies have found an indirect link between high BMI and not just lower cognitive capacities, but even an increased risk of dementia and Alzheimer's disease.

Any readers unfortunate enough to fall into the obese category may find this news rather daunting. While possible solutions to the various problems associated with temptation are described in a separate chapter (see Chapter 9, p. 219), in the interests of avoiding panic right now, here's an optimistic study demonstrating that help is at hand for those who truly have lost control of their eating behaviours. The rates of mild cognitive impairment were measured in a group of severely obese individuals. Half of these patients then underwent gastric band surgery. This shrinks the stomach to severely restrict the amount of food a person is physically able to eat, typically by half. Just one month later there were nearly 50 per cent fewer cases of mild cognitive impairment in those who underwent the surgery. Although surgery is an extreme option, it is one that could potentially rescue the brains of even the most chronically overweight individuals. There is always hope, provided a person is suitably determined to embrace change.

Irreversible?

Evidence has surfaced from imaging studies with chronically obese mice and rats that indicate changes in cellular morphology – the shape and size of brain cells – in regions of the hypothalamus that respond to the various hormones that signal the energetic state of body and brain. Specifically, these cells become less sensitive to hormones like CCK and leptin that signal to the brain when we're full. Under normal circumstances the impact of these substances on regions of the hypothalamus controlling appetite is to make us stop eating once sufficient calories have been taken on board. At the same time, the relevant hypothalamic compartments also exhibit an *increased* sensitivity to ghrelin and other chemical signals that indicate a calorie deficit, promoting the urge to seek out food.

While other impacts of obesity on health, such as the visceral fat and narrowing of blood vessels to the heart and brain, can be reversed with better dietary management and regular exercise, the malfunctions in the hypothalamus seem to be permanent. This presents an obese person with a much bigger challenge to contend with than the merely overweight person – they must control how much they eat despite impairments to their brain's appetite-regulating system. This suggests that ideally we really need to take action before people reach the stage of obesity in the first place, but given the nature of the food environment in modern developed-world countries, this is easier said than done.

You might be forgiven for thinking that a person either has obese genes or they don't. After all, a spot of people-watching on the high street can quickly lead to the observation that if parents are overweight then their kids are often on the tubby side too. Recent research suggests that parents are often completely blind to their children's excess pounds; they simply cannot see it. How much of obesity is nature (DNA inherited from our parents) versus nurture (eating habits passed by example from parent to child)? Although our general body shape is inherited from our parents, there is a lot more variability in the amount of flesh attached to that frame than can be accounted for by genetics alone. After all, those children don't just inherit the genetic makeup of their parents, but also their eating habits, coping systems, emotional responses to life events and values. We copy the behaviours of the people around us. Children emulate the example set by their parents and other influential figures in their lives. This is where their sense of what constitutes normal behaviour comes from in the first place. The death blow to the idea that obesity results from nature (genes) rather than nurture (experience) arises from the observation that, in recent times, each successive generation is heavier than the previous one. The genes passing from generation to generation are more or less the same. So that means that nurture is to blame.

People are exercising less, yet eating more, than any previous generation. The food we eat is more processed than ever before. Food processing involves stripping nutrients out of food and replacing them with high levels of sugar and fat to make the food last longer and taste better. The money spent on marketing junk food increases every year and the rise in advertising budgets mirror the increase in obesity. Take-aways, fast-food outlets and supermarkets compete to offer deals that allow less money to be spent, with less effort, to consume more calories than ever before. Supersize that? Oh, go on then! Would you like whipped cream on that? I shouldn't really, but seeing as you've offered...

The over-abundance of high-calorie, nutritionally empty food, cunningly designed to keep us riding high on the sugar roller coaster, ensures that multinational companies make a killing out of our mindless habit of snacking on treats throughout the day. This roller coaster involves creating a sugar high that is quickly followed (thanks to a good squirt of insulin) by a hunger-inducing sugar low, sending us scuttling towards the nearest available sweet fix, which sends those blood sugar levels rocketing again. For many, this perpetual cycle occurs each and every waking day. Eating habits picked up in youth inevitably follow us into adulthood, so the advertising has become targeted at younger and younger audiences. Toddlers across the world can now correctly identify

most of the major fast food brands long before they've
mastered the alphabet. No wonder obesity rates are rocketing.

The big picture
When the world's 20 million obese people in the year 1995
rocketed to 30 million by the year 2000 it became clear that
the global fight against obesity was going nowhere. During
the 1990s the emphasis of health campaigns aiming to address
this problem tended to revolve around eating less fat. However,
by placing so much emphasis on the scourge of high-fat foods
in increasing our waistlines, it temporarily derailed all hope of
communicating to the masses that excess carbohydrate in the
form of bread, cakes, sweets and sugary drinks is also converted
into fat. As long as people consumed the low-fat options they
generally felt justified in eating as much as they wanted.
Unfortunately the manufacturers were hard at work devising
'low-fat' options that often, if anyone had bothered to check
the labels, contained more calories overall than the 'normal
fat' options.

Children in the UK are eating three times (and adults
twice) the recommended daily intake of sugar. The primary
source of this is sugar-laden soft drinks. The recommended
daily amount of added sugar constitutes no more than 5 per
cent of your daily calorie intake, which works out as 30g for
anybody 11 years or older. Considering that there is more
than 30g of sugar in a single regular-sized (330ml) can of
Coca Cola or Pepsi (both 10.6g/100ml) it's plain to see how
the millions of pounds spent annually on advertising for soft
drinks alone has warped our intuitive sense of how much
extra sugar in our diets is acceptable.

Now that our dietary attentions have switched from a focus
on avoiding fat to avoiding excess sugar, there has been a drive
towards artificially sweetened low-calorie options. Sadly even
this seemingly sensible approach is doomed to failure. It turns
out that artificial sweeteners only lead us to seek out more
calorific foods. In a study in which experimental animals were
fed healthy food, or the same meal plus a popular artificial
sweetener, those animals that received the sweetener consumed

a third more calories overall. The sweeteners were also observed to cause insomnia and, as we know, poor sleep quality leads to an increased likelihood of opting for higher-calorie food options the next day. Although few of these studies have been replicated in human populations, these early insights should at least give people pause for thought when they next find themselves reaching for a 3-litre bottle of 'diet' fizzy drink. You may have been convinced by the tone of regularly encountered adverts that it's the healthier option, but your brain will spot the difference between the sweet taste and the lack of calories, and nudge your hypothalamus into food-finding mode in an effort to compensate.

As mentioned above, more often than not there's nothing wrong with the genetic makeup of obese families. The problem is the environment in which the parents themselves were raised and in which they raise their own kids. There is a deficit in education relating to an understanding of what foods we should be eating, how best to prepare meals, how much to consume each day, when and why. There is also a clear and well-evidenced marketing conspiracy that is intentionally brainwashing us all to one degree or another. Perceptions have been shifted to make consumption of many more calories than anyone could realistically burn on any typical day seem normal. Our only hope, if we don't want our healthcare systems to be crushed under the weight of obesity-related medical bills, is to counterbalance these unhealthy influences with easily accessed, clearly described messages about affordable alternatives to delicious, but nutritionally deficient food and drink.

Interventions are most effective when they target people early in life, before their behaviours settle down into a relatively fixed pattern. A surprisingly effective way of changing the average teenager's eating habits to avoid the delicious fatty and sugary stuff to which they are naturally drawn is to make them angry. Bringing their attention to the injustice associated with huge, well-funded multinational companies generating profits from the obesity epidemic and even doing everything in their power to encourage it actually has a positive impact on their

eating habits. Consuming fewer calories each day, combined
with interventions encouraging us to see daily exercise as an
essential part of life, are key to preventing the brain changes
that get us stuck on the sugar roller coaster. Moreover, the
sooner a person starts, the less likely they are to cross the
threshold into full-blown obesity. This is not the place to go
into detail about strategies we might choose to employ in an
effort to reduce temptation; there's a whole chapter devoted
to that (Chapter 9, p. 219). And anyway, we have many more
vices to consider before we have any hope of delivering
ourselves from evil.

The next capital vice we will consider is intimately related
to the sin of gluttony. As St Basil astutely observed: 'Through
the sense of touch in tasting – which is always seducing
toward gluttony by swallowing – the body, fattened up and
titillated by the soft humors bubbling uncontrollably inside, is
carried in a frenzy towards the touch of sexual intercourse.'

CHAPTER FOUR

Lust

Lust is to the other passions what the nervous fluid is to life; it supports them all, lends strength to them all: ambition, cruelty, avarice, revenge, are all founded on lust.

Marquis de Sade

L et's talk about sex. But first – a warning. This chapter is not for the faint-hearted. If you are prudish, squeamish or easily offended, you may wish to skip straight to sloth (Chapter 5, p. 115). I am a neurobiologist by training, in other words a biologist who chose to focus on the human body and, in particular, the brain. When a biologist describes the mechanisms of sexual arousal from an objective scientific perspective it is quite possible for what is intended to be a simple, no-nonsense, direct approach to conveying the facts to be mistaken for crude vulgarity. I have gone to great pains to adjust my language to minimise the possibility of causing offence but, despite my best efforts, for some people, parts of what follows might make for uncomfortable reading. Others will reach the end of the chapter and have no idea how anything I've said could possibly be construed as objectionable. I've done my very best to find a path through a veritable jungle of interesting and relevant material that I hope will keep all parties intrigued. I felt it was important not to shy away from some of the more inflammatory topics, tempting as it was to ditch them in order to avoid upsetting people. My intention is not to offend, simply to inform.

In exploring the science relating to the sin of lust our primary concern is sexual behaviour that might reasonably be considered anti-social from the perspective of a potential to cause harm; a force that drives people apart, rather than bringing them together. To fulfil this aim we'll be taking a look at which particular sexual practices religions consider to be inappropriate and examine how well such views have stood the test of time. We'll be thinking about what sexual arousal actually is, and we will assess several avenues of research into groups of people's physiological and neurological responses to a wide range of erotic stimuli. By the end of this journey we should have a clearer picture of what's going on when people do the sexual things they know they shouldn't.

Historical perspective

The major religions disagree on many things, but they all seem to share a dim view of adultery. Definitions of what actually qualifies as adultery vary considerably from one religion to another, but all seem to be united on the matter of cheating on a spouse: it is simply not on. Buddha was probably the least damning: 'Being dissatisfied with his wife, if one is seen with prostitutes or the wives of others, this is a cause of one's decline.' Hinduism's cautionary words are stronger: 'He who commits adultery is punished here and hereafter; for his days in this world are cut short, and when dead he falls into hell.' Islam prescribes severe punishments for sexual activities out of wedlock, providing a stark warning: 'And come not near unto adultery. Lo! it is an abomination and an evil way.' And of course the Judeo-Christian tradition has 'Thou shalt not commit adultery' as one of the Ten Commandments.

By the time St Gregory the Great came on to the scene, his list of the seven deadly sins featured *Luxuria*, a Latin term roughly translating as 'extravagance'. This wasn't just limited to lust in the sense of sexual behaviour, but involved lust directed at a wide range of targets. It forbade the act of lusting over other people's property, their wives, their slaves and any other luxury for that matter. The deadly sin of lust as we know it today only became focused specifically on sex acts in medieval times. By the thirteenth century when St Thomas Aquinas got involved, the sex acts that were explicitly forbidden were listed under the category of sodomy – the sixth species of the umbrella sin *Luxuria*. Sodomy forbade many things. No masturbation. No sex toys. No anal sex. No same-sex couplings. No sex with other species. Tracing back the reasoning behind why these particular sexual behaviours were considered to be diabolical takes us back to philosophical debates that took place many centuries earlier.

The earliest Christian writings on the topic of what constituted acceptable and unacceptable sexual practices were notoriously vague. Clement of Alexandria took it upon himself to simplify matters by inventing the Alexandrian Rule: sex is acceptable if the aim is procreation. Everything else is off the menu. The specific acts that ended up being forbidden under the heading of sodomy all seem to satisfy the Alexandrian Rule rather well, which itself evolved from the concept of sin *contra naturam* in Latin or *para physin* in Greek, that is, sins against nature. Clement's thinking is understood to have been ultimately influenced by another Alexandrian by the name of Philo, and *his* original motivation to write about sin *para physin* is thought to have stemmed from a heartfelt objection to pederasty – men having sex with boys – which was rife in his home town during that era.

These days, attitudes vary wildly regarding the potential harms that human sexual impulses can cause. To some, masturbation is an act of evil; to others it is not just harmless, but might even protect against cancer for those with a prostate gland.* Some believe that sex between a pair of unattached consenting adults is an abomination if they happen to be of the same gender. Others would argue that, given how widely homosexuality is documented in the animal kingdom, suggesting that it might be somehow 'against nature' is surely inconsistent with the facts. That said, I suspect that the vast majority of human beings on the entire planet, whatever their beliefs or upbringing, concur regarding paedophilia. When it comes to the potential to cause physical and long-lasting psychological damage, most people would agree that this particular sexual urge is the lowest of the low. This rather unpleasant topic will be our first port of call in this exploration of the sin of lust.

---

* Masturbating frequently between the ages of 20 and 50 is associated with a reduced incidence of prostate cancer.

Paedophilia

A study by Burns and Swerdlow (2003) describes the case of a
40-year-old married man who, despite a lifelong history of
perfectly civilised behaviour, started to develop uncharacteristic
sexual urges that ended up going beyond his control. Formerly
a US corrections (prison) officer, he went into teaching
after successfully completing a Master's degree in education.
Two years into a stable relationship with his second wife he
started visiting brothels and collecting child pornography.
After he had made sexual advances towards his pre-pubescent
step-daughter, she promptly told her mother about his
behaviour, who in turn reported him to the authorities. A
conviction of child molestation led him to a 12-step sex
offender rehabilitation programme in order to avoid a custodial
sentence. Even during rehabilitation he found himself unable
to resist his sexual urges. He requested sexual favours not only
from other female attendees at the programme, but even from
those who actually ran the groups. A formerly responsible
individual, with no prior history of inappropriate sexual
conduct, this man suddenly found himself possessed by
Asmodeus – the demon that Bishop Binsfeld (whom we first
met in Chapter 2) dedicated to the sin of lust. This man knew
that what he was doing was morally unacceptable, which is
why he kept his growing collection of paedophilic images as a
carefully guarded, guilty secret, yet he found himself powerless
to resist all the same.

The evening before he was due to appear in court to be
sentenced, he started experiencing terrible headaches and
difficulties with his balance. He was quickly taken to the
University of Virginia Hospital in Charlottesville, for
investigative brain scans. These revealed a huge tumour in
his right orbitofrontal cortex – a brain area just above the
eye socket. The egg-sized mass of tissue was surgically
removed and the dreadful headaches went away. Amazingly
his paedophilic urges also seemed to miraculously disappear
too. So thoroughly had his deviant sexual impulses been
abolished that the prison psychologist felt comfortable

testifying that, as a result of the surgery, the man was no longer a threat to children. He was released from prison and allowed to return home to live with his wife and step-daughter once again.

Within a few months, though, the desire to collect pornography returned and was accompanied by a return of the severe headaches. This prompted him to seek medical help and further brain scans revealed that the tumour had re-grown. Another operation not only abolished the inappropriate sexual urges once again, but this time various cognitive problems that he had been dealing with ever since the first operation improved too. His handwriting, formerly illegible, became readable again. His inability to accurately copy a clock-face was remedied, as were several other aspects of his previously impaired brain function. For paedophilic tendencies to be switched on and off like this was previously unheard of; this certainly wasn't a typical case.

Paedophiles typically develop a sexual interest in children much earlier than 40 years of age. It has been suggested that this man may have been a paedophile all along, and the tumour interfered with his ability to manage these sexual impulses. Whether or not this is true is a matter for debate. Certainly he was not solely attracted to children, as during his rehabilitation he made sexual advances towards adults too, so the tumour may have somehow ramped up his sex drive across the board. Either way the possibility that he had always been a paedophile, albeit one who could successfully inhibit his urges until the tumour interfered with this ability, raises an important point.

Many people out there in the world harbour sexual desires that are forbidden by cultural norms, specific laws and/or religious teachings. Knowing that these impulses are wrong, they are able to actively suppress them. They usually have a full comprehension of what society thinks of people who act on such impulses. Even in prisons, an environment not typically associated with a strong sense of morality, paedophiles are routinely housed separately from the rest of the prisoner population to protect them from attack. When paedophiles are identified in local communities, they often find themselves on the receiving end of verbal abuse, physical aggression and vandalism. Men and women who take advantage of vulnerable minors are reviled both in and out of prison.

We know statistically that a proportion of people in any given community will, for one reason or another, find themselves more sexually attracted to children than adults. Distasteful as this is to think about, what should we do with such knowledge? Most of us find ourselves so disgusted by these people that we bury our heads in the sand and try to pretend that it isn't happening. But ignoring the problem won't make it go away. It can be useful to look at it from their perspective. If a person feels the onset of paedophilic urges and wants to seek help in resisting such deviant desires, knowing that society, the law and religions all deem such impulses to be an abomination, what are their options? Given that public opinion generally involves a desire to see paedophiles punished in the harshest possible ways, it's easy to see why they don't seek help. Considering that child sex offenders, that is, those who actually get caught, are the tip of the iceberg, there will be many others out there feeling these impulses, but with no access to help in controlling them. This is a troubling prospect.

If society wants to deal with this problem head on, rather than leaving paedophiles to find like-minded others on the internet who will only make matters worse, shouldn't these people be offered some assistance? If not for their own benefit, at least in an effort to protect their potential future victims? In 1992 a telephone service was set up in Vermont, USA, to provide such assistance. Similar charities have since been set up in Germany (a community known as the Dunkelfeld, or 'darkfield') and beyond. In the UK, the office of Stop It Now! typically handles 700 to 800 calls per month, with an estimated double that number missed each month due to staff shortages.

As well as psychological counselling for those yet to commit offences, there are drugs available that are routinely used to help suppress the deviant urges of sex offenders. Both forms of therapy are far from perfect (see Chapter 9, p. 219), but they are much better than leaving these people to their own devices. If only we had a better understanding of what is actually going wrong in the brain of a paedophile, surely then we could find better ways to reduce the threat of serious harm to innocent children?

To understand exactly what we're dealing with, we cannot just rely on a single, one-off case study of our man with the bizarre tumour-related paedophilic tendencies. What we would need is a large group of paedophiles whose sexual interest in children has been consistent throughout adulthood, in order to compare the sexual responses in their brains to those of a control group of non-paedophile brains. Amazingly, thanks to over a decade of work by Dr James Cantor and colleagues, working across various scientific and medical institutions in Toronto, Canada, we now have a much better understanding of the average paedophile's brain.

In 2008, Cantor and colleagues published a fascinating discovery whereby they noted significant differences in the white matter tracts of the paedophile brains compared to non-paedophile controls. The brain's white matter consists of neuronal brain wires that connect distant areas all the way between front and back of the brain, between left hemisphere and right, and between the outer cortical surface and densely packed networks at its very core. High-speed electrical messages can be passed along these 'information superhighways' thanks to an insulating fatty wrapper called myelin that helps the signal hop, skip and jump along the brain wire at 150 metres per second, rather than the mere 10 metres per second possible in neurons without this myelin wrapper. It is these myelin go-faster wrappers that give the 'white' matter a paler appearance than the 'grey' mattter found on the brain's outer surface.

In the paedophiles, two of these white matter tracts in particular were less tightly packed than usual, suggesting a reduced capacity for carrying information between specific brain areas. You could think of these routes through the brain as being degraded from motorways to B-roads, or from hyperoptic broadband to dial-up internet connections. One of the two superhighways in which they observed a deficit passes through a part of the brain that would almost certainly have been compressed by the egg-sized tumour in the 40-year-old teacher we met earlier. This might just be a coincidence. On the other hand, it could suggest that this particular pathway was involved in suppressing the deviant sexual impulses for most of his life, but as the tumour grew it was later rendered ineffective. We'll never know for sure, but it's a distinct possibility pointing towards a potential target for future interventions.

In 2016, Cantor and colleagues went on to publish another large-scale MRI study. This time they focused on functional rather than structural connectivity between different brain areas while subjects were at rest in the scanner. Once again they were in search of consistent differences between the brains of paedophiles as compared to non-paedophile controls that might explain their aberrant sexual behaviours. Such studies often use subjective measures to establish participants' sexual preferences. This involves asking them to fill out questionnaires, an approach that is vulnerable to people intentionally giving misinformation, which can skew the results. This study avoided that problem by taking objective measures – namely monitoring blood flow to the penis while viewing erotic images – to confirm that the paedophile group were genuinely more sexually aroused by explicit images of children than adult images and the non-paedophile group were only sexually aroused by adult material. This was just to ensure that the paedophile group was exclusively comprised of real paedophiles and the non-paedophile group really was sexually disinterested in minors. Once the groups were established, they were not actually shown any erotic material while inside the scanner. Yet, of the 23 different brain areas that exhibited higher functional connectivity at rest in paedophiles compared to non-paedophiles, 20 were within the regions of the brain comprising the 'sexual response network'. This is a network of interacting regions known, on the basis of a large number of completely independent brain-scanning studies, to be involved in orchestrating sexual responses in healthy brains. Rarely does brain imaging research stack up so neatly. It suggests that the brains of paedophiles are fundamentally different from other people's in that, even at rest their Sexual Response Network is more tightly integrated.

It is important, when trying to deal with the problem of paedophiles in society, to realise that the structure and functional connectedness of their brains is different from everyone else's. The 'sexual response network' brain areas that govern healthy sexual responses in the rest of us seem to be hyperactive in the paedophile, even at rest, when they are lying in the MRI scanner, not required to do or think anything at all. In the rest of us these brain areas only tend to light up when we view erotic images or are being physically sexually stimulated in the scanner.

Like everyone else, paedophiles cannot control *what* produces a sexual response in their brains. Unlike everyone else, if they actually act upon such urges, children get hurt. While the impulses themselves are automatic, whether or not they act on their urges *is* entirely their own responsibility. It is important to grasp the difference. They absolutely must be held entirely responsible for their actions, but at the same time they cannot be blamed for the sexual excitement they feel. It is not just that it is unfair to hate people for something they cannot help, but more importantly it is unhelpful in trying to reduce the threat posed by the problem of paedophilia. There are almost certainly large numbers of people out there who have never committed a crime in their life, yet secretly harbour paedophilic impulses. Those impulses arise because their brains are different from other people's. Rather than allowing our disgust that such people have such impulses to drive them into the dark recesses of the internet, where they will probably find like-minded others who will make the struggle to resist these impulses harder, not easier, we should be doing everything in our power to help them manage their urges more successfully. With rates as high as 3 per cent of women and 1 per cent of men in the UK having been on the receiving end of rape or attempted rape by an adult during childhood, it is important that we start viewing early intervention with paedophiles as a form of child protection, rather than an act of showing sympathy for the devil incarnate.

OK, you can relax. The most unpleasant subject matter is now behind us. Before you continue, you might want to go and wash your hands. Several studies have shown that the brain responses to physical disgust and psychological disgust are very similar. As you may well be feeling slightly sullied by the subject matter we have just considered, the act of cleaning your hands – something that usually makes us feel more comfortable when we're covered in filth – may help to rid you of any residual psychological discomfort. It may sound odd, but there is good evidence to support this idea. Then when you return, you'll be ready to consider the joy of sex, as the next topic we are going to explore is the biology of everyday, healthy sexual arousal and a curious body of evidence that suggests it isn't as similar to sexual desire as you might have thought.

Sexual excitement

Triggering sexual arousal in the human brain can be achieved in a multiplicity of different ways. The main hub of sexual excitement, into which all these different triggers are ultimately channelled, resides within the hypothalamus and in particular a compartment known as the paraventricular nucleus. It is responsible for manufacturing various hormones that are released into the bloodstream from the pituitary gland, to be circulated all over body and brain. The hormones released from the pituitary in response to erotic stimuli stimulate the release of sex hormones from the ovaries in women and the testes in men. The sexual circuitry of the brain – the Sexual Response Network mentioned above – can be switched on by a whole array of different sensory stimuli. It could be tactile stimulation of the genitalia, the nipples or the breasts; a visual trigger, like catching a glimpse of an alluring body contour; olfactory: the whiff of a delicious fragrance as somebody wafts by; acoustic: the specific characteristics of a person's voice; even purely psychogenic activity (imagination alone) is perfectly adequate to do the job. One woman in the medical literature even experienced orgasm every time she brushed her teeth.speaking of orgasms, while the male orgasm has long been known to be a necessary part of reproduction in terms of fulfilling the vital role of successfully depositing sperm inside the vagina, the biological function of the female orgasm was always something of a mystery to science, until now. It turns out that the female orgasm causes rhythmic pulsing of the cilia – tiny hairs that line the fallopian tubes connecting the womb to each of the ovaries – in a way that selectively wafts the sperm into whichever fallopian tube actually contains an egg. So female orgasm may well serve the biological purpose of improving the odds of conception, partly through contractions of the vaginal wall that help to get the sperm into the womb in the first place, and partly through a Mexican wave from the cilia that sucks the sperm into the appropriate fallopian tube.

In both men and women the state of sexual arousal that precedes orgasm essentially involves genital vasocongestion. The aim is to increase blood pressure and this is achieved by dilating the blood vessels taking blood into the penis or vagina and constricting those that take blood away. It really is as simple as letting more blood *in* to the genitalia than is allowed back *out* again. The increase in blood pressure induces an erection in the male sexual apparatus, by causing the special spongy tissue inside the penis to fill with blood, increasing its length, width and rigidity. The increase in blood pressure in the female sexual apparatus causes the vagina to increase in length and width *and* induces the release of a lubricating fluid into the vaginal canal. It also engorges the clitoris* with blood to increase its surface area. These processes all use exactly the same biological trick to prepare the male and female genitalia for coitus. Many different types of sensory signal can trigger

---

* What most people think of as the clitoris is just the head of the structure; it also has an extensive structure under the surface along the length of the inner labia.

this process and no matter what anyone tells you, this reflex is
not under conscious control; it is entirely automatic.

  While many phenomena can trigger sexual arousal, when it
comes to what works for a certain individual, no two people
are exactly the same. As with most things, this comes down to
a mixture of nature and nurture. Biologically everyone's
genetic endowment is slightly different from everybody else's,
unless you happen to have an identical twin. Similarly,
everybody's accumulation of life experiences will differ too,
even compared to those of an identical twin. According to
each person's unique combination of nature (their genes) and
nurture (their life experience), what reliably turns one person
on may do nothing for someone else. Everyone is different.
Some women find that manipulation of the clitoris is the
most reliable path to orgasm. For others vaginal stimulation is
the only sure-fire route to sexual satisfaction. Some may find
that the cervix (the neck of the womb) is the critical body
part that must be probed to reach climax.* And for yet others
it is a combination of all three. As for men, some achieve
orgasm most readily through manual stimulation, others
through oral and while the majority of men have a preference
for vaginal sex, many are driven wild by anal sex, irrespective
of whether they are straight or gay. Exactly what triggers that
unmistakable sensation of vasocongestion between the legs
varies enormously from individual to individual. And as we
are about to see, studies investigating which kinds of erotic
stimuli lead to arousal in people of different sexual persuasions
is not as straightforward as it might seem...

  One particularly fascinating body of research investigated
how people of various sexual orientations responded to a
variety of erotic films. Three different types of pornography
were shown to all subjects depicting scenes of either heterosexual or homosexual sex, and the participants involved in the

---

* This was first discovered in pioneering sex studies with women
suffering spinal cord injuries that prevented touch information from
the clitoris and vagina reaching the brain, while the mechanisms
relaying information from the cervix were intact.

study were representatives of four different groups: straight men, straight women, gay men and lesbians. Sexual arousal was measured by plethysmography; quite possibly the most difficult-to-pronounce word in science. In men, penile plethysmography entails fitting an expandable collar around the base of the penis to measure changes in circumference. Photoplethysmography is used in women. A tampon-sized, light-emitting probe is inserted into the vagina to measure the strength of light reflected back from the vaginal wall. This changes according to blood vessel dilation: the more blood, the more light is reflected back. In both cases plethysmography measures changes in blood flow to the genitalia as a proxy for sexual arousal.

The results were as mind-boggling as they were unexpected. Male sexual arousal was very much focused on the target of their specific sexual orientation, that is, women for straight men, men for gay men. Straight men were turned on by women having sex. It really didn't matter what they were doing, straight sex, lesbian sex or anything else for that matter – so long as there was a naked woman in the scene it resulted in reliable, objectively measured, sexual arousal. No surprise there then. Gay men were turned on by men having sex together, but not if the sex involved women. In this case, whether the women featured in the erotic clips were having sex with a man, or with another woman, the plethysmography showed no increase in penile circumference. This is exactly what the researchers were expecting to find. The surprises started when they looked at the data of the female participants.

Irrespective of whether the erotic material matched their stated sexual preferences or not, *all* the women showed some degree of objectively measured sexual response to *every* different type of porn. Both straight and lesbian women were turned on – as in physiologically aroused – by heterosexual sex, lesbian sex and sex between gay men. This could be taken to indicate that genital vasocongestion has nothing to do with sexual arousal whatsoever, but that seems unlikely. The other interpretation is that vaginal lubrication, which is one of the consequences of vasocongestion, simply occurs whenever there is sex happening in the immediate environment, irrespective of whether it fits the tastes and sexual interests of the woman in question. In support of this interpretation, these studies also included a fourth category of material: monkeys having sex. None of the men, whether gay or straight, were sexually aroused by the monkey sex. All the women, on the other hand, showed increased responses in the objective measures of sexual arousal, again irrespective of their sexual preferences. This control condition helped to drive home the notion that the physiological responses to erotic stimuli are a separate issue to the psychological desire to have sex. It is clearly ridiculous to suggest that all these women *desired* monkey sex. Inter-species sexual attraction does happen, of course, but it is far too rare to explain these findings.

These data could suggest that the physiological component of female sexual arousal may be a reflex designed to protect the vaginal canal from damage. Rather being indicative of a willingness to have sex, these automatic responses may simply serve to minimise the chance of contracting a potentially deadly infection by protecting the vaginal wall from tearing. As therapists who counsel rape victims know only too well, the experience of vaginal lubrication, and sometimes even orgasm, during rape is not uncommon. When this occurs it is often a source of tremendous guilt and psychological turmoil. It can be mistaken for an indication that the victim might have somehow enjoyed the experience, or worse, that it constitutes some form of tacit consent. Viewed from a purely evolutionary perspective, it seems much more likely to be a health-preserving reflex designed to protect the vaginal canal from damage; an involuntary response to protect a particularly vulnerable part of the anatomy.

Another aspect of sexual responsiveness that heterosexual women have little or no control over is how the stage of their menstrual cycle influences how attractive they find stereotypically masculine men. The more testosterone a man has swimming around in his body, the more his biology will become masculinised in a way that can be seen and heard even from a distance. This is because high testosterone impacts on the development of several different parts of the male body. It gives a man a broader jaw than another who produces less testosterone. The impact on the larynx results in a deeper, more resonant voice. The shoulders will usually be broader and the body in general more muscular. He will usually have thicker hair and a coarser, denser beard. Research exposing heterosexual women to a variety of male faces, bodies and voice types at different stages of their menstrual cycles reveals a rhythm in the fluctuations observed in the rules of attraction. During the fertile phase of the cycle, the attractiveness ratings the women gave for more masculine-looking faces, bodies and deeper-sounding voices increased slightly. On the other hand, during the *non*-fertile weeks of the menstrual cycle, the attractiveness ratings for the more feminine male faces, bodies and voices increased slightly. Putting these observations together provides a logical explanation for why a small but significant proportion of men are raising another man's child without even realising it. The explanation is not straightforward, so take a deep breath and let's dive right in.

The first idea you need to grasp to follow the logic of this theory is that high testosterone is thought to be indicative of a strong immune system and therefore high-quality genes. The reason for equating high testosterone with strong genes is because testosterone suppresses the immune system. The idea is that if a man with all that testosterone in their system – as indicated by their tall and broad-shouldered stature, their deep voice and wide stubbly chin – is still fit, strong and healthy *despite* the chronic suppression of their immune system, then they must have a very powerful immune system in the first place. However, at the same time that those external signs of high testosterone may predict genetic benefits for any potential future offspring – in terms of being strong, attractive and having a strong immune system – they also predict certain disadvantages. High-testosterone men are likely to be more virile, impulsive and opportunistic relative to men with lower circulating testosterone, making them a poor choice for a long-term partnership.

For many thousands of years this was a vitally important consideration for our ancestors in terms of the ultimate survival prospects for any child conceived in a one-night stand. As the choice of sexual partner has stark implications for the likelihood of a person's genes being passed on through successive generations, instinctive predictions about the likelihood of a prospective lover sticking around to provide support in the rearing of any offspring is thought to have become factored in to the complex equation of female sexual attraction towards men.

Put this all together and it predicts the following optimal breeding strategy. The elevated attraction towards men whose physical features indicate lower testosterone – rounder, friendlier faces, for example – for the majority of each month, suggests that a long-term partnership will often be pursued with the archetypal nice guy: less virile, so more likely to be faithful. The increased attraction towards more masculine features – broad, stubbly jaw, athletic physique and so on – during the fertile few days of each month may encourage the occasional spontaneous sexual liaison with an archetypal stud: higher quality genes, but lower suitability as a long-term partner. From a stark, cold-hearted, biological perspective this would give the woman in question the best of both worlds: a reliable, long-term partner and the odd 'cuckoo' child[*] here and there with particularly strong genes that bears a striking resemblance to the handsome young gardener or handyman from down the lane.

Current estimates indicate that in Western Europe 1 to 2 per cent of men are raising a child that is not their own. Although odds of between 1 in 100 and 1 in 50 are much lower than *The Jeremy Kyle Show* might have led you to believe, it is not a negligible figure. While cheating on a partner is typically considered a predominantly male issue, recent estimates of the percentage of women who have ever

---

[*] Cuckoos routinely lay eggs in other birds' nests, leaving a completely different species to do all the chick-rearing.

committed adultery varies from 15 per cent to 50 per cent (not every sex act results in conception, of course). According to Dante such adulteresses, including famous ones like Cleopatra and Helen of Troy, would find themselves blown around by a blustery wind for all eternity, a pretty tame punishment by his standards. Tales of male adultery are still to come, but first we are going to dip into a scientific theory that attempts to account for how lust fits in with the intimately related, yet often competing, drives of romantic love and long-term commitment.

Triad

Biological anthropologist Helen Fisher has done a fantastic job in her efforts to simplify perspectives on the confusing intersection between sex, romantic love and long-term bonding. Her theory, which she developed based on early research conducted with Prof Arthur Aron of the State University of New York, describes how these behavioural phenomena are governed by three separate but overlapping brain systems. Each evolved to support a different aspect of the various processes that together help our species proliferate and thrive.

She notes that lust – driven primarily by sex hormones – is often relatively indiscriminate and short-sighted in terms of who is selected as a sexual partner and that the urge can often be successfully dealt with in just a few frantic minutes. The basic fundamental purpose it seems to serve is to ensure that we pass our genes on, by hook or by crook. Romantic love occurs much less frequently, but lasts considerably longer, with surveys investigating the matter concluding that the average duration ranges from 8 to 18 months. Love is considerably more selective than lust, inspiring us to synchronise our lives with a specially chosen person deemed to be superior to all the others. Finally, long-term commitment, which gradually takes over as the intensive romantic love phase recedes, is thought to be driven primarily by the neuropeptides oxytocin and vasopressin. This stage seems to confuse modern humans the most, but it serves the purpose of enabling couples to stay together for long enough to fulfil their parenting duties. As mentioned in the introduction this is a much longer-term project for humans than for any other primate. Looking at this phase purely from the perspective of the survival of our genes, long-term commitment provides a long-lasting platform of support which gives rise to major benefits. The offspring are more likely to fulfil their own potential and this in turn improves their prospects of passing on their genes to the next generation. The idea is that the support of two parents over many decades improves the children's prospects of developing into adults able to secure strong, healthy, supportive partners of their own. This logic can be extended even further in our modern era if the grandparents choose to provide support with childcare (another project easier to fulfil as a pair) to help the third generation fulfil *their* potential,* loading the dice for a favourable outcome when it comes to seeing one's genes passed onto the great-grandchildren.

Despite being tightly interwoven, these three systems of lust, romantic love and long-term commitment can nonetheless operate relatively independently. This may explain some of the bizarre situations people find themselves in when it comes to episodes of sex, love and long-term bonding over the course of a lifetime. A person can find themselves wanting to have sex with someone they are neither in love with, nor have any long-term interest in. They can find themselves falling in love with someone they are not particularly sexually attracted to, and with whom they do not have any kind of committed long-term relationship. And they can form deep, long-term social bonds with people to whom they are not sexually attracted, and towards whom they have no romantic feelings. Hence, bizarre combinations of libido, love and long-term commitment can form. A person may feel intense lust towards a co-worker and fall head-over-heels in love with their

---

* Helen Fisher, to my knowledge, never mentioned this part. It's just the logical extension to her theory.

favourite movie star, all while being in a fully committed long-term relationship with someone else entirely.

Out of control

When it comes to the independent nature of lust, love and long-term bonding pulling people in different directions, rather than all settling neatly on a unique individual, men are notorious for being the worst offenders when it comes to adultery. Recent genetic research has suggested that Genghis Khan, supreme ruler of the Mongol Empire – which by the year 1225 stretched the entire width of Asia from the Caspian Sea to the Sea of Japan – now has around 12 million direct living descendants. It seems fair to presume he had sex on the brain. For a relatively modern-day example of a prolific sexual appetite we need look no further than Cuba. In an interview for a documentary, an aide to Fidel Castro estimated that the former revolutionary leader had had sex with 35,000 different women: 'He slept with at least two women a day for more than four decades – one for lunch and one for supper.' That is an awful lot of adultery.

Gossip columns of the tabloid media love to document the alleged 'sex addictions' of today's celebrities. Actor Michael Douglas's tales of sexual conquest brought the concept of being addicted to, rather than just highly motivated to pursue, sexual escapades into the public forum. A short while later, Tiger Woods's highly publicised extra-marital affairs reinforced the concept that 'sex addiction' might be a medical condition rather than merely a moral weakness. By the time Harvey Weinstein started trying to blame his conduct on sex addiction, the term may have become so familiar that it had the ring of a genuine psychiatric condition, but in reality the jury is still out. An addiction to sex, pornography and combinations thereof have been considered for inclusion in the DSM over the years but, at the time of writing, 'sex addiction' still has yet to be recognised as a genuine psychiatric condition. So, for the time being at least, philandering men can't use it as a *bona fide* excuse for their poor decision-making.

The sexual arousal they feel may be involuntary and beyond their control. Choosing to act on that sexual arousal is another matter entirely.

The best currently available scientific research into a condition that approximates to what people typically think of as sex addiction – an obsession with sex that damages their psychological wellbeing and ability to live a normal productive life – is Compulsive Sexual Behaviour (CSB). A growing body of research has attempted to establish what, if anything, is different in the brains of those who seem incapable of exerting control over their sexual impulses.

Dopamine is a neurotransmitter we encountered in the previous chapter that has long been known to play an important role in sexual arousal in a wide variety of mammalian species. During adolescence there is a well-documented increase in sensitivity to dopamine that is often cited in scientific explanations for teenagers' enhanced appetite for high-risk behaviours. This is a vital part of the process that sends the adolescent appetite for sex into overdrive. The trouble is, dopamine is involved in so many different brain processes that, in order to be sure it plays a role in out-of-control sexual behaviours, some cunning experimental manipulations are required.

In the hunt for science that is relevant to understanding what makes lust spiral from impulsiveness into compulsiveness,* there are several interesting avenues to pursue. One surprising source of insight comes from people being treated for Parkinson's disease. This is an illness in which damage to dopamine neurons deep inside the brain causes difficulties with movement. The characteristic rhythmic hand tremor, for example, makes it hard to perform simple day-to-day activities like drinking a cup of tea without spilling it. Difficulty initiating voluntary movements eventually leads to a shuffling

---

* Impulsiveness describes the temptation to do something because it feels good; compulsiveness describes the urge to do something no matter whether it makes you feel good, bad or indifferent.

walking style rather than their usual purposeful strides. When Parkinson's sufferers are given dopamine-boosting drug therapies, it helps them to regain control over their voluntary movements, but in 3.5 to 7 per cent of cases this is accompanied by an undesirable side effect: hypersexuality.

The small proportion of patients affected in this way will typically pester their partners incessantly for sex. They start to show an increased interest in pornography and masturbate frequently. In many cases this libidinous surge leads to visiting prostitutes, even in cases where this would previously have been unthinkable. Such unsavoury behaviours often lead to divorce, damaged reputations and even the occasional brush with the law. This phenomenon has led to an excess of dopamine being considered as a likely cause of hyperactive expressions of sexuality in other conditions too.

In the general population, rates of CSB range between 3 and 6 per cent. The cause of this perpetually elevated interest in sex could be accounted for by a stronger than usual libido, a weaker than normal capacity for self-regulation, or both. Functional MRI studies comparing the brain activations of people, usually men, exhibiting the characteristic features of CSB with those of non-sex-obsessed, healthy volunteers reveal significantly elevated responses to pornographic stimuli in three key structures: the ventral striatum, the amygdala and the dorsal anterior cingulate cortex (dACC).

The ventral striatum contains the nucleus accumbens (which we first met in Chapter 3, p. 57), a key hub in the reward pathway implicated by countless brain imaging studies in generating feelings of pleasure and governing vital processes involved in decision-making. This dovetails nicely with the observation that dopamine-enhancing drugs can trigger hypersexuality in patients, as dopamine is well known to be the main neurotransmitter used in the synapses of this particular pathway.

The amygdala is involved in amplifying all sorts of different emotional responses, not just negative ones associated with detecting threats for which it is famed. It has many sub-compartments, each involved in many different emotional experiences, positive ones included. The enhanced response to sexual images in the CSB patients' amygdala has been interpreted as reflecting an exaggerated positive emotional response to erotic images.

We have also encountered the dACC before (see Chapter 2, p. 46) in terms of its involvement in painful experiences – whether physical or social in nature – and in the context of conflict. It was also the most consistently activated part of the Sexual Response Network in a meta-analysis of 58 separate MRI studies investigating the brain's responses to erotic stimulation. One possible explanation for its involvement here revolves around the conflict arising when a person in the MRI scanner becomes sexually aroused by the images they are looking at, while being under strict instructions not to move! Any movement during an MRI scan corrupts the brain data and so one of the most over-emphasised instructions given to volunteers participating in all studies is to keep still. Under normal circumstances, when somebody with CSB looks at pornography they will usually do so in the context of touching themselves. The dACC activity in this study, to my mind at least, almost certainly reflects the battle to resist this temptation, which is likely to be tougher for CSB sufferers than for non-CSB people.

The dynamics of the dACC activations were scrutinised more closely in this study, and it was revealed that they diminished more quickly in CSB people than others when repeatedly exposed to the same erotic images. This may indicate that CSB people get bored with each erotic clip faster than the controls, perhaps explaining their compulsion to seek out novel pornographic material.

Together these observations argue that people with CSB clearly have an exaggerated positive drive towards erotic stimuli than others, helping to account for the tendency for sexual thoughts to intrude with great frequency into their daily lives. What more can we learn about the difficulties CSB people have exerting self-control over their sexual impulses?

Structural MRI studies have tried to understand whether the brains of people with CSB are physically, as well as functionally, different from those whose sexual appetites fall into the normal range. When 23 CSB brains were compared to those of 69 healthy volunteers, the left amygdala was found on average to be significantly larger in the CSB brains. A separate study investigating the functional connectivity of different brain areas at rest observed that the left amygdala and dorsolateral prefrontal cortex (dlPFC) had a reduced capacity for influencing each other in CSB brains compared to non-CSB brains. Critically, the dlPFC area in question is often associated with exerting conscious control over all sorts of impulsive behaviours, perhaps accounting for the difficulties CSB people have in this regard. As well as exhibiting a more powerful emotional response to sexually stimulating images, CSB brains also show the hallmarks of a reduced capacity to suppress libidinous feelings.

A recent study with Parkinson's patients known to be susceptible to the hypersexuality side effect presented a unique opportunity to test out the hypothesis that elevated dopamine might be involved in triggering CSB-like brain activations. This MRI study compared the brain activations of the same Parkinson's patients when they were on or off their medication, enabling their brains' responses to erotic material when they were and were not experiencing the side effects of hypersexuality. This study found that the ventral striatum and dACC were more active in the hypersexuality-prone Parkinson's patients when they were on versus off their medication; the same areas identified in the CSB patients. This strongly implicates elevated dopamine in the ventral striatum as a likely cause of hypersexual behaviour.

The irresistible compulsion to over-indulge in sexually stimulating behaviour is not limited to adults. The ubiquitous availability of internet pornography – freely accessible, anytime, anywhere there is a smartphone, tablet or desktop computer – is starting to have a major impact on adolescents too.

Internet porn addiction

In this, the final section of this chapter, we will explore the potential for pornography to cause harm and thus qualify as a sin of lust from two perspectives: the impact of over-consumption on brain function and its effect on cultural norms.

What happens when teenage boys over-consume pornography has perhaps been best summarised by the head of the Italian Society of Andrology and Sexual Medicine, Dr Carlo Foresta. Commenting on the results of a huge survey investigating the use of pornography and the real-life sexual experiences of adolescent boys, he outlined the progression towards sexual dysfunction that is being observed with increasing frequency. To start with, porn sites gradually begin to elicit less sexual arousal than usual; then it develops into a general reduction in libido and can eventually result in the inability to get an erection at all.

Binge-watching pornography induces these behavioural changes by altering the responsiveness of the ventral striatum, not just to sexually explicit materials, but to any rewarding stimulus. To properly understand how the responsiveness of the ventral striatum becomes compromised we first need to take a step back and look at how it usually responds.

Brain imaging studies have demonstrated that the responses of the ventral striatum are more nuanced in humans than in other mammals. If a person in the scanner views an attractive face, a stronger activation is induced in the ventral striatum than that elicited by a less attractive face, reflecting the greater appeal of the former over the latter. A smiling facial expression induces a stronger 'predicted reward' activation in the ventral striatum than the same face presented with a neutral facial expression.* If the smiling face happened to be attached to an

---

* The reward pathway is a brain system that gives us an intuition regarding the best decision in any situation requiring us to choose one course of action over another. It does this by generating predictions about how each choice might turn out later on, on the basis of how similar decisions have turned out in the past. Usually the decisions we make, all other things being equal, are governed by

attractive naked body (of the preferred gender), then the ventral striatum would generate an even stronger response, reflecting a further enhancement of its predicted reward value. These differences in activation strength within the ventral striatum underlie the general preference for a smiling attractive naked version over the smiling attractive version, and for both of these over the unsmiling version. It is these preferences, manifested in the size of responses in the ventral striatum, that steer our decisions.

Neurons originating in the ventral striatum send projections into the medial orbitofrontal cortex (mOFC). The mOFC was originally suspected to be involved in decision-making because people with brain damage affecting this area often have great difficulty making choices. They tend to go round and round in circles, without being able to make a final call, because the mOFC enables all the predicted reward values coming out of the ventral striatum to be considered in the light of other relevant factors (more on this in the following chapter, p. 115). These include current priorities, recent events, available time, prevailing mood, plans for later in the day, what's going on in the immediate environment, and so on. The ventral striatum and mOFC help us to work out the relative value of each choice of food, erotic film clip, etc., in light of prevailing circumstances *and* reach a final decision regarding which option is most likely to deliver the greatest reward and feelings of pleasure (see Figure 5).

The latest scientific papers to lay out the evidence relating to pornography addiction account for the behavioural changes observed in those who overconsume it by borrowing from the drug addiction and internet addiction literature. The large surges of dopamine triggered on a daily basis in response to regular exposure to explicit hardcore sex scenes is thought to induce regulatory mechanisms that try to

---

whichever option induces the greatest activation in the ventral striatum, a brain signal traditionally referred to in the neuroscience literature as its 'predicted reward value'.

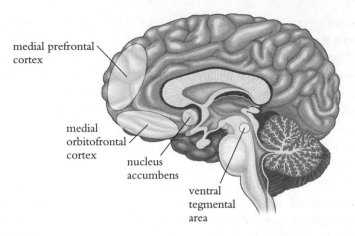

medial prefrontal cortex

medial orbitofrontal cortex

nucleus accumbens

ventral tegmental area

Figure 5 Part of the reward pathway called the nucleus accumbens, which resides in the ventral striatum, assigns a predicted reward value to any potentially rewarding stimuli. The part of the medial prefrontal cortex sitting above the eye orbits, known as the medial orbitofrontal cortex, helps us to make choices by evaluating these predictions in light of other relevant contextual information.

rebalance the system. An opiate peptide called dynorphin is released to suppress dopamine release in the overstimulated reward pathway. This reduces the impact of dopamine in the reward system, diminishing the potency of responses to previously rewarding stimuli, resulting in a blunted experience of pleasure overall. As well as reducing the pleasures derived from non-erotic stimuli, it also results in the reward pathway building up a tolerance to erotic images; or in the words of Dr Carlo Foresta: 'It starts with lower reactions to porn sites'. Pornography that previously delivered the desired feelings of satisfaction becomes ineffective at generating and maintaining sexual arousal, so the porn watcher typically starts to click through the various available categories until they find something that 'works'. For most it will involve something more unusual or shocking, to compensate for the blunting of their pleasure response. Genres of pornography deemed to be distasteful when first encountered may eventually become the only material that turns them on.

Over the course of many months of daily exposure to porn, teens and adults alike are inadvertently training their brains to exclusively produce sexual responses to supernormal stimuli only. 'Supernormal' means bigger, brighter and more shocking than those normally encountered in real life. This might involve footage of men with huge penises, women with huge bums and breasts performing erotic practices that, although par for the course in pornography, are unlikely to be encountered in the course of most people's everyday life. Although, as we will see shortly, early evidence suggests that attitudes seem to be changing in this regard.

This phenomenon has been likened to the work of Nikolaas Tinbergen, who won a Nobel Prize for his work with herring gulls. His birds also learned to prefer supernormal artificial stimuli over and above the real thing. His research involved creating artificial eggs that were larger or much more colourful than the birds' own eggs. The gulls often chose to sit on the supersized or vividly coloured eggs, rather than the real ones that actually contained their offspring. This was the first demonstration of the development of a preference for supernormal, artificial options over the natural biological versions.

The main concern is that both the internet porn addicts and Professor Tinbergen's birds end up developing a preference for the fake over the real. The birds attempt to hatch eggs made of plaster of Paris meant that their abandoned eggs ended up not hatching. The problem posed to the internet porn addict is that it displaces the time, effort and inclination that they could be investing in their real sex life and, even when they do partake, their porn habit can cause havoc with their ability to perform between the sheets. Such a long term outcome, of what might otherwise seem a harmless bit of fun, has clear potential to have a negative impact on their ability to form a meaningful partnership – driving people apart rather than bringing them together. Sex plays a vital role in developing intimacy in a partnership and long-term partnerships offer much more than just sex. It is in everyone's best interests that people keep an eye on how much pornography they consume and simply be careful not to let their fondness for erotica get out of hand.

No sex please, we're British

For much of the twentieth century we British were famous for our ultra-conservative attitudes towards sex. This appears to have become a thing of the past. Brits currently enjoy the dubious distinction of having the most liberal attitudes to sex of all the Organisation for Economic Cooperation and Development (OECD) nations. According to survey responses to the Sociosexual Orientation Inventory of sexual attitudes from 14,000 people across 48 different countries, from Argentina to Zimbabwe, the UK came top of the 35 OECD nations. The UK was followed by Germany, the Netherlands, the Czech Republic and then Australia. (Including the non-OECD countries, Finland topped the list overall.)

Explaining this shift in our attitudes to sex is not straightforward, but the invention of the condom and other forms of contraception has certainly played a role. In terms of the potential harms caused by casual sex, barrier-method contraception comes with the twin benefits of vastly reducing the likelihood of unplanned pregnancy and contracting a sexually transmitted infection. At the same time, reductions in infection risk and inconvenient conception only make casual sexual encounters seem more appealing. Another part of the equation is the rise of freely available pornography.

Before the internet, the availability of pornography was relatively restricted. Horny teenagers had to summon the courage to pick up a magazine from the top shelf of the local newsagent or walk through the doors of a sex shop. Now they can pull out their smartphones and instantly access a full A–Z of porn films, all the way from the relative innocence of softcore 1970s pornography, right up to the latest hardcore sado-masochistic, pseudo-rape scenes – all completely unrestricted and free. Systematic exploration of each 'category' quickly provides a good idea of the depth and breadth of what is on offer from each genre. Those who choose to educate themselves in this regard often find themselves shocked to realise how many freely available films feature scenes of aggression, victimisation and sometimes violence, with no restrictions whatsoever to prevent underage access.

The impact on pre-pubescent children who, purely out of curiosity, end up browsing the full spectrum of human sexual practices online, often before they have had a chance to experiment themselves, is concerning. In the absence of any personal experience of what sex is really like to help contextualise what they view, it is hard to see how their fledgling concepts of what sex *is* could avoid being fundamentally altered. Compared to the tamer introduction to the forbidden world of adult sexual behaviour of previous generations, an acceptance of whatever extreme erotic practices they regularly encounter online as normal is surely inevitable. Indeed, there is mounting evidence to suggest that attitudes to sex among young people in the UK and beyond have dramatically shifted over the past 50 years. While some of these changes have been liberating, freeing us from traditionally conservative sexual attitudes, other aspects are proving to be distinctly unsettling.

One large survey of the sexual behaviours of adolescent boys between the ages of 14 and 17 across five European countries concluded that a regular diet of pornography is associated with an increased incidence of sexual coercion and victimisation, increased acceptance of aggressively themed sexual activities as normal and reduced condom use. Humans are accomplished copycats. We learn best from the example of other people. As mentioned in Chapter 1 (p. 12), to learn a new skill primates like us typically observe the actions of others and then try to reproduce the same movements with our own bodies. Indeed, we have a specialised set of brain cells, known as mirror neurons, which are thought to facilitate these fundamental processes of mimicry. It is no wonder that intensive exposure to pornography leads to fantasies about recreating those same sexual behaviours through the instinctive urge to copy other people – our brains are built to do this. We set goals according to what we see others do.

Evidence to support this concept comes from another recent survey of sexual practices. This time the participants were 393 16-year-old Swedish schoolgirls. One of the main findings was that, while 30 per cent of regular porn watchers had tried anal sex, the figure was 15 per cent for the girls who did not regularly watch porn. It's all too easy to be distracted by the implication that watching pornography doubles the likelihood that the average Swedish girl will have experienced anal sex by the age of 16. Another way of looking at these findings is to focus on the 15 per cent who do not regularly watch porn. That 3 out of every 20 girls who don't watch porn have tried anal sex at such a young age seems surprisingly high. Might this suggest that pornography has an impact on attitudes to sex, whether or not an individual is exposed to it personally? In other words, even if a person does not watch porn themselves, if everyone else in their social group does, then their attitudes to what sexual practices are and are not acceptable may still be shaped by the general consensus.

The impact of mass consumption of pornography on the general consensus within a culture is sometimes referred to as 'pornification'. In some parts of the world there is evidence that this may be causing relationship problems even among adults. Evidence is accumulating to suggest that excessive consumption of online porn is breeding a culture of acceptance of stereotypical male dominance and aggressive sexual practices. A study of over 50 women seeking to extract themselves from unhealthy relationships in rural Ohio, under circumstances where they felt victimised by their partner's intimate violence, cited the pornification of culture as a major contributing factor. With so many men immersed daily in free online sex films, what constitutes 'normal' and acceptable treatment of women is being warped to the extent that they are increasingly being viewed as sex objects.

Jerry Springer's final words...

In terms of the potential to cause harm, pornography is neither completely good nor completely bad. As with many phenomena there are relatively harmless aspects of pornography as well as the very harmful. The totally unrestricted, instant accessibility of free online pornography, and particularly the hardcore material, is starting to prove problematic. Excessive use of pornography is impacting on healthy sexual behaviours. Regularly encountering footage featuring themes of male domination and female victimisation seems to be warping attitudes towards what constitutes acceptable practices in a way that is causing serious harm. Another unfortunate influence of pornification is the omission of behaviours that are strongly associated with a healthy sex life, but rarely make the cut in pornography.

The tactile sensations generated through the panoply of intimate behaviours involved in the sex act are extremely powerful in cementing and reinforcing the most intimate of social bonds between humans. Touching, stroking, caressing, hugging and kissing – all these activities induce the release of powerful neuropeptides that are fundamental to creating feelings of trust, comfort, safety and contentment between two human beings. One of these – oxytocin – is fundamentally involved in all sorts of social bonding. It is essential to the bond formed between mother and child. * It also cements the bonds between unrelated people involved in an intimate relationship too. In fact, oxytocin is released into the bloodstream by the pituitary gland and into the reward pathway by neurons projecting out of the hypothalamus whenever physical affection is shared between any pair of trusted individuals, whether friends, peers or relatives. Even the psychological support we receive from others impacts on our oxytocin levels. The most powerful source of physical and psychological reassurance comes from our lovers. Most of the pornography that vast numbers of people are viewing on a daily basis, and thereby fundamentally influencing collective perceptions of what is 'normal', places the emphasis squarely

---

* It triggers the process of labour and then is involved in releasing the milk from the breast in response to suckling. It is also fundamental to producing feelings of safety and security, playing a huge role in social bonding throughout life.

on the stimulation of the erogenous zones. With such a strong focus on the dopamine high of penetrative sex and orgasm, porn watchers have a tendency to overlook the importance of more affectionate behaviours that result in neuropeptide release and strengthened social bonds. In pornography the tender caresses involved in the act of sex, the bit that usually comes under the heading of foreplay, is either omitted or fast-forwarded through. Yet this is the part that is fundamental to the psychological benefits of a healthy sex life. When it comes to the virtuous influence of libido – a force that brings people closer together rather than pushing them apart – oxytocin is second only to its molecular cousin vasopressin. This particular neuropeptide is usually considered in the context of monogamy thanks to a large body of research investigating the love life of voles. While the prairie vole is monogamous, mating for life with whichever prairie vole they first have sex with, a closely related species is polygamous, mating with a different partner each breeding season. Inject vasopressin into the brain of the polygamous type and they enter into a monogamous partnership with the animal they first breed with. This research is usually discussed in terms of the debate over whether humans are fundamentally monogamous or polygamous. Considering the role vasopressin could play in loyalty this may be a more interesting angle to consider. The reason so many different religions forbid adultery is surely that once loyalty is betrayed and trust is broken, it can never really, truly, be fully recovered. My hunch is that the neuropeptides are fundamental to loyalty. We are born into the world alone and ultimately we depart this world alone. In between these two inevitable life events, our quality of life can be vastly improved if we manage to connect ourselves with an InGroup that makes us feel accepted and valued. Best of all, if we can find ourselves a specially chosen individual with whom to cooperate on a more intimate level, we can take on the world as a dedicated partnership; a much less daunting approach than to take on the world going solo.

Lifelong partnerships may seem rare in this day and age, but I would argue this is less about whether it is in our nature to be monogamous or polygamous* and much more to do with the warping of expectations. We've seen how porn might have contributed to this over the past few decades, but films, novels and love songs have been filling our heads with nonsense for centuries. Add modern technology into the mix and no wonder sex, love and long-term relationships all seem to be so transient and disposable these days. People can get divorced one week and start dating the next, simply by signing up to a smartphone app specifically designed to make finding potential dates as easy as swiping right. People looking for the 'perfect partner' and a 'love that lasts forever' have developed cultural expectations that place them on a collision course with reality. What is a more achievable goal is to use the knowledge that kind words and affectionate actions can induce the release of oxytocin and vasopressin in the recipient's brain. These substances actively promote trust, perhaps even loyalty, which together are the enduring characteristics of every successful long-term relationship. This knowledge places the reinforcement of social bonds under our control. People will always find themselves feeling sexually aroused by attractive strangers. Sexual arousal, after all, is not under conscious control whatever your sexual orientation, but acting on these urges is. Rarely are the passing pleasures of illicit sexual dalliances worth the penalties of betrayal when infidelity is ultimately revealed. Forgoing the fleeting excitement of dopamine releases associated with adulterous affairs, instead doing the simple things that reinforce mutual trust and feelings of security, continuously strengthens rather than erodes the bond between a couple and leads to far greater benefits in the long run. Yes – it is hard work, as all worthwhile pursuits in life tend to be, but when it comes to the positive impacts of having one person in your life that you can completely rely on, it's surely worth all the effort.

---

* The biological take on this is that, compared to other monogamous and polygamous primates, our features are intermediate between the two: we are both and neither. For more on this try *Behave: The Biology of Humans at our Best and Worst* by Robert Sapolsky.

If Pride is the mother of the deadly sins, then Gluttony and Lust are the impulsive twins in this despicable family of seven. As we've seen, from the perspective of neuroscience, these twins have a serious issue with controlling their urges. While they can be voracious in their appetites for food and sex respectively, the next deadly sin has the opposite problem. Sloth can't even be bothered to get out of bed in the morning.

CHAPTER FIVE

Sloth

Idleness and lack of occupation tend—nay are dragged—towards evil

Hippocrates

Three-toed sloths spend the vast majority of their lives upside-down. They can be found throughout Central and South America, hanging from the branches of trees by specially adapted, elongated claws, spending between 15 and 20 hours per day sound asleep. Even their digestion is lazy: it takes a full fortnight for them to digest a single meal. In their defence, in addition to shoots and fruits, their diet consists of toxic leaves that require multiple stomachs to break them down safely. Not only do sloths have the slowest digestion of any mammal, but when they do move, they do so at a snail's pace. Descending from the trees once a week to defecate, they spend most of the rest of their time in the canopy completely motionless – so much so that their fur is home to a menagerie of other creatures, including moths, beetles, fungi and algae. The latter give their coat a greenish tinge, helping them to blend into the foliage. The combination of motionlessness and symbiotic camouflage helps to keep them safely hidden from predators.

Are sloths lazy? Well, it really depends on your frame of reference. The sloth's behaviour fits perfectly the repertoire of skills necessary for sloth survival. Their entire biology evolved to support a leisurely pace of life. Their limbs are designed for it. Their digestion is designed for it. It's a prerequisite for success in the ecological niche in which they evolved.

The same cannot be said for humans. Our biology evolved under very different environmental pressures. Our bodies are adapted for movement. Our hearts, muscles, bones and brains need to be exercised on a regular basis to stay in good repair.

You could be forgiven for having no concept of this unassailable fact given our increasing reliance on labour-saving devices. Whether it's using delivery services to save a 10-minute walk to the local take-away, driving to a location a few hundred metres down the road or taking a lift to reach the first floor of a building, many of us simply cannot resist the temptation to take a shortcut to save time. That said, even the laziest of humans can't compete with a real sloth; but many give it their best shot.

Take Paul Railton, for example. Paul, from County Durham in the north of England, decided to take his dog for a walk in the countryside one fine day in 2010. Evidently feeling acutely lazy, he contemplated how to achieve this goal with the minimum possible expenditure of energy. His dubious stroke of genius involved holding his pet lurcher's lead through the open window of his Nissan Navara so that he could walk the dog down a narrow country road without even having to set foot outside. An appalled cyclist who happened to be passing at the time witnessed the dog being dragged along beside the car and promptly reported the incident to the police. Mr Railton ended up in court, where he pleaded guilty to a charge of not being in proper control of his vehicle. The witness's testimony described how he was 'hanging onto the dog's lead through the driver's window, approaching a blind summit'. He was fined £65, plus court charges, and banned from driving for six months. Mr Railton, unemployed at the time, was reportedly 'not bothered' by the driving ban, explaining: 'I might save myself some money not having a car.' Every cloud...

The available evidence suggests that all sorts of creatures usually opt for whichever course of action minimises the amount of effort required of them. We're not the only species that likes a short cut. That said, under certain circumstances, we can be perfectly happy to do work even in the absence of any material return to reward our efforts. What makes the critical difference is whether we do the work in the context of a 'social contract' – where all we stand to earn is gratitude – or a 'financial contract' – where the rewards are more tangible. Performing a menial task, litter picking in a local park for example, we tend to find the experience much more satisfying when it is done out of the goodness of our own hearts as opposed to doing exactly the same work for minimum wage. When working for remuneration, the motivation to put in the effort is extrinsic – inspired by the goal of getting something that we want from the outside world, i.e. cash. Intrinsic motivation, on the other hand, describes a willingness to work that derives from the satisfaction of seeing a worthwhile job through to completion and helping others. When the motivation to work is purely extrinsic it usually has a negative impact on a person's willingness to put in any extra effort in the absence of an additional incentive; this is not the case with intrinsic motivation. Intrinsic motivation can be seen in action in people giving up their time freely for charity or volunteer work and those investing tremendous energy in their hobbies. Sometimes the journey *is* the destination.

Given the choice between receiving a small sum of money in return for a few hours spent performing a relatively straightforward task, or receiving the same sum of money for no effort whatsoever – the pragmatic choice seems clear. There is no point expending energy for no reason. From the perspective of biological efficiency, we should surely always try to perform tasks with the minimum of effort, so long as it results in an acceptable outcome – right?

Wrong. It may seem strange, but there is even research to suggest that we gain more pleasure when we've had to put in more rather than less effort to earn a given reward. Counter-intuitive as it may be, the seemingly pragmatic approach of conserving energy wherever possible is not only less satisfying but, as we will see below, can even be dire news for our health. Avoiding exertion at all costs reduces our wellbeing overall. Unfortunately, many people go through life without learning that the satisfaction of a job well done improves quality of life more effectively than the seemingly logical approach of reducing effort wherever possible.

It goes even further than that. Humans, unlike the sloth, simply didn't evolve to hang around all day. For evidence to support this view you need look no further than your own foot.* Compared to our non-human primate cousins, it is clearly specialised for long-distance running. For thousands of years our ancestors supplemented their diets by chasing down huge meaty animals until they more or less collapsed with exhaustion. If the very morphology of our bodies evolved to make us good at running, and working for our rewards is more satisfying than sitting around waiting for them to fall into our laps, then why is it that some people love to keep active while others do everything in their power to avoid exerting themselves? Why do gym bunnies feel motivated to work out at every available opportunity, while couch potatoes spend as much time as possible lazing around at home in their slippers?

In this chapter, we'll explore the roles of habit and opportunity in influencing the degree to which different people keep active. We'll examine what the sin of sloth meant in ancient times and how it manifests itself today. And, of course, we'll meet the brain areas that fundamentally govern our motivation levels.

Historical perspectives

When caught in the grip of most of the deadly sins people usually find themselves unable to resist the temptation to do something that they know they shouldn't. Sloth immediately differentiates itself from all the other capital vices by residing right at the opposite end of the spectrum. It comprises the desire to slack off when we know we should be doing something useful. It is all about ducking our responsibilities. The temptation to do absolutely nothing is sometimes the very vice that we try, and fail, to resist.

Jacques Collin de Plancy's *Dictionnaire Infernal,* first published in 1818, described Belphegor as the demon charged with the responsibility for those falling foul of the sin of sloth. Art featuring Belphegor typically depicts him sitting on the

---

* There's a great podcast on this topic, highly recommended: www. freakonomics.com/podcast/shoes/

porcelain throne. Sitting on the toilet is, apparently, the perfect posture for anyone seeking to win his favour, according to ancient lore. Belphegor started out by tempting lazy people to part with their hard-earned cash in return for exciting and innovative madcap inventions.

Many of the world's most popular religions are highly critical of those who try to keep their expenditure of energy to an absolute minimum at all times. If you think about it, no religion that tolerated excessive sloth could possibly thrive. Banishing apathy from its followers is a vital part of ensuring any religion's survival. Religions generally require some form of daily, or at least weekly, ritual. If they want to have a strong influence in their followers' lives they must have the opportunity to provide regular reminders of the religion's core messages and entrain certain habits, all of which might sound like far too much effort for those preferring the path of perpetual laziness. If the congregation didn't bother turning up to temple, synagogue, church or mosque each week, how else would the religion in question be able to make a meaningful impact on the fate of their souls?

Even Buddhism, arguably one of the more tolerant belief systems, is damning of sloth. The sanskrit dictionary translates *kausīdya* as 'sloth' or 'indolence' and it is one of the five obstacles to meditation and so considered a serious hindrance to achieving transcendence. Buddhism warns against the temptation to give in to the lure of lying down, stretching out and indulging in extended periods of unproductive inertia. The Islamic equivalent is *kasal*. The requirements for Muslims to pray five times per day and fast during Ramadan are both powerful influences for promoting the eradication of the universal human tendency towards sloth through the entrainment of virtuous habits.

From the Christian perspective, Evagrius of Pontus went as far as to describe sloth* as 'the most burdensome of all' the eight evil thoughts or *logismoi* that he assembled to guide the

---

* Or *acedia* as it was known in the late fourth century.

pious. When it came to temptations likely to lure people away from their daily spiritual duties, sloth was presumably a particularly troublesome source of distraction for solitary monks holed up in the sweltering heat of the desert.

Interestingly, when St Gregory the Great first assembled his seven deadly sins, he opted for the term *tristitia* rather than sloth. This describes a more melancholy form of habitual disinclination to perform one's duties, evoked more through sadness or despair than the absence of emotion implied by sloth. Given the negative impact of clinical depression on a person's motivation levels, this could constitute the identification of apathy as a symptom of depression centuries before psychology came onto the scene. By the time of St Thomas Aquinas the term sloth was substituted for *tristitia*, but it was still described in terms of a 'sorrow about spiritual good'.

As the centuries rolled by the definition of sloth started to shed its ecclesiastical connotations. Shirking work, family or community duties, rather than spiritual idleness, is the anti-social temptation modern society tends to frown upon. And as twenty-first-century living has us penned in on all sides by labour-saving devices and services, opportunities for sloth abound like never before. Gone are the days when we had to graze our knuckles on the washboard, peg the washing out on the line and bring it all back in again a few hours later. The modern washer/drier is now at hand for anyone who wants to eliminate all that hassle and at prices most people can afford. Long journeys can now be completed in a few hours on a plane, rather than the weeks or months it used to take on foot or by boat. Automated vehicles now sweep elegantly around factories and warehouses, displacing much of the modern day's muscle into the gym – demoted from serving a vital function to mere aesthetics. Robots of one form or another are becoming increasingly visible, not just outside the home, but inside it too. People have graduated from feeling disinclined to summon the energy to wash and dry the dishes to being reluctant to get off their lazy bums to stack the dishwasher. Before you know it vacuum-cleaning robots like iRobot's 'Roomba' and Dyson's '360 Eye' will have taken over cleaning

duties in most homes. For some, all of these conveniences free
up more time to idly surf the internet or stare at the television,
for others they are nothing short of a life-saver in terms of
enabling already time-pressured individuals to get through an
overwhelmingly packed 'to do' list. Now that these energy
conserving wonders have progressed from the 'drive-thru'
fast-food restaurant to having food delivered to your door at
the tap of a smartphone app, it's a small step to walking a dog
through the open window of a moving car. Worse still, it has
actually reached the point where our obsession with any and
all labour-saving devices and services is actually killing us.

'Lack of exercise as deadly as smoking' screamed headlines
in the summer of 2012. An influential study had just been
published in *The Lancet* – one of the world's oldest and best-
known medical journals – indicating that laziness is causing
millions of avoidable deaths worldwide, each and every year.
Simply stated, if we don't take regular exercise, our health
rapidly declines. According to this study, Britain holds the
ignominious title of Europe's third laziest country when
ranked by the proportion of the population regularly failing to
take enough exercise. With an embarrassingly high 63.3 per
cent of UK adults failing to take the recommended 20 minutes
of moderate exercise per day, only Malta and Serbia have a
greater proportion of adults who simply can't be bothered to
take a brisk daily walk.

We all know deep down that we should exercise. Of course
we do. It's been known to improve health and life expectancy
since 4,000 BC in East Asia and since at least 300 BC in Western
Europe. Yet we still can't summon the energy. A study published
in 2015 monitored more than 300,000 Europeans over an
average period of 12 years, measuring various lifestyle choices.
It concluded that the primary cause of death was inactivity. To
put this into perspective, this is twice the number of people
killed each year by obesity and so, in terms of the threat the
seven deadly sins pose to humanity, sloth is officially more
lethal than gluttony. The major non-communicable diseases
that lead to premature death as a result of sloth are coronary
heart disease (clogged-up blood vessels that supply the

energy-hungry heart muscle), type 2 diabetes, colon and breast cancer. The take-home message is that all these diseases are made considerably more likely by an inactive lifestyle, whether you are obese or not.

Brain Basis of Apathy

You'll recall from the previous chapter (Chapter 4, p. 101) that when people with Parkinson's were given dopamine-boosting drugs to improve their ability to perform smooth fluid movements, some of them developed side effects. As dopamine levels were raised across the whole brain it impacted not just on the movement triggering pathways, but on non-target pathways too, accidentally increasing the patients' motivation to engage in sexual activity and turning a minority into sex pests. These dopamine-boosting Parkinson's treatments can induce other side effects too. In some people, rather than having an impact on their sex drives, it instead produces other powerful compulsions. Some go gambling every day; others go off on extensive shopping sprees, often racking up huge debts in the process. Taken together these side effects clearly suggest that increasing dopamine levels across the whole brain has the potential to dramatically *increase* people's motivation levels.

Damage to the striatum – the main target of dopamine in the brain – on the other hand, usually results in vastly reduced levels of motivation. The word *striatum* itself derives from the Latin word for *grooved*, because this incredibly important chunk of brain meat looks stripy to the naked eye in post-mortem examination. Chop through the brain in a horizontal plane, about level with the bridge of the nose, and just before the knife reaches the very centre of the brain it would pass straight through the corpus striatum, which is located just below the corpus callosum and either side of the thalamus (see Figure 6).*

_____

* The thalamus is the centrally located junction box through which the many millions of neurons residing in the crinkly outer surface of the brain – the cortex – share information with each other and coordinate with the body via the spinal cord.

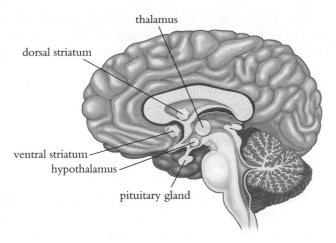

Figure 6 This illustration shows the location of the thalamus, hypothalamus and pituitary gland on a medial view of the human brain. Relative positions of ventral and dorsal striatum are indicated by the dashed circles. The left and right sides of the striatum actually extend right the way around the thalamus. This means that the ventral and dorsal striatum are in fact located deeper than the plane of this particular image, which has been used here for the sake of consistency with the other figures.

The involvement of the striatum in reinforcing important behaviours such as those involved in finding and eating food (see Chapter 3, p. 68) or seeking out and engaging in sexual behaviours (see Chapter 4, p. 101) has already been described. The striatum is also vital for initiating movements and a wide range of other behaviours. When the blood supply to specific parts of the striatum is cut off – in other words, the person has a stroke – the damage caused can often result in apathy, a lack of motivation. Formally, apathy is described as a 'quantitative reduction in voluntary, goal-driven behaviour' and can be induced by strokes for different reasons according to exactly which part of the striatum has been damaged.

The striatum is usually discussed as a tale of two halves. As we know, the ventral (lower) striatum is densely interconnected with the medial orbitofrontal cortex (mOFC) to form a primary conduit of the reward pathway. Strokes that damage either this lower portion of the striatum or the mOFC interfere with motivation by destroying the person's capacity to evaluate which is the best option given the prevailing conditions, making it almost impossible to choose one course of action over another.

The dorsal (upper) part of the striatum is tightly interconnected with the dorsolateral prefrontal cortex (see Figure 7). If either of these areas are damaged by a stroke, apathy also results, but for slightly different reasons. This time the person has no problem working out which option is best, but they can't take action on the decision because damage to this brain circuitry abolishes the capacity to plan an appropriate sequence of actions to achieve that goal.

Damage to the former set of brain regions results in *emotional-affective* deficits: the person concerned lacks a strong urge to do one thing rather than another. When the latter brain regions are impaired the resulting *cognitive* deficits leave the person unable to figure out how to carry out the desired action. Either way motivation grinds to a halt. To bring the differences to life we'll consider an everyday example of how these pathways work, but first we need to dig a little bit deeper into the characteristic features of the circuitry.

The striatum is merely the puppet-master pulling the strings of a group of interconnected deep brain structures that comprise the rest of the basal ganglia (BG). Painstaking investigations into the mind-bogglingly complex circuit diagrams of this network reveal that the key to grasping how motivation works revolves around the concept of *disinhibition*. Disinhibition is similar to the idea of releasing the handbrake on a car parked on a hill. The action of releasing the handbrake involves removing (dis-) the brakes (-inhibition) that were preventing the wheels from moving. Once the handbrake is released, only then can the car start to roll.

Brain circuits in the BG use interlocking circuits of disinhibition to set neural processes in motion. Chains of neurons each have an inhibitory impact on the next in line. Once a certain threshold is passed at a critical point in the chain, the inhibition is taken away, creating a domino effect

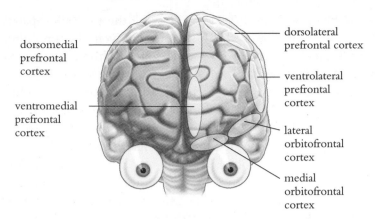

dorsomedial
prefrontal
cortex

ventromedial
prefrontal
cortex

dorsolateral
prefrontal cortex

ventrolateral
prefrontal
cortex

lateral
orbitofrontal
cortex

medial
orbitofrontal
cortex

Figure 7 This illustration shows the different segments of the prefrontal cortex that sit directly behind the forehead: the ventral striatum is densely connected with the medial orbitofrontal cortex and the dorsal striatum with the dorsolateral prefrontal cortex, respectively.

through the rest of the circuit to enable the command to exert its influence. Dopamine plays a crucial role in controlling the interactions between the neurons in this system.

As the BG is effectively an elaborate system of interlocking brakes, it can be helpful to imagine that it is constantly on the verge of triggering all sorts of actions that might be relevant to what you are doing at any given moment. In a highly motivated person the different pathways in this network are constantly vying with each other to get the chance to release the brakes (disinhibition) at strategic points along the network circuitry, to initiate a certain action sequence. In an unmotivated person, lacking the drive to get things done, this brain system may well be chronically underactive.

In defence of laziness
Samuel Johnson, author of the world's most famous early English dictionary, quipped that 'the happiest part of a man's

life is what he passes lying awake in bed in the morning'. In the context of a busy and productive life, this can indeed be not just pleasurable, but perfectly wholesome. A little bit of laziness here and there is a right we should all feel entitled to. It's entirely pragmatic to allow ourselves to step back periodically from the breakneck pace of modern life. People who don't are prone to run themselves ragged, leaving their bodies no alternative than to force a complete shutdown to make the necessary repairs.

One of cortisol's many roles is to suppress the immune system until the cause of stress has been dealt with. Fighting disease-causing agents is an energetically expensive business. Were our bodies to divert energy into the immune system every single time an invading pathogen was detected, we'd never get anything done. On the other hand, if we are constantly rushing around, forever postponing rest, the spikes of cortisol perpetually triggered throughout each and every day lead to stress levels that never subside sufficiently to allow the invading pathogens to be kept in check. Eventually our immune system will be forced to take matters into its own hands, triggering full-blown sickness behaviour to force the issue, leaving us feeling weak, pathetic and utterly incapable of work. Some people only rest if they feel completely wiped out, and the immune system is perfectly capable of actively creating these feelings if absolutely necessary. A much healthier approach is to stop before we get to this stage.

Cancelling social engagements at the last minute in favour of doing absolutely nothing is sometimes the very best thing we can do when we're worn down. Sometimes, when we find ourselves committing this heinous social crime, it's because we can sense that we're coming down with something. We instinctively know that our body will have a better chance of dealing with the lurgy more swiftly if we go straight to bed. This conserves energy that would otherwise be squandered on less important matters and instead would be better invested in fighting off the bug before it overwhelms us. Serial offenders may well find themselves getting a bad reputation for being anti-social, but the occasional bout of 'flaking out' is absolutely fine. Sloth is sometimes sensible.

This is not the only benefit that giving in to a bit of idleness every now and again can offer. There's strong evidence, for example, to support the tradition – once extremely popular throughout the Mediterranean – that a short afternoon nap is not only hugely restorative, but can even enhance creative problem solving.

Our soft spot for sloth is even starting to be exploited in the modern work place. The promise of future opportunities to be lazy, in return for extra effort right now, can be extremely motivating. Pillow days – where a person calls in to work to inform the boss they will be coming in late, usually to get some extra shut-eye – are becoming increasingly popular. What better way to reimburse employees for going the extra mile when a company with limited funds needs to get all hands on deck? In a similar vein, offering staff an additional day's annual holiday can be quite sufficient to entice them into willingly doing overtime when a business really needs it. Many companies now allow staff to give back a portion of their salary in return for extra days of annual leave and a surprisingly large number of employees are willing to accept a reduction in annual income in return for more time off.

So, as with all the deadly sins, a little bit of sloth can be good. It can even be virtuous when the promise of future sloth incentivises us to work harder right now. Under circumstances where we have been overexerting ourselves over lengthy periods of time, taking some hard-earned time out allows weary bodies and brains to recover. This can help us avoid the false economy of constantly trying to work as hard as possible, despite this ultimately being counter-productive in the long run. And that's just as well, because one manifestation of this – sleep deprivation – has been calculated to cost UK businesses £40 billion each year in lost productivity.

Some people just do nothing

Not everybody is so motivated. There are plenty of people in the world who seem perpetually inactive, but not all deserve Belphegor's attentions in the afterlife. When looking for practitioners of sloth, there are several factors that need to be taken into consideration.

Take the unemployed, for example. With no job, they're much less likely to be making a meaningful contribution to their community, unless they pursue the commendable option of working on a voluntary basis. With no earned income, the unemployed are limited in terms of available funds to spend on activities that might enable them to get out and about, to stay positively engaged within the community. The stereotypical long-term unemployed person spends steadily decreasing amounts of time actually looking for work and increasingly focuses on finding inexpensive ways to kill time and boredom. The most cost-effective ways to do this in this day and age are to watch television, play video games, surf the internet and hang around watching the world go by. It looks a lot like sloth and so many people view long-term unemployment as a sign of a poor work ethic – a preference for doing nothing over the concerted effort it takes to get up and go to work. This is rarely the case.

A study conducted in 2013 measured the impact of the length of time spent out of employment on the call-back rate, that is, whether a person who has applied for a job is called for an interview. It seems that, in the USA at least, once a person's CV shows that they've been out of work for six months or more, they're very rarely contacted for interview, regardless of their level of experience and skill set. Extended time outside the workplace seems to create the perception that the prospective employees are somehow out of the loop, which then prevents them getting the very job that would enable them to get back into the loop – an unfortunate vicious cycle.

Research conducted at the University of Stirling has shown that long-term unemployment can actually have a negative impact on a personality trait that is highly relevant to being a productive member of society. The Five Factor Model, a personality questionnaire, was completed by 6,769 German adults twice, a few years apart. During this time the employment status of several of the participants happened, quite by chance, to change. When the impact of unemployment on these measures of personality were analysed, they found that 'conscientiousness' among the men in the sample had declined in a manner proportional to the number of years spent out of work. For women the results were a little more complicated: there was a decrease in conscientiousness in years two and three of unemployment, but for some reason it bounced back after four years.

People who have to get up and go to work every day are more likely to be in the habit of conscientiously fulfilling their duties. Those who have nobody actively assigning them tasks will probably not be in the routine of getting a 'to do' list ticked off each day. Unless they set themselves up with a self-imposed routine during periods of unemployment in order to maintain their discipline, it is clear to see how levels of conscientiousness might decline. When people find themselves unemployed and thus free to get out of bed at a time of their choosing, most will tend to linger for longer than those who have a specific start time to make. It's easy to see how this could gradually slip, with people getting up later and later in the day, leading to increasingly sloth-like habits.

Brain circuitry that is used regularly and intensively over long periods of time is strengthened and reinforced; this is the process of neuroplasticity described in Chapter 1 (see p. 7). Brain circuitry that is used infrequently, or not particularly intensively, falls into relative disrepair. Could this be the fate of the striatum in the long-term unemployed? Applying the principles of neuroplasticity to the striatum, it may be that these very brain circuits of motivation become less able to generate get-up-and-go in people who haven't had to use them regularly and intensively to get work done. Such studies comparing the structure and function of the striatum in the same brains after long periods of employment and unemployment have never been done. But it certainly seems feasible.

Back in the USA, in 2016 the Executive Office of the White House released some disheartening figures on the long-term impacts of unemployment. These demonstrated that the number of prime work-aged men not currently in work, and who didn't work a single day for the entire duration of the previous year, steadily increased from 1988 to the present day. This may reflect a form of *learned helplessness* known as the discouraged worker effect. It essentially describes a phenomenon whereby the longer a person is out of work, the more likely they are to conclude that efforts to find work usually turn out to be a waste of time.

The inactivity of homeless people could easily be mistaken for sloth too. You walk past the same person, day in, day out, and they're sitting on the same paving stone, begging for loose change. What do you think of them? Are they lazy? Or do you assume that they would probably happily throw themselves into work, if only they could extract themselves from the cycle of poverty? The chances are, you probably don't give it much thought at all. This is the conclusion of a study conducted by Princeton University social psychologist Susan Fiske. It turns out that your brain probably doesn't even register a homeless person as being a human. Her work clearly shows that a specific part of the medial prefrontal cortex, normally activated whenever we lay eyes on a human but not when we look at other animals or inanimate objects, does *not* kick in when we see the dishevelled appearance of a homeless person. Exactly why this happens is unclear. It may have something to do with wanting to spare ourselves from fully engaging with the heart-breaking nature of their predicament, *i.e.* a way of saving ourselves from feeling the social pain of another person's suffering. No one really knows for sure. The good news is that when the same people whose brains failed to respond to photos of homeless people as if they were actually human spent a weekend volunteering to help homeless people in a soup kitchen, their brains changed almost overnight. When re-scanned the following week, the empathy circuits came back online when viewing generic photos of the homeless. This suggests that simply interacting with the homeless, reminding us of our shared humanity, can reverse the dehumanisation inherent in how most people regard the homeless.

The reality is that homeless people do *not* freely choose to live on the street. They invariably find themselves forced to sleep rough due to circumstances beyond their control and a lack of alternatives. They may have run away from abuse, family problems or crushing debt; a life of perpetual uncertainty is sometimes, for many unfortunate souls, a better prospect than the certainty of suffering. And 25 to 30 per cent of homeless people are struggling with a serious mental illness – in which case they're certainly not plain lazy, just not getting the help they so desperately need.

False alarms

If someone is in a coma, you can hardly accuse them of the sin of sloth; it goes without saying that a person must be fully conscious before they can be held morally responsible for their inaction. By the same token, if parts of the striatum – the very epicentre of a person's capacity to be proactive – are knocked out by a stroke or a bang on the head, their apathy clearly does not reflect an inherent laziness either. The point is that only freely chosen inactivity can be reasonably attributed to sloth. If it is *not* freely chosen, it is not sloth.

According to this logic, when someone finds themselves out of work or with nowhere to live for long periods of time, their idleness usually reflects a lack of opportunity. This cannot reasonably be attributed to sloth. Even if long periods of inactivity and lack of opportunity eventually lead to bad habits, so long as the original period of inactivity was forced upon them, rather than being freely chosen, accusations of sloth would be quite unfair.

From a purely neurobiological standpoint, apathy involves problems with the striatum's capacity to release the handbrake on the basal ganglia (BG) circuitry that enables a person to spring into action. As we've seen, various life circumstances can make it harder for some people to take off the BG handbrake and get themselves moving than others. These circumstances can range from brain damage to conditions that deplete dopamine levels. For instance, a person may take recreational drugs so frequently that the striatum becomes structurally reorganised to make acquiring and taking that drug their primary motivation, over and above all other things.

People struggle to become motivated to get meaningful, useful work done for many reasons, but the brain area that always seems to be implicated is the striatum, so this may prove to be the best target for therapeutic interventions (see Chapter 9, p. 242).

Freeloaders

With so many false alarms, you may be starting to wonder who actually *does* qualify for an accusation of sloth. As always we are looking for something that has anti-social impacts that either drive people apart, or prevent them from being brought closer together. In the case of sloth the opportunity to do something productive must have been shirked willingly, under circumstances where not bothering was a choice freely made. If you are devoutly religious then sloth might take the form of staying in bed rather than going to your place of worship. If you're a teenager it might involve avoiding homework until the very last minute, or saying you'll do the household chores knowing full well that you have no intention of getting round to them. In sport it would be the glory-seeker who's keen as mustard when there might be a chance to score, but completely loses interest the very second possession is lost and it's time to race back down the field to defend. In the workplace, if one team member can't be bothered to do their part, then everyone else's efforts might go to waste, or else the others will have to pick up the slack to avoid ending up with a dissatisfied customer.

Social penalties for defaulting on duties can be harsh, from getting thrown off the team to being kicked out of the house, or even losing your job. Other people in the group who are negatively affected by your laziness will make their displeasure known eventually, by leaving you on the bench, refusing to renew your contract, or ensuring you're the first for the chop when the next round of redundancies are on the horizon. It may not be the most destructive form of anti-social behaviour, but sloth is a sure-fire way to fall out of favour with the InGroup and find yourself left out in the cold.

There will always be people who try to play the system, and of course we all cut corners from time to time. There can be folly in always trying to be a perfectionist; sometimes pragmatism requires that you do the best job you can given whatever time and resources are available. But some people seem absolutely determined to expend as little effort as humanly possible, as a matter of course. This is not so much a tendency as a way of life. Whether it's working with someone who always does the absolute minimum on any project; co-habiting with someone who takes no interest in cleaning up after themselves, leaving their dirty dishes piling up in the sink; or coping with a neighbour whose garden is an overgrown tangle of weeds and rubbish that winds you up every time you walk past – why does this generate such fury?

Chronically lazy people break a sacred but unspoken truth: social bonds are reinforced when everyone chips in and does their bit in a communal enterprise. On the other hand, these bonds are severed when someone routinely defaults on doing their share of the work. It offends our sense of fairness when other people don't seem to realise, or care about, the frustration they cause others when they don't pull their weight. We will often become indignant and outraged by the slackers' behaviour, moaning about it to anyone who'll listen. This isn't just about blowing off steam. It also acts as a sanity check. If others agree with our sentiment, then we feel entitled to be angry and may be more likely to assert ourselves. But then again, the third party might offer information which provides a different perspective. If we discover that the person causing us so much aggravation is struggling with some kind of mental illness, that they are not just lazy but neurologically incapacitated, this may help to soothe our ire. If the person living next door is the one in a thousand people who suffer with schizophrenia, we might be able to reframe the situation in our mind. Rather than blaming it on sloth, we might realise that the reason their garden is in such a disgraceful state is not because they are neglecting their social duties out of choice, but because their motivation levels have been suppressed by the very same drugs that help to suppress their delusions.* You may ultimately conclude that, rather than bitching about what a terrible neighbour they are to anyone who'll listen, a more constructive course of action might be to offer them a helping hand? Better still, offer up your lazy teenager's gardening services...

When there are no mitigating circumstances to prevent someone from freely choosing and pursuing constructive goals, then it is perfectly reasonable to feel aggrieved by their apathy. At that point it can reasonably be considered akin to the sin of sloth. If we feel utterly convinced that the laziness is freely chosen, that might be the time to wheel out the social penalties. Those who don't do their fair share of the work will find themselves gossiped about and bad-mouthed behind their back. It may seem petty, but spreading the news that a certain person has a tendency to shirk their duties could even be considered a moral duty; it could help others to avoid having to find out the hard way.

Couch potatoes

There's one very modern tribe of humans whose unmitigated sloth often slips under the radar. The worse offenders are rarely seen in public and so the abhorrence they feel when contemplating the fulfillment of their duties remains largely hidden from view; from everyone but those who happen to live with them. Should you happen to walk in on one of their number, you'll likely find them sitting motionless and transfixed. Their prolific laziness may well be cunningly

---

* 'Negative' symptoms that sap a schizophrenic person's motivation are part of the condition anyway, but there's a suspicion that the dopamine-blocking drugs that reduce delusions and hallucinations may make the apathy worse.

obscured behind a façade of intense concentration, but don't be fooled.

Come Judgement Day such individuals may find themselves being bullied and cajoled into the eternal marathon by Belphegor, the infernal PE teacher himself. These people freely choose to spend disproportionate quantities of their short time on Earth in a fierce pursuit of purely illusory goals. These are goals that, once fulfilled, achieve nothing of any value whatsoever for themselves, nor for the society of which they are a part. Those who *do* manage to hold down a job can be found hiding in plain sight, squinting into their screens on buses, planes and trains across the length and breadth of the planet.

These are the slaves to technology: the Candy Crushers, the Facebook fanatics, the Insta-idlers, the Snapchat servants and Twitter twiddlers who spend every spare minute absorbed by their screens. These are the fully grown adults who spend every free moment they can find engaged in virtual battle with ogres, dwarves, robots and space pirates, plugged into one of the many Massively Multiplayer Online Games (MMOGs). This clan also includes the parents who sacrifice precious hours of sleep, after the kids have finally gone to bed, by burning the midnight oil playing online bingo, spinning virtual roulette wheels and entering poker tournaments from the comfort of their living rooms. All these digital distractions displace thousands of hours of valuable time that could otherwise have been spent doing something useful.

Steam, a huge online gaming company, helpfully logs the number of hours its users spend playing their suite of games. All of the top 10 on this 'Wall of Shame' have accumulated in excess of 50,000 hours of game play with annual averages in excess of 5,000 hours. Bearing in mind that even if you played eight hours per day, 365 days per year, you wouldn't even hit the 3,000 hour mark, clearly there are some people out there playing video games at the expense of *all* other activities. Just as those who over-consume internet pornography rewire their striatum in a manner that biases motivation towards the pursuit of erotica over and above all other things, the same thing can happen with those who

plough this many hours per year into video gaming. If similar
charts to the Steam 'Wall of Shame' were compiled to point
the finger at people who willingly squander thousands of
hours per year compulsively surfing porn sites, YouTube
videos of kittens or their favourite form of social media, we
might find that sloth is not just one of the more deadly sins of
our age but also the most prevalent.

Not everyone who uses these apps, online casinos and
spectacularly absorbing computer games is guilty of the sin of
sloth. In the context of an otherwise productive life, if a person
wants to spend *some* of their spare time glued to their
smartphones, tablets and computer monitors, it's quite up to
them. There is even a growing body of evidence supporting
the idea that playing 'first person shoot 'em up' games can
actually improve all sorts of cognitive capabilities. But there are
always plenty of people who end up overindulging. Given that
these digital creations are specifically designed to encourage
the development of compulsive engagement, only the most
disciplined will manage to control their use. Sadly, many end
up idling away such a large proportion of their spare time on
what might be viewed, from an objective perspective, as utterly
pointless digital pursuits that it can end up having a negative
net impact on their overall quality of life.

The worst offenders when it comes to falling foul of sloth
in this day and age, despite the illusion of tremendous industry,
are those who spend every spare moment of every day and
night fiddling with their screens. These hyper-consumers of
digital idolatry usually have no pre-existing bugs in their
striatal circuitry, neither were their dopamine levels running at
a deficit when they started out. As the vast majority of these
people freely choose to slavishly squander their precious free
time whilst achieving little of worth in the grand scheme of
things, they are truly are the children of Belphegor.

While there's nothing wrong with using the digital tools of
entertainment in moderation, most people don't stop to give
serious consideration to the potential negative impacts of
having so much spare time used up in these sedentary pursuits.
It may simply be because these technologies are so young and

were so quick to appear on the scene that we've had no time to appraise the situation or adjust our behaviours to avoid the negative consequences. It is quite possible that the next generation will strike a better balance. But as science and society are still getting to grips with where the benefits end and the disadvantages begin, in the meantime we are the experimental generation, the unwitting guinea pigs in a grand global study of gargantuan proportions.

Computer game designers must share some of the blame. Arguably, they understand the dynamics of the human reward pathway (albeit implicitly) better than any scientist studying the striatum. They have more data available to them than any international collaboration between scientific laboratories and they are financially incentivised to get as many of us hooked on their wares as possible. No entity on the planet knows better than the gaming industry how to create a non-drug-related experience that is so moreish that people come back again and again, daily, and often give it priority over all other activities. You may feel that this rant is over the top, that gaming is harmless, but the truth is – it has already led to fatalities. If the USA is the canary in the coal mine for narcissism and obesity, warning the rest of the world of what's to come, when it comes to over-engagement with technology East Asia is the crystal ball giving us a heads-up on what the future holds.

In 2005 a couple in South Korea accidentally starved their three-month-old child to death because, in a horrible twist of irony, they were completely absorbed in a game that involved caring for a virtual infant. In 2007, a Mr Zhang died in China after playing *World of Warcraft* – an MMOG that allows different players from across the world to collaborate with each other in fighting teams – for 50 hours straight. On 4 February 2012, the *Taipei Times* ran an article reporting on a 23-year-old man who was found dead in an internet café after gaming for 10 straight hours directly after a long shift at work. The article expressed surprise, not that someone might game themselves to death – by 2012 such a case was not unusual by East Asian standards – but that none of the other customers even noticed they were sitting alongside a dead body until it turned blue and rigid with rigor mortis.

Tremendous quantities of time and energy that could have been used to do something meaningful and useful are wasted on activities that achieve absolutely nothing. Some people might be addicted to gaming now,[*] but nobody starts out like that. Before the brain changes that entrain addictions kick in, during the period when people willingly give in to the impulse to over-indulge purely because they derive great pleasure from it, they are guilty of the sin of sloth. Once a person pours enough hours into their passion – like the glutton who becomes morbidly obese, or the fan of erotica who indulges their lust so much that they reach the stage of full-blown internet porn addiction – it becomes less clear-cut. The striatum shifts into a different gear when the gaming becomes compulsive rather than impulsive, so it's harder to tell whether a person is guilty of a deadly sin, or just another helpless addict.

Certain segments of society can be very harsh in their attitudes towards the lack of motivation apparent among homeless, long-term unemployed and/or mentally ill people, but none of these people chose their fates freely. Accusations of sloth should be reserved for those who *freely* choose to fritter away all their spare time and energy on frivolous distractions.

Forget religion. The App Store contains the opium of the masses. And the future heroin of the masses –Virtual Reality – will soon find its way into our homes. Let's hope we've learned our lessons from the first wave of the silicon revolution, or else we might all find ourselves being sucked into Belphegor's digital black hole.

---

[*] According to the BBC4 Storyville documentary *Web Junkies* there are 400+ internet addiction centres in China alone.

CHAPTER SIX

Greed

It is easier for a camel to go through the eye of a needle than for a rich person to enter the kingdom of God.

Mark 10:25; Matthew 19:24

A historical perspective

Christianity, Islam and Buddhism all warn against the dangers of greed. In Buddhism it is taken very seriously indeed. Greed is one of the three mind poisons, which, along with anger and ignorance, are considered major obstacles to enlightenment. Islam warns against the 'ruin and destruction' that will ultimately result from the greedy pursuit of wealth. In Christianity, despite the 'eye of the needle' quote being familiar to most, the case against greed was made most succinctly by St Paul.

Born in Tarsus, near the Mediterranean coast of modern-day Turkey, Paul started out as a tent maker called Saul who was a Roman citizen and a devout Jew. At first he was no fan of the Jesus cult but, according to his letters, he underwent a dramatic conversion on the road to Damascus. So deep was his new-found faith in the teachings of Jesus that he ended up being credited with writing 13 of the 27 books of the Bible. St Paul was one of the earliest Christian writers to point an accusatory finger at those whose entire lives seem to revolve around the pursuit of wealth. He is credited with penning the Latin phrase '*Radix Omnium Malorum Avaritia*', which translates as 'The root (radix) of all (omnium) evils (malorum) is the pursuit of wealth (avaritia).' As the first letter of each word spells out R.O.M.A. (meaning Rome), it seems his exposure to ancient Rome's infatuation with wealth and opulence may well have inspired this insight.

The word 'avarice' derives from the Latin word *avaritia,* which translates as 'the inordinate desire for more'. 'Inordinate' is the critical word here. The desire for wealth and material possessions is not the problem, in and of itself. Greed's status as a capital vice is all about banishing *excessive* desire for wealth from society. When the acquisition of wealth becomes a person's primary purpose in life it can inspire a rich variety of anti-social behaviours. So while St Gregory the Great placed pride front and centre as the ultimate cause of all the seven deadly sins, a few centuries earlier St Paul had already suggested that they actually all stemmed from greed.

The ancient Greeks, forever ahead of the game, had some fantastic words in their lexicon that beautifully capture the essence of greed. *Pleonexia* describes an 'obsession with acquiring more'. *Philargyria* describes an 'excessive desire for money'. Building on these ideas, St Paul's conception of the sin of greed may be best described as a combination of the two: an obsession with acquiring more money, regardless of how much a person already has.

Mammon is the Prince of Hell that Bishop Peter Binsfeld assigned to greed, and in Jacques Collin de Plancy's *Dictionnaire Infernal* he is depicted as a withered old man protectively clutching bags of money in his lap. This introduces us to another important aspect of greed: it often inspires penny-pinching stinginess. Another great work of art, George Frederic Watts's painting of Mammon, shows a hugely fat man, crown perched on head, bags of cash piled up in his lap, pushing the head of a supplicant down with one hand and stepping on the head of another. This brings us to the idea that once someone has great wealth, they often use the power that comes with it to subordinate others. And as we will see as this chapter unfolds, a person's wealth does seem to skew the balance between pro-self and pro-social influences on financial decision-making towards selfishness.

The latest statistics on the distribution of global wealth indicate that greed may be thriving better than ever before in the history of our species. According to a recent report by Credit Suisse, 0.7 per cent of the global population are US dollar millionaires, collectively accounting for 45 per cent of the world's total material wealth. Another way this has been framed is that the richest 1 per cent of people own as much of the planet's total wealth as the remaining 99 per cent. And, as we'll see, the 1 per cent truly excel when it comes to maintaining this imbalance year on year.

When it comes to the anti-social impact of greed it's not just about a small number of people hogging the wealth that could otherwise be shared more equitably. Convincing arguments have been made to suggest that greed is the ultimate cause of all fraud, corruption and theft. Finance and fraud have been intimate bedfellows ever since humans first invented money, and we've been swindling, bribing, defrauding, embezzling, racketeering and conning each other ever since. That said, despite warnings about the anti-social influence greed has in society, many people seem to find it highly aspirational all the same.

'Greed, for lack of a better word, is good'

These words, uttered by the fictitious billionaire Gordon Gekko during a speech to shareholders in the 1987 Hollywood film *Wall Street,* couldn't fly more squarely in the face of the concept of greed as a sin. This sentiment resonated so thoroughly with the atmosphere of the late eighties stock-market boom that his performance won Michael Douglas an Oscar for Best Actor. The character he played so brilliantly was, by then, a familiar figure: the hyper-aggressive businessperson whose sole motivation in life is to continue increasing their wealth and power no matter how much they have accumulated to date. Thousands have since succeeded in emulating Gordon Gekko's example across the globe. In Donald Trump's best-selling book, *The Art of the Deal,* which sold over a million copies when it hit the shelves in 1987, he explicitly states: 'The point is you can't be too greedy.'

Gordon Gekko and Donald Trump weren't the first to extol greed as a virtue. It had been argued that greed can be a force for good in certain circumstances long before they came onto the scene. In fact, over two millennia ago, the Athenian general and historian Thucydides (460–400 BC) conceded that, for all the negative consequences of individual greed he had observed throughout his life, it also had an undeniably positive role in terms of its capacity to motivate people. Indeed, many people since then have argued that it is nothing less than a vital ingredient in the receipe for a thriving economy. The economist Adam Smith famously pointed out that: 'It is not from the benevolence of the butcher, the brewer, or the baker that we expect our dinner, but from their regard to their own self-interest.'

In 1987, I was more into cartoons than business books or Hollywood movies, so my first exposure to the concept of greed was Scrooge McDuck. Scrooge is a pivotal character in Disney's *Duck Tales* – a successful businessman with a vast fortune, yet utterly miserly when it comes to his huge vault of gold coins and always hungry to pounce on any opportunity to increase his wealth. Despite his prosperity he steadfastly refuses to share the wealth with his beloved great-nephews Huey, Dewey and Louie, no matter how much they try to coerce him into financing their various hair-brained schemes. *Duck Tales* narratives also often involve great-uncle McDuck fighting beak and claw to increase the profitability of one shadowy deal or another, showing no concern whatsoever for any collateral damage that might be suffered by others, their communities or the local environment as a result. This returns our attention to the core antisocial impact of the sin of greed: whether taking too much means depriving others of their fair share, or actually causes them harm, as far as the greedy are concerned it makes no difference; to them it's like water off a duck's back.

In the world of commerce, judging whether decisions are diabolical or perfectly reasonable is a tricky business. At the very pinnacle of the Forbes Rich List we find Bill Gates with an estimated net worth in excess of $75 billion. It is interesting to consider to what extent greed was an intrinsic factor in helping him reach such heady heights of personal wealth. He founded Microsoft back in 1975 together with Paul Allen who, at number 40 in the Rich List, has a mere $17.5 billion to his name. There is good reason to believe that they were willing to intentionally put others out of business to drive their own profits. The evidence that they wanted to crush their competitors out of existence comes from a 1998 law suit in which Microsoft was taken to court by the United States of America over allegations of business strategies specifically designed to 'extinguish' the competition and 'cut off air supply'. At the time, they had just expanded from being junior partners with pioneering computing firms like MITS, Digital Research and IBM into one of the most powerful and all-conquering corporations the world has ever seen. But was this greed or fair game? Some people would view this behaviour as a supreme, sustained example of greed. Others would view it as the shrewd strategy of two of the greatest businessmen the world has ever seen. As we will see, this grey area in defining the threshold between virtuous and vicious aspects of greed in the financial world is particularly damaging. While the case of Microsoft's business conduct may be slightly ambiguous in terms of whether the co-founders did right or wrong, the Bernie Madoff scandal is a different kettle of fish all together.

Bernie Madoff became infamous for defrauding a whopping $65 billion from investors over the course of several decades. But how in the world did he manage to get away with it for so long? Could it have been his infectious charisma, the famous bonhomie? Certainly it would have had something to do with the exclusivity he cultivated in selecting who did and did not get the chance to become a member of his inner circle. Madoff wouldn't take money from just anyone. It was impossible to become a part of the scheme unless you could find a way to get introduced to him by someone already involved in the investment. Wannabe investors were excited to finally gain access to this exclusive club, which presumably helped get them to drop their guard.

Another factor that kept Madoff under the radar was that, unlike the eponymous Ponzi of the original 1920s scam, he wasn't offering a spectacular get-rich-quick scheme. At 1 per cent growth per month – a relatively modest rate of appreciation by the standards of the time – he offered stability, but not huge profits, in a notoriously erratic stock market. As a result he tended to attract the more prudent investors and the involvement of such risk-averse folk no doubt served to further reassure newcomers to the scheme. The fact that Madoff served as non-executive chairman of the NASDAQ from 1991 to 1993 probably also allayed any suspicions that he might be a crook. The investors he enticed into the scam started out as friends and associates from his country club, progressing eventually to well-endowed hedge funds and major charities. They were issued with professional-looking monthly reports detailing sales and purchases of shares in well-respected blue chip companies. Yet every single 'transaction' was a complete fiction. Had the 2008 financial meltdown not occurred, spurring many of his investors to request a return of their money, he might never have been rumbled. Incidentally, if you've wondered why the actor Kevin Bacon has been in some high-profile advertising campaigns of late, it may have something to do with him losing an absolute fortune in the Madoff scam. An extensive list of the people and institutions affected was published by the *Washington Post*, including details of the size of their investments, which really helps to convey the sheer scale of this fraud.

From maximising profit on a deal regardless of the collateral damage to others, all the way up to spinning a web of lies in an effort to get people to invest in fraudulent schemes, those who fall into the clutches of greed have no trouble acting in an incredibly self-centred manner when money is at stake. Why they do this seems clear: they are driven by an insatiable desire to maximise profits at all costs. The question is, are some people just born greedy? Or do they develop the habit of greed over time?

Where does greed come from?
Neuroeconomics is a branch of neuroscience that investigates how brains make value-based decisions. Usually these studies involve humans making some type of financial decision while their brains are being scanned, typically using MRI. A recent meta-analysis, looking for consistencies across 200 neuroeconomic studies, identified two brain areas that are

always activated more strongly for the option perceived to be of greater value than the others. The areas that always seem to prefer more over less are two that we have encountered before: the ventral striatum and the medial orbitofrontal cortex (OFC). People always choose the option with the highest *predicted reward value*, that is, the one that causes the strongest response in these reward pathway structures, all other things being equal. Could the very wiring of the reward pathway account for people's inordinate desire for more?

Give a hungry person a whiff of banana whilst starving and certain parts of the OFC respond with great enthusiasm. Stuff them full of bananas and then give them another whiff of banana and a response will barely register. This is because activation levels do not respond to the absolute, objective value of a banana (20p at the time of writing in your average London high street supermarket), but to the relative, subjective value that takes into account the person's current state. Although such brain areas originally evolved to help us maximise our access to various primary rewards that help to keep us alive, like food and drink, they can also be trained to respond to secondary rewards, such as money, that we know can be exchanged for food, drink and other commodities of value. Some studies have suggested that the parts of the OFC towards the front of the brain have become specialised in humans to respond to money, whereas those a little further back prefer rewards that we can actually consume directly. Either way, while the reward pathway's evaluation of primary rewards changes according to our current state – our levels of hunger or thirst – when it comes to money, we almost always prefer the option that gives us more over less, regardless of how much we have to start with.* Preferring it is one thing, but as we shall see shortly, if choosing the option of

---

* There is an exception to this rule of thumb. When money is taken away from us and given to a worthy charitable cause, reward pathway activations increase, despite this being a financial loss to the individual. Happily this suggests that giving really is its own reward. More on this later.

maximising financial gain means wronging others, we may be discouraged.

Why did we evolve a brain that seems to prefer more to less in most situations? Brain circuitry with an in-built preference for more over less may have improved our ancestors' survival prospects by encouraging the accumulation of an excess of resources. Back in pre-history, when finding enough resources during the warmer seasons to withstand the long, cold winter defined the yearly rhythm, a decent surplus could have made the difference between life and death. If supplies ran out before the spring thaw made it possible to go out and top them back up again, then what? When bad luck on the seasonal hunts and foraging trips led to shortages of food, medicinal plants and materials that could be used to feed the fire or keep out the cold, those who had hoarded sufficient spare provisions would have a better chance of surviving than those who had not. So it is easy to imagine how the greedier ancestral humans might have managed to pass on their genes, while the less greedy ones bit the dust. When it comes to the survival value of greed in the context of dangerous and unforgiving environments, perhaps characters like Gordon, Scrooge and Donald are simply an inevitable and unfortunate product of evolution?

The trouble with this over-simplistic outlook on greed is that if our Stone Age ancestors *always* behaved in a way that was excessively greedy then it would have ended up causing them problems in the long run. For creatures as highly dependent on the cooperation of others as humans, getting a bad reputation for always taking more than their fair share could be lethal for all but the most dominant member of any pre-historic clan. If accumulating a surplus was always achieved at the expense of other people, some of them might eventually tire of the selfish behaviour and take steps to punish the offender. This could eventually involve casting them out of the InGroup into the wilderness to fend for themselves. Such a fate, back then, would have made the ultimate goal of raising offspring to maturity so that *they* might pass on *your* genes less likely. So a balance had to be struck between the pro-self desire to acquire more and the pro-social instincts that ensured membership of the InGroup.

A cooperative of individuals is much more likely to successfully establish and maintain an excess of resources, to see everyone through the lean times together, than any given individual on their own. Even looking at it from the perspective of the strongest, fastest, biggest and most cunning hunter in the group, a surplus is best defended against scavengers and raiders with the help of trusted collaborators. For a socially dependent species like ourselves the desire for more had to be balanced against the perils of social isolation. A pre-requisite of this is an intrinsic sense of how our share of the spoils compares with that of others, and whether or not it is fair.

Equity and the art of deception

A general preference for more over less is not unique to humans. It's not even restricted to mammals. It's fairly ubiquitous across the animal kingdom. Given the choice between two options, where one option consists of a greater number of tasty morsels than the other, a wide variety of animals – from chimpanzees, lions and hyenas to birds and even cuttlefish* – have demonstrated the ability to count and show a preference for the larger number. What is far rarer in the animal kingdom is a sense of fairness.

Evidence has been collected from 10 different species of primates and a handful of birds indicating a brilliant capacity to rapidly judge what constitutes a 'fair share' of the spoils. Like us, these other species have a distinct tendency to throw their proverbial toys out of the pram whenever they find themselves getting a smaller share than their peers. Greedy creatures will always try to push their luck and social sanctions are used to discourage them from trying to overstep the mark again in the future.[†]

---

* Believe it or not, cuttlefish can count up to five.

† While dominance in animal social hierarchies can give certain individuals privileged access to a greedy and unequal share, it invariably causes trouble among those at the same level of the pecking order.

In humans, this sense of equity arises during the second year of life. Should an infant find themselves on the thin end of an unequal share, a temper tantrum often ensues. This may help them secure a share of the pie that is equal to others in the future. Of course at that age they often get it wrong – their sense of fairness has yet to be properly calibrated.

The ability to get away with wangling a bit more for themselves than others, without getting caught in the act, takes much longer to develop. Several different brain areas, each playing a different role, must mature before all the relevant components are in place to ensure such acts of greed remain undetected. Even at the age of three, a human child is still largely locked into the first-person perspective. At this age they simply cannot fully put themselves in another person's shoes. If they pick up a bunch of keys that their mum has left on the kitchen table and place them in a drawer while she's out of the room, when she comes back in looking for them, they won't understand why she doesn't go straight to the drawer. Their capacity to comprehend the world from another person's perspective, even that of their own mother, simply hasn't kicked in yet. It's obvious to us as fully grown adults that if the mother wasn't in the room when the keys were moved, she could not possibly know where they are now. By the age of four, this impressive feat of perspective-taking suddenly emerges, but only after significant work has gone into finessing certain brain pathways.

The brain changes that support this capacity usually take place between the ages of three and four. They involve maturation of a specific bundle of white matter fibres – the neuronal cabling that ferries electrical impulses from one brain area to another – called the arcuate fascicle. This particular information superhighway connects the temporo-parietal junction (or TPJ) with specific regions of the ventrolateral prefrontal cortex (vlPFC). While the TPJ

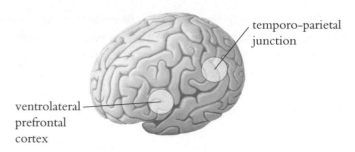

ventrolateral
prefrontal
cortex

temporo-parietal
junction

Figure 8 Theory of Mind describes the ability to fully grasp what other people are thinking and feeling, a skill now thought to be dependent on maturation of the arcuate fascicle – a white matter tract connecting the temporo-parietal junction with the ventrolateral prefrontal cortex.

enables us to understand the world from another person's perspective, the patch of vlPFC in question is critical for factoring in differences between our perspective and theirs when making decisions (see Figure 8). This capacity is known as 'Theory of Mind' (ToM). Once it starts functioning properly, it becomes instrumental in helping us to ensure that the urge to maximise our own selfish gains doesn't jeopardise our relationships. And one way of doing that, of course, is to bend the truth.

We all use these ToM capacities every day. They are invaluable for helping to ensure that we interact with others in a way that tends to please rather than displease them. Sometimes to achieve this goal we need to use deception in order not to hurt people's feelings. What do you say if somebody asks you: 'Does my bum look big in this?' Most people would answer that it all depends on how the person in question would react to the response 'yes' versus 'no'. Different people want to hear different things, so you first have to consider how each possible answer is likely to go down. Weighing up the potential social penalties that might come your way if you tell them the truth versus telling them whatever they really want to hear relies heavily on ToM. Most people with a fully developed TPJ will conclude that, if the truth is likely to hurt their feelings, then it is probably safer to tell a 'white' lie.

Young infants, by virtue of having vastly underdeveloped ToM pathways and therefore a complete inability to take other people's point of view into consideration, are terrible liars. This leaves them prone to experimenting with deception under circumstances where their chances of success are minimal. For instance, having wilfully ignored the instruction 'Don't touch the cake!' when left alone in the kitchen for a few minutes, young children will happily try to deny having done anything wrong despite being plastered head-to-toe in chocolate. This is a 'primary lie'. It is a straightforward deception that takes no heed of what others can and can't see, nor what they do and do not know. Once brain areas supporting the capacity for ToM kick in, humans can start telling 'secondary lies' – where the other person's point of view *is* taken into consideration. By the age of seven or eight a child will graduate to 'tertiary lies' where, in addition to factoring in other people's perspectives, they also make sure that what they say when hiding the truth is consistent with whatever other facts and evidence are likely to be available to the other person.

As these skills of deception are being developed, children will often experiment with trying to maximise their share, in other words, to be greedy without getting caught in the act. That way both the Stone Age imperatives from earlier can be satisfied: maximise self-interest and maintain group membership. That said, we also develop social skills enabling us to detect deception and any child who does get caught being greedy too often will soon find that there are social penalties to pay. While they won't be left out in the wilderness, they may find themselves being spurned by others. Under normal circumstances such experiences naturally temper a child's greediness so they can maintain their friendships. This delicate balancing act of trying to maximise self-interest, while simultaneously taking steps to preserve membership of the InGroup, is practised every day, honed via trial and error, in

nurseries and schools all over the world. And depending on
the social norms of the culture a child happens to be raised in,
those small humans will turn into adults with varying degrees
of tolerance to inequality in the distribution of rewards.

Greed on the brain

Behavioural economics has developed a wide variety of
tools that focus on decision-making that requires participants
to trade off their desire to maximise profit against the
repercussions that might arise from acting unfairly. These
include the Ultimatum Game, the Dictator Game, Public
Goods Games, the Prisoner's Dilemma and numerous others.
Whole books have been written on the insights that have
emerged from neuroeconomic studies investigating what
happens in the brains of people as they play such trading
games, but we will be focusing on some of the most interesting
findings from just one – the Ultimatum Game.

The Ultimatum Game couldn't be more straightforward. A
prize fund of, say, £100 is up for grabs and must be split
between two players. One person decides how the proceeds
will be split. The other either accepts the offer, in which case
the funds are divided as agreed, or they reject the offer and
neither party gets anything. When such studies were first
undertaken, it was expected that people would generally accept
any split so long as they got something. After all, even £10 out
of £100 is better than nothing. At least that is what was
predicted by the prevailing economic theories of the time. In
actual fact, not only did those on the receiving end of the
propositions almost always reject splits of the pot that were
deemed too greedy (e.g. £90/£10, £80/£20, £70/£30), but
more often than not such unfair splits were rarely offered in the
first place. The upshot? Humans would rather turn down free
money than let another person get away with acting unfairly.

Let's take a moment to put this into perspective. People are
effectively willing to 'spend' up to £30 (assuming a pot size
of £100, split £30/£70) to stop others being excessively
greedy. Proposers – those who suggest how the pot is split –
demonstrated an intrinsic awareness of other people's willingness

to punish a complete stranger for being greedy, even when it costs them money to do so, by proposing the greediest splits less often than the fairer ones. When players are up against a computer, on the other hand, this effect disappears. People only feel compelled to punish greed if they believe they are interacting with a human.

Scrooge McDuck, Gordon Gekko, Donald Trump, Bill Gates and Bernie Madoff have one important thing in common: their brains just don't work like this. They all seem to have a much greater tolerance for making financial decisions that leave others worse off. The million-dollar question is – why? The natural instinct to share fairly that discourages most people from taking advantage of others is clearly rendered ineffective. The children of Mammon may be utterly impervious to the unpleasant social emotions like guilt that usually assail people when they consider doing something morally dubious, such as making decisions that short-change or even harm others. The threat of social sanctions has no impact on them. Even legislation designed to prevent such behaviour is, more often than not, completely ineffective in discouraging them. It seems as if nothing will stand between the greedy and their pursuit of greater profit.

To reconcile our general proclivity towards fairness with the insight that people are also usually motivated to maximise their wealth wherever possible, it was presumed for many years that we are instinctively motivated towards selfishness, but certain brain areas can step in to inhibit these anti-social urges to help us avoid the social penalties if there is a good chance we'll get caught. Then, in 2012 David Rand and colleagues at Harvard University published a remarkable study describing 10 separate experiments in which people had to decide whether they would act selfishly or cooperate under a variety of different time constraints. The aim was to establish whether we are indeed hardwired to be selfish and need to suppress this tendency to be cooperative, or *vice versa*. Reassuringly, whenever people had to register their responses very quickly, before they had time to think their choices through, they tended to behave more fairly. When they were given longer to reach their decision, on the other hand, they tended to be more selfish. This, together with complementary research from other laboratories around the world, strongly indicates that our default setting is to share with others fairly. In other words, greed is not instinctive but instead requires some measure of conscious deliberation. Only when people took time to mull their decision over did they end up choosing the selfish route.

The notion that we have to put in extra cognitive effort to make greedy choices has since been bolstered by a brilliant study that used bursts of magnetic stimulation to disrupt regions of the dorsolateral prefrontal cortex (dlPFC) from which these greedy influences were thought to arise. When the area in question was magnetically deactivated, the offers that were made were more generous than usual, making the person more likely to engage in 'costly sharing' than when the dlPFC was left undisturbed. Greed distinguishes itself from the other sins of excessive appetite right there: while the PFC mechanisms implicated in lust and gluttony appear to rein in those temptations, the PFC regions implicated in greed seem to stimulate it.

A meta-analysis of over 20 neuroeconomic studies that have all independently investigated brain responses while volunteers played the Ultimatum Game identified two key brain areas that were consistently activated whenever people were confronted by the prospect of an unfair split. The anterior insula (AI) responded to the inequity irrespective of which party was left at a disadvantage. It seemed to be sensitive to any violation of fairness, regardless of whether that meant a larger or smaller share for the individual concerned. The other consistent activation was found in the dorsal anterior cingulate cortex (dACC). Increased activation was only observed here when the *other* person stood to gain from the unequal split in proceeds. Given the role of the dACC in feelings of social pain and processing conflict (see Chapter 2, p. 31), these activations could be interpreted in terms of the unpleasant, conflicted feelings that usually arise when we find ourselves being taken advantage of by others.

A brand new tool has come onto the scene very recently that enables people's relative levels of greediness to be measured, giving them a 'dispositional greed' score. It comprises a questionnaire that can reliably identify whether people have a strong or weak tendency towards greed. This is a vital precursor to any study aiming to establish how the brains of greedy people differ from those who prefer to be more equitable. Sadly this research hasn't been done yet. On the basis of the neuroscience we have considered so far, we could predict that those with a high dispositional greed score may have an overdeveloped dlPFC compared to the non-greedy and that something fishy might be going on in their AI and/or dACC. Only time will tell…

Building tolerance to inequity

Given the preference most people have for avoiding the unfair division of rewards across a variety of neuroeconomic games, it seems almost surprising that greed has managed to become such a familiar phenomenon in many modern societies. In the absence of functional imaging studies to illuminate what's going on in the brains of greedy versus non-greedy people, we'll have to look elsewhere to establish what the key influences might be that make people deviate from a default preference for fairness.

Several studies have indicated that those with a formal education in economics are likely to keep more money for themselves in economic games, behave uncooperatively and lie more often. Their knowledge of economics may help them formulate rational arguments to make any antisocial decisions made in the context of maximising profit feel justified. This could be achieved in a number of ways. Through practice they may be able to decrease the production of unpleasant social emotions, perhaps by gradually suppressing the AI and/or dACC responses to inequality through repetition. The precedent for such a phenomenon has been set by a recent MRI study that demonstrated how lying can feel less and less uncomfortable the more a person repeats their self-serving behaviour. The dlPFC brain area deactivated by magnetic pulses in the previously described study, which made people more likely to choose the less greedy options, may also be involved. It could provide the source of a signal that suppresses the discomfort that non-greedy people, without a formal education in economics, feel when making greedy choices. However it is achieved, the knowledge of economic theories seems to boost the likelihood of a person opting to increase their own personal wealth irrespective of the cost to others, even if it means being actively dishonest.

Aside from a formal education in economics, being wealthy also seems to have an impact on people's tendencies towards greed. Having a vast fortune may foster a sense of being insulated from the usual social or legal consequences of getting caught out. Given that the rich can afford the most expensive lawyers, and expensive lawyers routinely help people evade the consequences of any profit-making activities that contravene the laws of the land, this makes sense. Presumably the peace of mind that comes from being able to afford the best legal eagles makes illegal methods of generating or retaining wealth seem less intimidating. And, as we shall see, this isn't limited to those who grew up in an atmosphere of wealth and privilege.

Take Lionel Messi, for example, the only footballer in the world to have won FIFA's coveted Ballon d'Or award five times. His father worked in a steel factory and his mother worked on a magnet-manufacturing production line to support 'Leo' and his three siblings during their childhood in Rosaria, Argentina. Hardly what most people would call a privileged upbringing by today's standards. Yet Lionel and his father Jorge (who became his agent when Lionel hit the big time) got into a spot of bother in 2016 while living in Spain when it was revealed that they had dodged a large chunk of tax between 2007 and 2009. Having been caught defrauding the Spanish government of an estimated €4,100,000-worth of income tax (£3,600,000) and despite the presence of both their signatures on the incriminating documents, Leo got clean off the hook. He claimed to have had no knowledge of the corporate structures, stretching from Uruguay to

Switzerland, that reduced the tax burden on income from his image rights (completely illegally as it turns out). No doubt a very bright and costly lawyer helped to convince the jury of this point.

Tax evasion may deprive a nation's coffers of much needed revenue, but the perpetrators of such manoeuvring often claim it is a victimless crime in that no individual goes hungry or is finanically ruined as a direct result. In other circumstances acts of greed carried out by the rich and powerful have left millions to suffer the consequences. We will briefly consider two.

Take, for example, one of the many high-profile bankers whose perfectly legal acts of greed contributed directly to the 2008 global financial meltdown. Stanley O'Neal was CEO of Merrill Lynch until 2007. Under his guidance the bank pursued extensive investments in the risky subprime mortgage market.* As a direct consequence the bank was left so overexposed to bad debt that it went bust and had to be bought out by the Bank of America. Several reports indicated that O'Neal's decision to allow the risky investments that increased the likelihood of driving the bank into the ground was made quite intentionally. In fact, it was thought to have been inadvertently incentivised, as it ended up making his overall severance package (in excess of $100 million) much larger than it would have been otherwise. Clearly he felt sufficiently well insulated from any punishment that might arise from bankrupting his own firm that he allowed his inner Mammon to run wild.

Ali Bongo Ondimba had a similar indifference to the suffering his selfishly motivated financial decisions might cause others. Ali, Gabon's president since 2009, was born into a rich and powerful family and took over the presidency from his father, who had ruled from 1969 until his death in 2009. It has been alleged that Ali took it upon himself to siphon

---

* 'Subprime' essentially means loaning money to people who probably can't afford to pay back what they've borrowed.

25 per cent of the country's entire GDP into his personal coffers, despite more than a third of the country's people living in poverty. A disciple of Mammon, if ever there was one, and still in power in 2018.

The final and particularly cold-hearted example of vicious greed is the tale of what happened to the money raised by the 1985 Live Aid charity campaign. The aim was to feed millions of starving men, women and children who were suffering the consequences of a terrible famine in Ethiopia and the campaign led to an unprecedented outpouring of charitable donations from across the UK. It turns out that the vast majority of the aid money ultimately ended up being spent on weapons and attempts to overthrow the government. Claims backed up by declassified CIA documentation in 2010.

How can such people live with themselves when their greed results in so much human suffering? 'Higher social class predicts increased unethical behaviour', thundered the verdict of a study published in a highly respected science journal in 2012. The implication of this study was that those from the upper echelons of socioeconomic status (SES) tend to be more greedy. SES describes where someone is in the socioeconomic pecking order, according to factors like profession, wealth and educational attainment. This study indicated that, relative to lower SES people, upper SES individuals were found to consistently demonstrate anti-social tendencies. They were far more self-centred and less cognisant of other perspectives. They also struggled with empathy, showing clear deficits in their capacity to identify emotions felt by others.

The tendency for wealthier people to behave more antisocially than the less well-off has also been demonstrated simply by monitoring different types of car at a busy intersection. Expensive cars, a proxy for drivers of higher socioeconomic status, were significantly more likely to contravene the highway code, blocking other cars at junctions and pedestrians at crossings, than cars typically driven by middle or lower socioeconomic status individuals.

People from the lower socioeconomic brackets tend to live in environments defined by fewer resources, more threats to their security and greater uncertainty in general, so it could have been reasonable to expect that they would be the ones to deviate from the instinct to act fairly more often, purely through desperation. This seems not to be the case. The tendency to cheat others out of their fair share appears to depend on the perception of how serious the consequences of getting caught are likely to be. In other words, lower-class individuals may feel more vulnerable to any social sanctions that might be levelled at them should they get caught in the act of being too greedy. Anyone whose greed is exposed and then later finds themselves in a tight spot, in need of a helping hand, may find themselves isolated, with others unwilling to provide any assistance. Those from the upper SES echelons, on the other hand, may simply feel protected by their greater wealth, in the sense that they could use it to cushion the fall should they ever get caught red-handed in an act of greed and find themselves facing social or legal penalties.

Greed on a grand scale

Behavioural dynamics modelling is a branch of science that examines how multiple exchanges operate across large groups of people. It has created an effective approach to modelling how greed operates on a larger scale than the one-on-one studies used in most neuroeconomic studies. Greed on this grander scale is boiled down to multiple iterations of choosing either to exploit partners – to gain a larger proportion of the profit at their expense – or to cooperate and split the profits more equitably.

This is not dissimilar to a common plot twist in your average pirate story whereby, once they've finally managed to locate the buried treasure, one of them considers whether or not to increase their own share of the plunder by killing one or more of their confederates. In the world of commerce, such backstabbing acts of skulduggery are usually executed with greater subtlety, yet the basic drive – to maximise profits irrespective of the negative impact on partners – is essentially the same.

Greedy behaviour, in business or in piracy, is often inspired by the fear that if you don't make the first move against the others, then they might screw you over first. Both parties know that if they try to take advantage of each other at the same time, neither gets anything, so the evaluation of trustworthiness becomes central to the ultimate decision.

Trust levels between two people, institutions or even nations weigh in heavily on brain mechanisms governing decisions over whether to act cooperatively or greedily. Sometimes, seemingly greedy behaviour is actually stimulated by anxiety about the trading partner's lack of trustworthiness rather than raw, unflinching greed. Could it be that much of what looks like greed and selfishness in the modern world is really fundamentally driven by fear?

Computer simulations modelling these kinds of large-scale economic interactions indicate that the choice to cooperate is typically eliminated after a few rounds of being on the receiving end of trading partners who routinely default on the mutually beneficial option. The choice to consistently defect quickly marches across the patchwork quilt of interacting agents, with one exception. Wherever there are large homogenous clusters of cooperators, where those in the centre of the cluster are surrounded by other cooperators with minimal exposure to defectors, cooperation can thrive. In other words, isolated pockets of cooperators can survive in round after round of exchanges. So there is hope for an economy driven by cooperation rather than pure unadulterated greed. This is just as well, because if we continue on our current trajectory, we are headed for a global catastrophe.

Long-term Consequences of Global Greed

Focusing on short-term profits in a system that will inevitably go horribly wrong in the long run is possibly one of the most worrying aspects of the sin of greed operating on a global scale. The Tragedy of the Commons is a theoretical scenario described by William Forster Lloyd in 1833, whereby if all people took advantage of their right to graze their livestock on the Commons – grassland shared by the whole community – the pasture would soon be overgrazed to the point that there was no grass left for anyone. If everyone in a collective perpetually focuses on getting what they want, without thinking about the long-term consequences of everyone behaving that way, the shared commodity ends up ruined for everyone.

Our collective greed is currently killing the planet. Overfishing in various parts of the world has led to the permanent destruction of fish stocks. Coral reefs around the world are dying off at an unprecedented rate. Felling rainforests to make room for highly profitable cash crops strips delicate soils of their capacity to replace nutrients, leaving it unable to support plant life ever again. Each time we take a plastic bag, we contribute to the process of gradually filling our oceans with plastic to the extent that by 2050 there will be more plastic in our seas than fish. Small individual acts of self-centred greed are multiplying into devastating global consequences. We need to take inspiration from Walter Mischel's Marshmallow Test and try to be more like the kids who managed their primal urge for instant gratification in favour of behaviours that work out better in the long run.

Extremes of greed notwithstanding, most humans find themselves motivated to distribute wealth fairly when the relevant social circuitry of the brain fires up. There are many examples of common areas across the world where local communities have organised themselves to protect pastures from over-grazing and fishing grounds from over-fishing. This system works only when greedy urges are reined in by the knowledge that the negative consequences of not doing so affect everybody in the community.

If outsiders intervene, upsetting this delicate balance then promptly disappear to leave everyone else to deal with the consequences, the whole system breaks down. Globalisation interferes with the local mechanisms that operate to control individual greed on a smaller scale, rendering them ineffective. When people find themselves on the receiving end of an act of generosity, it generates a strong urge to reciprocate. But when people repeatedly experience betrayals of trust, they soon end up concluding that if you can't beat them, you may as well join them. The behavioural dynamics modelling research we considered earlier (p. 158) seems to support this folk wisdom unequivocally.

Neuroeconomic studies clearly demonstrate that unfair division of wealth activates brain areas usually implicated when people feel discomfort or disgust (e.g. AI) and social pain (dACC). This can, in turn, motivate people to want to see the anti-social behaviour punished. Witnessing a greedy person being penalised for transgressing the rules of fair behaviour can induce a surge of activity in the reward pathway, suggesting that many people take pleasure from seeing cheats punished.* The problems arise when cheats *aren't* punished and when greedy people are allowed to get away with benefiting from an unequal share over and over again.

As a species, if we are to survive the existential threat posed by greed on a global scale, we will need to take steps to better legislate against corruption and hold the modern Mammons of our world accountable for the decisions that directly cause suffering to others. If more Bernie Madoffs were punished for their greed and fewer Stanley O'Neals got away with making huge profits from the decisions that leave millions suffering the consequences of economic collapse, then, in future, the greedy might pause to think before intentionally screwing everyone else over.

When it comes to the capacity of the planet to sustain human life, our fates really are inextricably intertwined, whether our socioeconomic status is high, low or intermediate. Might this some day help to mitigate against excessive greed? If the legal insulation the rich can purchase with their exorbitant wealth was no longer available, removing the sense of being impervious to punishment, modern-day Mammons

---

* Interestingly, this was observed in the brains of male but not female participants.

might choose to rein in their insatiable desire for more and begin to favour decisions that benefit everyone. In the meantime, economic bubbles will continue to grow, the greedy will continue to profit and banks will continue to go bust as a result of investing in risky ventures, safe in the knowledge that they will always be bailed out because we know of no other system capable of sustaining a global economy. So round and round we go…

CHAPTER SEVEN

Envy

Comparison is the death of joy.

Mark Twain

Of all the behaviours described by the capital vices, envy is surely the least fun. Lust and gluttony are undeniably pleasurable. Feeling free to hit the snooze button as many times as you like when on holiday is one of life's great joys, so there is definitely pleasure to be taken in sloth. Given how pleased people always seem to be when they win games like Monopoly it's easy to extrapolate the feelings of smug satisfaction associated with feats of real-life greed. The ego-boost that comes from being showered with praise for a job well done is an undeniably great feeling, so that would be the joy in pride. Satisfaction can also be gained, albeit fleetingly, when we hurl abuse at someone who has wronged us, so even wrath can have its pleasures (see Chapter 8, p. 191). But nobody enjoys feeling worse off than others – there's no gratification to be had from feelings of envy.

Nobody wants to see a more delicious-looking plate of food set down in front of another person, nor hear about how sizzling other people's sex lives are if we are not getting any ourselves. It brings no joy to hear of others getting more days of annual leave *and* a bigger pay packet. Discovering how much more impressive other people's houses, cars and home entertainment systems are than our own is unlikely to induce a surge of satisfaction.

Envy *always* feels unpleasant, varying mainly in the degree and character of the discomfort experienced. It varies from the prickle of envy we feel when hearing how great the party was that we weren't invited to, through the waves of envy when we hear of a school friend's far greater wealth, happiness and success, all the way up to the stab of envy suffered when finding ourselves outshone by a professional rival who wins praise and recognition despite their work being nothing special. Exactly where the envy lands on the sliding scale of prickle to stab depends largely on who we compare ourselves with *and* how big the gap between them and ourselves is perceived to be.

Over the best part of two decades, Professor Susan Fiske and colleagues at Princeton University have conducted dozens of social psychology experiments in the USA and several other countries across the world. Together these demonstrate that the primary dimensions across which people judge others tends to focus on two key criteria: competence and warmth. Those regarded as low in both competence and warmth tend to become targets of our scorn. Those high in both competence and warmth tend to earn our respect. Those high in warmth but low in competence receive our pity. Envy is reserved for those we perceive to be high in competence, but low in warmth.

Envy always looks upwards to those we perceive to have superior competence, but not so much if they are deemed to be way beyond our station. We tend to feel the fangs of envy sink in most palpably when we consider those with advantages over us, but with whom we otherwise feel more or less on a par. Neighbours, peers and friends from school, college or university, family members, work colleagues and sporting team mates – these are the usual suspects. Envy is best triggered across relatively small gaps of disparity: when a work colleague gets a more comfortable office chair, a neighbour gets a slick new gadget that you'd love to get your hands on, or an old friend posts photographs of their luxurious lifestyle on Facebook.

While greed is infinite, forever reaching for more regardless of current wealth, envy is entirely relative. Whenever envious feelings are unleashed, the trigger always involves a direct comparison between a specific person and ourselves. In the absence of someone in the outside world with whom we can make a direct comparison, there is no envy. This means that another key difference between envy and others in the malevolent septet is that it is driven by external rather than purely internal factors. It requires a rival's lovelier clothes, better holidays, more exciting hobbies, greater successes and superior access to privilege to create a contrast between what they have and we don't.

An extensive body of psychological research indicates that there are four basic prerequisites for feelings of envy to be triggered. First, the person with whom we compare ourselves must be more or less comparable in social status. Unless a person is themselves a member of the aristocracy, they are very unlikely to feel envious of the lifestyle of members of the royal family. The differences between the lives of royalty versus everyday people are too great for envy to really take hold. Second, the comparison we make between ourselves and another must be directly relevant to our own situation. Unless we happen to be an actor ourselves, the emotions we experience are very unlikely to involve envy when we discover that an acquaintance has managed to score a leading role in a blockbuster movie. The mega-rich may enviously eye up each other's super-yachts, but for someone who is not even a boat owner, let alone a member of the yacht club, envy will not be among the emotions felt when they spy a luxury vessel moored in the harbour. Admiration, resentment, ambivalence or stunned incomprehension – perhaps, but not envy. The third prerequisite is that whatever is envied must be hard to attain. The fourth is that the advantage must be perceived to be undeserved.

Mary Konye and Naomi Oni went to the same school in Forest Gate, east London, from the age of 12 and became good friends. As in many teenage friendships, Mary was said to be envious of Naomi's beauty and popularity with the boys. While the intensity of adolescent envy tends to mellow when people progress into adulthood, in this case, according to a mutual friend, it developed into something of a full blown obsession. Mary began to imitate her friend in many ways, leading Naomi to later claim that she had 'copied my entire life'.

It all came to a head in 2011, when Mary Konye sent a series of text messages to Naomi Oni's then boyfriend. This did not go down well at all. After an exchange of insults they didn't speak for months, during which time Mary Konye hatched a devilish plot. On 30th December 2012, now aged 21, Mary waited outside the Stratford branch of Victoria's Secret where Naomi worked. Wearing a veil to hide her face, Mary Konye followed Naomi all the way back to her home in Dagenham, Essex. As they passed through a relatively quiet and secluded area, Mary took out a jar and splashed the contents into her rival's face. The concentrated sulphuric acid seared Naomi's skin, causing painful chemical burns all over her face and chest, resulting in permanent disfigurement. While Mary Konye was clearly under the influence of a range of emotions when she plotted and carried out this dreadful act of violence, envy was at the heart of this terrible crime. How envy could inspire such a devastating, premeditated attack is not a straightforward matter. Perhaps the religious and philosophical perspectives on this particular deadly sin might provide some important clues.

Historical perspectives

Most of the world's major religions caution against letting envy off the leash. The Islamic Hadith, which describes the concept of Muslim brotherhood, says: 'Do not hate each other, do not envy each other, do not turn away from each other, but rather be servants of Allah as brothers.' The Hindu holy book, the Bhagavad Gita, quotes Lord Krishna's words: 'Those devotees are very dear to me who are free from envy towards all living beings...' Buddhism has *irshya,* translating as 'envy' or 'jealousy', which, along with desire, anger, ignorance and pride, is one of the five poisons described by the Mahayana tradition as obstacles to enlightenment.

Despite being used more or less interchangeably in common parlance, envy and jealousy are fundamentally different concepts. Jealousy relates to the emotions experienced when you are already in possession of something that you are desperate not to lose to another person, while envy relates to the emotions experienced when another person has something that you want for yourself.

So jealousy, the green-eyed monster,* involves feelings that make a person act protectively over something they already have, such as someone guarding their lover against the romantic interests of a rival, or a child who won't let others play with their toys. Envy, on the other hand, involves wanting what other people have. This brings us to one of the Ten Commandments: 'Thou shalt not covet thy neighbour's house, thou shalt not covet thy neighbour's wife, nor his maidservant, nor his ox, nor his ass, nor anything that is thy neighbour's.'

St Thomas Aquinas said that at its heart, envy is 'sorrow over another's good' – a definition that is as accurate as it is concise. Long before him, St Augustine provided a more thorough explanation, helpfully including a list of ways the invidious emotions can inspire people harm to others: 'From envy are born hatred, detraction, calumny, joy caused by the misfortune of a neighbour and displeasure caused by his prosperity.'

Fast forward from ancient religious texts to more modern philosophical perspectives, and we find some wonderful insights into not just *which* regretful behaviours envy can inspire, but more importantly *why*. Arthur Schopenhauer pointed out that 'a human being, at the sight of another's pleasure and possessions, would feel his own deficiency with more bitterness'.

The contrast provided by what they have, compared to what we have, makes us feel inferior. In terms of understanding how this could lead to dreadful acts of spite like that committed by Mary Konye, Immanuel Kant surely framed it best when he described envious people finding themselves 'intent on the destruction of the happiness of others'.

---

* The term 'green-eyed monster' is credited to Shakespeare: the phrase 'green-eyed jealousy' is mentioned in *The Merchant of Venice* and the 'green-eyed monster' phrase itself is first uttered by Iago as he tries to discourage Othello from acting on his jealous rage. More on this below.

Incidentally, Dante may have been hoping to ease suffering, rather than making it worse (for once), when he wrote that those falling foul of the sin of envy would end up having their eyes sewn shut with leaden wire. If we have no idea what others are up to, we can't compare ourselves to them, which defangs the viper of envy.

Sadly, Mary Konye's eyes were wide open. Naomi Oni's beauty seems to have made her feel her 'own deficiency with more bitterness' over the course of many years. As a consequence of her overpowering envy she ended up becoming 'intent on the destruction' of Mary Konye's happiness by taking away her beauty and thereby, in her distorted thinking, making herself the more beautiful one. This is the *malicious* consequence of envy and classic works of literature are full of it.

Mirror, mirror

Evil stepmother characters from the Grimm brothers' fairy tales are infamous for their envy. When the magic mirror's predictable and reassuring reply to the oft-asked question: 'Who is the most beautiful of them all?' unexpectedly switches from the usual 'You are' to the judgment that Snow White had matured into a woman 'one thousand times more beautiful than you', envy flares up into murderous rage. After a few failed attempts to eliminate the competition, the evil Queen eventually succeeds in tricking poor Snow White into eating a poisoned apple.

Othello, a general of the Venetian army, promotes a less worthy soldier to a more senior rank than his standard-bearer Iago. The envy this provokes in Iago inspires a typically convoluted Shakespearean plot of deadly revenge. Iago cunningly harnesses the power of jealousy to trick Othello into strangling his wife Desdemona, on the basis of ridiculously circumstantial evidence of adultery. Only the Bard could weave a tale of envy *and* jealousy together with such effortless grace.

From envy-fuelled power struggles to spiteful destruction of a rival's reputation (that's the 'calumny' St Augustine was referring to above), tales of such wrongdoing fill our newspapers, social media newsfeeds and local gossip networks every day. In day-to-day life, the extremes to which otherwise perfectly normal healthy people will go to when in the clutches of envy know no bounds. They range from casual acts of malicious envy, like dragging a key along the paintwork of a neighbour's expensive car, to despicable acts of evil like plotting to cause a rival permanent disfigurement. Whether the response is petty or devastating, envy can inspire people to engage in totally irrational behaviours, purely to ruin the other person's advantage and even, it seems, when it comes at a significant cost to themselves.

Consider this. If you were offered a choice between earning £50k per year, under circumstances where everyone else in your neighbourhood earned no more than £40k, or £60k where everybody else in your neighbourhood earned £70k, what would *you* choose? One fascinating study demonstrated that, given a similar choice between two salaries of differing size, people were happy to accept the smaller one, just so long as it meant that they got more than everyone else in their neighbourhood. People are literally willing to throw money down the drain if it ensures that others won't enjoy an advantage over them.

The neuroscience of envy

One of the most influential brain imaging studies investigating envy was conducted by Hidehiko Takahashi and colleagues from various scientific institutions across Japan and published in 2009 in the prestigious *Science* journal. They found that, when people in the MRI scanner were confronted with a description of a more successful rival, the more envy that person felt, the greater the activity generated in the dorsal or upper part of the dorsal anterior cingulate cortex (dACC). Ring any bells? We've encountered it previously in circumstances such as the narcissists' excessive feelings of discomfort when experiencing social rejection and when people find themselves in the uncomfortable predicament of being offered an unfairly small slice of the proverbial pie.

Whenever a social interaction delivers a result that falls short of a person's expectations, the so-called 'cognitive dissonance' that this induces always seems to trigger a reliable response in this particular brain region.

The most likely conflict being detected by the dACC in this particular study involve the contrast created by the positive descriptions of their superior rival in direct comparison to how the person feels about themselves. Whether or not the dACC is the source of unpleasant feelings associated with being at a relative disadvantage to others remains to be seen. As activations in this area were observed to be stronger in those scoring higher in the Narcissistic Personality Inventory test and who experienced more social pain while being socially excluded, it's certainly possible. In support of this interpretation, as well as the increased dACC activity, this study also observed reduced activity in the ventral striatum. We've met the ventral striatum several times before, in the context of the predicted reward value activations associated with food, erotic images and winning money (see Chapter 3, Chapter 4 and Chapter 6). Reduced responses in the ventral striatum often occur when an expected reward is not delivered. In this case, it might reflect feelings of inadequacy induced by the description of a superior rival.

We have all experienced feelings of envy at some point in our lives. The occasional experience of the invidious emotions are referred to as 'episodic envy'. 'Dispositional envy' is different. Rather than fleeting, sporadic bouts of mild envy, it occurs with greater frequency, lingers for longer and cuts deeper. People who score highly on the dispositional envy scale will typically agree with the following statements: 'No matter what I do, envy always plagues me' or 'Feelings of envy constantly torment me'. The handy thing about having a well-established scale to capture the degree to which different people are afflicted by envy on a daily basis is that it lends itself very well to brain imaging studies. Yanhui Xiang and colleagues at the South China Normal University in Guangzhou, China, conducted an MRI study looking for structural brain differences that varied according to the individuals' dispositional envy scores, publishing their findings in a highly regarded *Nature* journal called *Scientific Reports*. Getting to the bottom of what happens in the brains of those with a chronic tendency to be envious is important work because it is associated with all sorts of negative outcomes including depression, low self-esteem and poor attendance at work.

The study found a significant difference in the size of a region of the dorsolateral prefrontal cortex (dlPFC) that is just about level with where the forehead meets the average person's hairline on the right-hand side. The more envy each person experienced on a daily basis, as measured by their dispositional envy scores, the smaller this patch of dlPFC was observed to be. Having observed this in the data of 73 brain scans, they went on to confirm it by repeating the experiment with 27 completely different people. In both studies they also administered a test to measure emotional intelligence (EQ*) and found that the higher a person's EQ, the larger the volume of space occupied by this patch of dlPFC. Regions throughout the vast area of cortex that falls under the label of dlPFC are often implicated in the ability to self-regulate emotions and impulsive behaviours. The particular part of the dlPFC implicated here seems to confer the ability to suppress nagging feelings of envy and this important cognitive capacity appears to be affected by the size of this particular brain structure.

Those who scored lower on the dispositional envy score, perhaps unsurprisingly, tended to get better EQ scores. These

---

* It's often referred to as EQ – Emotional Quotient – in counterpoint to IQ, which stands for Intelligence Quotient. The term EQ has been coined to capture other aspects of intelligence that are simply not captured by IQ. The IQ measurement involves tests of crystalline and fluid intelligence, i.e. the extent and depth of a person's knowledge and their ability to find solutions to problems the likes of which have not been encountered before. EQ, on the other hand, measures a person's capacity to identify and regulate their own moods and impulses, read other people's emotional states and generally use all of this emotional information to make good decisions and have positive social interactions with others.

people with a high EQ seem to be better able to exert a self-soothing influence to calm any feelings of envy triggered by exposure to information about their more successful peers. The implication is that the source of this envy-quelling influence is a better-developed dlPFC.

We now have a handle on the critical brain areas involved in generating envy and others that dampen it down. We've seen the circumstances under which it arises and the lengths people will go to when plagued by its destructive influence on a daily basis. It is tempting to speculate that Mary Konye's envy-driven assault on her childhood friend involved an overactive dACC, a shrunken envy-suppressing patch of dlPFC and a very low EQ. Without scanning her brain we will never know for sure. The big question is, given the trouble it can cause, why in the world would us humans have evolved the capacity to feel envious in the first place?

Origins of envy

As we read in earlier chapters, while basic emotions like happiness and sadness tend to emerge around nine months after leaving the womb, the social ones take much longer, kicking in at around 3 years of age. The reason for this is that envy, like guilt, embarrassment and shame, require three important neural systems to be sculpted before it is possible for them to be generated.

One prerequisite for being able to manifest envy is a sense of self. The evidence suggests that this usually kicks in around eighteen months after birth. Second, the little person also needs to have developed the capacity to grasp that other people also have their own sense of self, complete with their own unique set of feelings, priorities, intentions and desires. We met this one briefly in the previous chapter, the phenomenon known as Theory of Mind, which develops around the age of 4. Third, the fledgling human must have figured out the relevant social norms – the range of behaviours expected of them by their family, guardians and the society in which they live. Knowing exactly what behaviours are expected of us by a certain InGroup is a necessary prerequisite for being able to feel guilt, embarrassment, shame or envy at the appropriate times. This third step can vary widely according to where in the world we happen to be raised, or indeed which particular InGroup we seek approval from, while the first two steps are universal.

The experience of the social emotions – guilt, embarrassment, shame and envy – are somewhat distressing, and for good reason. If they were pleasant, then they wouldn't be very useful in discouraging inappropriate social behaviours. They serve as a barometer through which we can measure our anti-social proclivities. We feel shame and guilt when we realise our behaviour has fallen short of other people's expectations: shame as an emotional punishment for breaking the prevailing social rules, for example, or guilt when we transgress moral boundaries. We evolved to feel unpleasant self-conscious emotions like these because they help us to maintain the goodwill of whichever InGroup we find ourselves born into, or are trying to curry favour with. They help to mitigate against the possibility of incurring social penalties that might otherwise result from our misbehaviour. They help us to learn from each social faux pas, discouraging us from repeating antisocial decisions, to strengthen rather than weaken our membership of the InGroup. Envy, on the other hand, is slightly different.

Given its intrinsically comparative nature, envy is known as a 'fortune of others' emotion. We feel envy when we notice a disparity between ourselves and others that leaves us at a disadvantage. The role that envy plays is usually less to do with keeping our own antisocial behaviour in check and more to do with keeping tabs on what others are up to, particularly how they are faring in comparison with ourselves. It alerts us when we might be lagging behind our peers – the social emotion that drives people in their efforts to 'keep up with the Joneses'.

Envy can be regarded as an emotional beacon warning us of an inequality that leaves us worse off. This unpleasant experience – a type of social pain triggered by other people's superiority – acts as a thorn in our side, providing the impetus to take action. There are various courses of action available to correct the imbalance, not all of them destructive. For example, feelings of envy may inspire us to assert our right to an equal share. So long as we kick up enough of a fuss, this may be quite sufficient to help ensure that we're not taken advantage of by others in the future; it works by compelling us to become a thorn in *their* side. While most of the social emotions primarily help us to adapt our behaviour to avoid falling out of favour with the InGroup, envy goes the other way. It helps to ensure that we enjoy the same benefits from InGroup membership as everyone else. In all these scenarios we are compelled to take action to reduce our suffering, whether that means improving our conduct or, if we are being treated unfairly, getting others to improve theirs.

The existence of envious feelings in others can also help *us* to regulate our own behaviour. It can serve to help us balance the selfish, greedy instincts to constantly maximise our gains against the need to avoid displeasing our closest allies. We may try to take steps to alter our own behaviour to avoid inspiring envy in others. The ancient Greeks had some clever tricks up their sleeve in this regard (see Chapter 9, p. 219). So another function of envy is to help us find the equilibrium point between self-interest and group interest in an effort to avoid ending up on the receiving end of the malevolent intentions of others.

Where this equilibrium point is set can change from country to country and from region to region within a country, according to the social rules that prevail in each given sub-culture. Wherever the balance is set, the envy of others can play an important role in signalling perceived imbalances. In some societies people actually revel in the envy of others, sometimes even taking steps to emphasise any inequality that favours them. In other cultures people would find such inequality humiliating, and so immediately take steps to disguise or redress it.

Feelings of envy, guilt, shame and embarrassment are all part of a cunning neurological system of carrot and stick. The experience of these self-conscious emotions motivates us to avoid repeating whatever act induced the unpleasant state of mind in question. And because we know from personal experience how unpleasant feelings of envy are and the lengths others might be prepared to go to as a result, it may help to keep our own behaviour in check. All of the self-conscious emotions, but particularly envy, are vital to our capacity to regulate collective human behaviour, nudging it towards pro-social ends: 'leading us not into temptation, but delivering us from evil.' This system works pretty well overall, but it's far from flawless.

Not fair

Envy usually has a sense of injustice at its core. Our brains have the impressive capacity to be able to judge value almost instantaneously. As we saw earlier (see Chapter 6, p. 145), responses in the reward pathway are more strongly stimulated by a highly valued commodity than one of lesser value. The same neural machinery can be focused on other people's possessions or life circumstances, establishing rapidly how well they are doing compared to ourselves. At a glance we can tell when our slice of cake differs in size to that of others, triggering responses in the AI and perhaps also the dACC. If our slice is bigger – great! A warm glow of self-satisfied smugness may creep over us. If it's smaller, the cogs of envy may start to turn, resulting in a powerful urge to find a way to correct the imbalance one way or another.*

Envy is triggered by any *perceived* disparity that leaves us with the impression that we're worse off. Take the example of food envy, something we can all relate to. It usually starts with seeing a plate of food being placed in front of someone else that looks and smells more appetising than our own. We envy not just the prospect of our dining rival getting to eat a more satisfying meal, but also their superior decision-making skills. Once envy brings the perceived inequality to our

---

* Assuming both parties occupy a similar rung in the pecking order, that is.

attention, we may start mulling over how we might neutralise it, perhaps by trying to convince them to swap meals. If we are successful then we get to be the ones that enjoy the superior dining experience. The discomfort of food envy can often be quickly remedied if the people we are dealing with are cooperative and agreeable. Such envy would also quickly dissipate if the other person offered to go halves instead. Once both prospective culinary experiences are rendered identical, the inequality, and therefore the envy, miraculously disappears. In this way, envy can be a social force for equality.

Infants don't always get it right. They are often quick to fly into an invidious rage when they feel another child is hogging the best toy, when their portion of treats is smaller than everybody else's, or if a sibling seems to be getting more of something than they are. Adults learn, also through negative reinforcement, that if they want a bit of peace and quiet, they'll need to avoid (or at least disguise) flagrant envy-inducing disparities in future. Certainly my goddaughter's two-and-a-half-year-old brother has got this nailed. On her birthday I'm not allowed to give her a gift in his presence, or the ensuing tantrum might bring the roof tumbling down. His fledgling sense of fairness regarding what he gets relative to his big sister is so acute that his envy-induced outrage seems to be on a permanent hair trigger. He's got the sense of self, and a very rudimentary sense of other people's perspectives, but at the tender age of not-quite-three his sense of what's 'fair' is very much a work in progress. Until that gets up to speed, gift-giving in their household must be covert, to avoid toddler Armageddon.

At its heart, sibling rivalry usually boils down to envy. Despite the nerve-frazzling nature of all those tears, this too can be adaptive. A younger sibling, less capable of controlling their fledgling emotions than the older one, will tend to demand more attention, which you might argue they actually need. As well as getting the younger sibling more parental focus, it also gives the older sibling practice in accepting some of life's inevitable inequalities. Sibling rivalries, and in particular envy over a sibling's perceived advantages, usually mellow by adulthood. Under certain circumstances they can persist and, occasionally, get blown totally out of proportion.

One night in February 2002 a British man, Jonathon Griffin of Church Farm, Batcombe, Dorset, donned black clothing, applied camouflage paint to his face, grabbed a pair of night-vision goggles and had a friend drop him off near his brother's farm in the village of Fifehead St Quintin. He sneaked through the fields, broke into farm buildings and proceeded to cause an estimated £7,000 worth of damage to several tractors by rupturing their fuel pipes, knifing their tyres and adding contaminants to their radiators. This was just the beginning of what turned out to be a six-year campaign of destruction that comprised various acts of vandalism ranging from hacking open bags of silage and fertiliser to supergluing padlocks, damaging metal gates and brutalising a mechanical digger. What inspired this medley of devastation? Nobody knows for sure, but being cut out of his father's will may well have been a factor. Jonathon's father Frank had died in 1994, eight years before the first incident took place. His last will and testament had stated that his farm – Skinner's Farm in Stoke Wake, near Blandford, Dorset – should be equally divided between his widow Florence and Jonathon's older brother David. Jonathon himself got nothing, despite having worked there for six years. In 2008, Jonathon was found guilty of two separate charges of criminal damage, but maintained his innocence throughout:

Before my father died I got married and moved onto another farm and I let David run Skinner's Farm like he had been doing. I had no problem with the will; that is a complete red herring. David would ring my mother up and tell her that I'd been doing things and ask her to tell me to stop doing them. I'd discuss it with people I worked with and later those things I said turned into 'admissions'. They said I had night-vision goggles, but I've never owned any. Police took all my tools and searched my home and found nothing linking me with any crime. But mud sticks and they threw a lot of it at me. I haven't really fallen out with my brother, he's just got it in for

me. In court I tried to point out all the lies but it just made me
look obsessive. I suppose I'll just have to take the punishment. *

For the sake of argument, despite his protestations of innocence,
let's assume that for a court of law to have decided there was
enough evidence for Jonathon Griffin to be handed down a
twelve-month sentence for damage to the tractors and an
additional three months for a variety of other acts of criminal
damage, he probably *did* commit these crimes. Why would
someone to go to all that effort, over so many years, sneaking
around at night, procuring (and, it seems, carefully hiding)
camouflage gear and night-vision goggles, just to make their
brother's life more difficult?

Inheritance disputes are notorious for their potential to tear
families apart. Ostensibly, the squabbling is all about the money.
In reality, deep down, it all comes down to envy. It has all
the essential ingredients. Comparison with a specific person
that leaves one party at a clear disadvantage? Check. The
circumstances being directly relevant to the person's own life?
Check. The rival being of similar socioeconomic status?
Check. The advantage being perceived as difficult to achieve,
unfair and undeserved? Check. Check. Check.

The money is just a way of keeping score. The much more
important metrics, those that really get under people's skin but
are almost impossible to quantify objectively, are the social
currencies of love and approval. When a parent's last will and
testament leaves money or possessions to one relative and not
to another, the envy-inducing undertones are clear to all: they
loved and approved of one more than the other. As a result of
what is read between the lines, envy-fuelled acts of viciousness
between family members over disputed wills are frighteningly
common and can lead to absolutely devastating consequences.
During the time this book was being written, a young man
was reported to have stabbed both his mother and sister to

---

* This statement was printed on 18th August 2008 in the *Evening
Standard*.

death shortly after he found out his late father – one of the founders of London's famous 24-hour snack shop, Beigel Bake on Brick Lane – had excluded him from the will. A few years earlier, after the owner of the exclusive Annabel's nightclub on Mayfair's Berkeley Square passed away, it transpired that he had left his two-year-old grandson £103 million, while his son got a mere £1 million. The son immediately launched a lawsuit to contest the will. The list of such tales goes on and on...

Inheritance squabbles are so apt to cause heartache and pain among the family members who survive the deceased that many high-profile individuals have opted to make it completely clear, right from the outset, that their children will be left nothing after they die. Anita Roddick, founder of the Body Shop, famously gave all her money away to charity. The rock star Sting has gone on the record stating that his three daughters and three sons will not get a single penny from his estimated £180 million fortune. Bill and Melinda Gates will leave just $10 million to each of their children, peanuts given the billions they have in the bank. Given the power of malicious envy to inspire behaviour ranging from the merely irritating to the downright murderous, it seems entirely sensible to take steps to mitigate against it. Yet its capacity to inspire malevolent behaviour is just envy's dark side. It has a lighter side too...

Benign envy

Envy might not feel nice, but the behaviour it inspires does not always end in tears. Closing the gap between you and a peer who enjoys some kind of advantage over you can always be achieved in one of two ways: elevate yourself, or pull them down.

Aristotle, as ever, was among the first to describe a virtuous form of envy where, having noted the other person's advantages, a person may be inspired to study them and try to emulate their example. This form of envy may compel us to imitate the admirable qualities of peers we feel are our betters. A handful of studies have chipped in over the past few decades to demonstrate this phenomenon in action in the workplace. Envious feelings have been found to increase work motivation, improve job performance and lead to admiration of and desire to learn from the target of envy. This is benign envy. It can spur us into action, focus our efforts on areas where our skills fall short and motivate us to elevate ourselves through hard graft. So long as it ends up compelling us to redouble our efforts to reach the same level as those with whom we compare ourselves, envy *can* be a virtue.

But even benign envy can have negative repercussions if it goes too far. In some people, usually the hypercompetitive ones, it can inspire a level of motivation that spills over into workaholism. The overall outcomes are rarely ideal for those who prioritise work to the detriment of all other aspects of their life. That said, for the many people who find the prospect of hard work repellent (see Chapter 5), benign envy could prove to be very useful. It might actually provide the impetus they need to knuckle down and get to work. If the response to feelings of envy in the lazy is extra motivation, it could be wielded as a cosh with which to beat Belphegor round the head and keep the temptations of sloth at bay. Owing to these complexities, envy is among the more confusing of all the cardinal vices.

Fortunately it doesn't kick in every time we notice a disparity between ourselves and others. This is just as well because, as Max Ehrmann points out in his poem 'Desiderata': 'for always there will be greater and lesser persons than yourself' (you can find this poem in the Appendices, p. 279). To be envious of many different people all the time would be exhausting and quite possibly catastrophic. Powerful influences in the modern media know this only too well and do everything they can to profit from this highly motivating force of human nature.

Advertising, bragbook and consumer spending
Envy is leveraged to drive profits all over the world on a daily basis. The advertising industry has been at it for centuries. Their flagrant tactics for stimulating covetousness in the

masses include displaying their wares on outrageously beautiful models, unutterably cool film and music stars, as well as careful product placement on the sets of films and popular television series. Getting our favourite celebrities to endorse certain products encourages us to view the goods in question more favourably. It capitalises on the motivating power of benign envy. The implicit message in big-budget advertising campaigns is that, by buying whatever desirable commodity the celebrities happen to be brandishing, we can close the gap between them and us. And although envy is generally more powerfully generated across a narrow disparity in wealth and status, when comparing ourselves to people from a similar background, the advantage of using celebrities is that some of our affection towards them can be displaced onto the watch, clothing line or luxury commodity.

Celebrity endorsement is nothing new. The British monarchy has been helping to peddle crockery since the 1760s when Wedgwood first earned its royal seal of approval. Fast-forward two and a half centuries and we find Hollywood actor George Clooney (all the men want to be him, all the women want to be with him) signing a $40 million deal with Nespresso to be their brand ambassador. Men secretly envy his charm, sophistication and good looks; all we need to do to close the gap between him and us is buy a coffee machine. Even if that doesn't work out at least we achieve the dream of barista-quality coffee in our very own home or office. Women lust after his good looks and charm, so either way his association with the brand helps to differentiate it from others the next time they find themselves browsing for a new coffee maker. In the late twentieth century the world of celebrity endorsement was dominated by such stars of music, sport and stage, but of late the trend has been shifting. These days the most sought-after 'influencers' are the stars of social media. But before we examine this phenomenon, we first need to explore the capacity for social media to stimulate envy in and of itself.

While advertising seems to do everything in its power to intentionally stoke the fires of envy, in social media it is more an accident of design. As with anything social, people have a natural tendency to present themselves in a favourable light. If we are going to a party then we'll tend to dress up in our best clothes, rather than turning up in whatever we usually throw on to loaf around the house on a Sunday morning. The bias towards wanting to make a positive impression means that there is a natural tendency to exaggerate when using social media channels to connect with friends and peers – Facebook being the most obvious example. These inherent biases effectively make people's social media feeds more of a life highlights showreel than a faithful representation of what is really going on in their lives. This can leave people with the false impression that everyone else is enjoying a much better quality of life than they really are. They post eagerly when there is good news to share, an amusing observation, or some kind of success to boast about. They go quiet when all the news is dull, the observations mundane or they find themselves beset by failure. And to make matters worse, when they *do* post, they frame photos of exciting nights out, delicious meals, holiday accommodation and activities in a way that makes it all seem far better than it actually was. All the bad bits are carefully omitted. With social media filtering real life in this way, sieving out the bad and amplifying the good, it can end up leaving people with the distinct, yet false, impression that everyone else's lives are vastly superior to their own.

As we know, envy is most powerfully stimulated by upwards comparison across a narrow rather than a vast gap. In this regard, social media services that connect us with our friends and family – like Facebook – should be more effective at stimulating envy than those used to connect with people beyond our social circles – like Twitter. Certainly Facebook has the potential to be far more potent in its capacity for generating envy than tabloid newspapers and magazines documenting celebrity escapades. Given how dramatically social networking warps reality through people's natural tendency to make themselves appear to be more successful, popular and/or happy than they really are, it is difficult to think of a tool better suited to catalysing envy. But is this suspicion actually supported by some hard data?

Some people who spend a lot of time on Facebook, thereby overexposing themselves to other people's life-highlights, are more prone to feeling depressed, but this doesn't happen to everyone. It seems to depend on how people actually use it. For those who use Facebook interactively, to stay in more regular touch with friends and family members than they would do otherwise, the psychological impact can even be broadly positive. If it genuinely makes them feel *more* socially connected, it can also boost self-esteem. This is not the case for those who spend time on Facebook as spectators, looking at other people's Facebook updates without actually participating much themselves. These are the lurkers, the stalkers and the voyeurs. Such people end up feeling depressed when their use of Facebook regularly results in the experience of envious feelings. Presumably this is particularly problematic for those scoring high on the dispositional envy scale, regardless of how interactive they are in their use of social media.

Whether or not the positive correlation between Facebook envy and depression among the lurkers means that intensive engagement with social networking actually causes an increase in symptoms of depression remains to be seen. It is possible that both are caused by something completely different. It is a topic that is currently being researched and fiercely debated, but it's certainly not beyond the realms of possibility. While we wait for the hard evidence from longitudinal studies that would be required to prove cause and effect, all we really have to go on in the meantime is anecdotal evidence.

A few years ago a couple of good friends of mine deleted their Facebook accounts when the constant comparison with others started to get them down, and it improved matters for them considerably. The best advice for those who've reached the stage of compulsively checking social media feeds, looking them up several times per hour without any particular reason for doing so, is that they might want to experiment with reducing engagement. If you're not feeling terribly happy about your life, any effort to reduce the number of incidents of social comparison per day should, in theory, help to reduce the envy and therefore the social pain experienced overall. Give it a go. Go cold turkey and see what happens.

In January 2017, *Marketing Week* published a list of the top 20 most sought-after Influencers of 2016. Personally, I recognised only one of the top 10, and that was only because it was the queen of selfies herself – Kendall Jenner. Let's see how you do: 1) Hailey Baldwin, 2) Vogue Williams, 3) Kendall Jenner, 4) Iris Apfel, 5) Karlie Kloss, 6) Gigi Hadid, 7) Bella Hadid, 8) Stephen Curry, 9) Emily Ratajkowski, 10) Ashley Graham. So... how many of these names did you recognise? Where are the movie stars? Not a single pop star, how can that be? Well, these days it's all about social media power. If you have a few hundred thousand Twitter and Facebook followers then the contract is yours. Model Hailey Baldwin, descendant of the Baldwin acting dynasty, has over a million followers on Twitter and more than 300,000 on Facebook, and appeared in advertising campaigns for Guess, Tommy Hilfiger, H&M and Ugg over the course of 2016. Vogue Williams is an Irish model who shot to social media fame through a variety of reality TV appearances on shows like *Dancing with the Stars* and *Bear Grylls: Mission Survive*.

Exactly why the stars of social media, predominantly models it seems, have started to displace traditional celebrities in the influence stakes is up for debate. Sports idols, who for years were the go-to role models to influence consumers, have been pushed down the rankings by the purebred social media ninjas. British swimming star Rebecca Adlington was in 11th place on this list, footballer Christiano Ronaldo in 17th and basketballers Stephen Curry and Shaquille O'Neal in 8th and 19th place, respectively. It doesn't just come down to the sheer numbers of followers. It has much more to do with how effectively the stars conjure up the illusion of intimacy with their followers through a constant feed of updates on their daily activities. If they can effectively reduce the perception of the gap between us and them it achieves three things. They feel more familiar, they are liked more *and* the power of envy is enhanced, all in one fell swoop. The implicit promise is the same as it always was: by owning whatever desirable objects they have, we can close the gap between them and us. The difference is that the effective use of social media has made the gap between the star and the consumer narrower than ever, which means the feelings of envy are stronger and so anything they're photographed holding, wearing or using just flies off the virtual shelves.

Epic fail

A popular form of entertainment in the world of social media is the 'epic fail'. This describes everyday people attempting to present themselves in a positive light on social media, yet falling flat on their face, often literally. Slapstick comedy has been popular for centuries. In mediaeval times, when the jester pretended to hurt himself, those assembled in the royal court would roar with laughter, having empathically experienced some of the fool's pain, followed by a surge of relief that it wasn't them suffering the humiliation of leaping around like an idiot. The pleasure we take from witnessing the misfortune of others was exploited from the 1920s onwards in the films of the Marx Brothers and Charlie Chaplin, and live in theatres for centuries before the movie camera was invented. From the late 1940s onwards even members of the public could become the star of the show. Using elaborate set-ups and hidden cameras, TV series like *Candid Camera* captured the humiliation of everyday people to the delight of families watching in their living rooms. The ubiquitous availability of the home video camera in the late twentieth century meant that people at home could start getting in on the act too, by sending footage of their domestic mishaps to TV shows like *You've Been Framed*. And now that everybody is constantly filming everything on their smartphones and posting the clips online, TV shows like *RudeTube* feature the most-watched YouTube clips, which more often than not involve people inadvertently causing themselves some kind of injury. We just can't get enough of it.

This brings us back to St Augustine's list of the evils associated with envy, which included the 'joy caused by the misfortune of a neighbour'. In this day and age, rather than this being something people vigilantly do their best to avoid to save their souls, it now seems to have become one of our most loved forms of entertainment. The pleasure that comes from witnessing other people's misfortune is known as 'schadenfreude'. The literal translation from German to English is 'harm-joy'. While the envy we feel when witnessing a rival's success involves feelings of displeasure, schadenfreude reflects delight at their failure.

Arthur Schopenhauer was of the opinion that, 'To feel envy is human, to savour schadenfreude is diabolic'; yet not everybody thinks this way. While we readily laugh at anyone that suffers a minor accident that could so easily have befallen ourselves, it can be especially satisfying when people we envy – those who cause us feelings of social pain by virtue of their superiority – experience a stroke of misfortune. Personally, I get a kick out of hearing that Chelsea FC have lost a match, even though the team I support is more often than not wallowing in the league below and so not even involved in that particular competition. This is probably because, no matter how much we might sing 'We're by far the greatest team, the world has ever seen' the simple truth is that Chelsea are *much* better. So it is schadenfreude that makes me smile when I hear our local rivals have suffered an embarrassing defeat. This is not atypical. Passionate sports fans across the globe delight at news that a rival team has suffered losses, embarrassments and misfortunes, particularly when their own team is the underdog. Equally, for anyone who works outside of the banking industry and earning a modest wage, it can be intensely satisfying to hear of crooked financiers being punished for dishonest working practices. After the fall of Enron* millions of North Americans rejoiced at the news that its board members had been given lengthy prison sentences for cooking the books to disguise heavy losses and create the

---

* A multi-billion-dollar US energy company that famously collapsed in 2001 after revelations of major accountancy fraud.

illusion that it was generating huge profits. We do like to see those at the top take a tumble.

From the perspective of evolutionary psychology, taking pleasure from the misfortune of someone higher up the pecking order makes sense. For most of human history, when we lived in groups of a more manageable size, life was defined by limited access to scant resources and there was a constant battle for survival. Under these circumstances, more for a dominant member of the InGroup meant less for you. If someone higher up the pecking order suffered a misfortune, it could be great news for you and yours. This is how evolutionary psychology accounts for how this diabolical pleasure came to be.

A major difference between envy and schadenfreude is that while envy tends to operate across smaller gaps in the pecking order, schadenfreude is possible across much larger disparities in wealth. This may be how the tabloid press has turned our voracious appetite for the misfortune of others into big business. Detailing the fall from grace of sportsmen, pop stars and anyone else the general public might perceive as being vastly and unfairly better off than everyone else is bound to go down well with the readership given how much pleasure it provokes. Nevertheless, envy and schadenfreude still share an intimate bond.

Neuroscience studies investigating schadenfreude have revealed that, when we learn that a rival's fortunes have taken a turn for the worse, an increase in ventral striatum activity occurs. This is generally interpreted to be the source of the satisfaction people feel when learning of the misfortune of others. At the same time that the ventral striatum becomes more active, a reduction in activity is also observed in the anterior insula (AI). So far we have considered the AI primarily in terms of its responses to aversive stimuli. But many MRI studies investigating the brain areas involved in generating our powers of empathy have also consistently implicated AI activations in the ability to feel the emotional state of others. So to experience the harm-joys of schadenfreude the AI may first need to be suppressed – to reduce our capacity to empathise with others – before it is possible to experience pleasure at another's misfortune.

The original envy study we considered earlier also investigated the degree to which the same 100 volunteers experienced schadenfreude upon learning of a rival's misfortune. It concluded that the stronger the degree of envy a given person experienced when hearing descriptions of a rival's superiority, the greater the strength of the schadenfreude-triggered activity in the ventral striatum on hearing of their downfall.

Experiencing pleasure from a rival's chance misfortune is one thing, but actively bringing about their downfall is quite another. We will conclude this chapter with a sad real-life tale of how dispositional envy can inspire diabolical acts of violence. Over the past few decades the USA has been hit by a spate of copy-cat mass murders. These attacks are usually characterised by disturbed individuals arming themselves with several weapons and going out with the express intention of killing large numbers of innocent people, more or less indiscriminately. In 2014, Elliot Rodger killed his three housemates and then drove around town, calmly shooting young people in and around the University of California Santa Barbara campus. According to a 100,000 word 'manifesto' he sent to friends, family members and his psychotherapist, he claimed to have been driven to this horrifying act of violence by overwhelming feelings of envy.

When a rival's advantage is perceived to be unfair – whether in terms of their superior appearance as in Snow White and her wicked stepmother, their position of authority as in Othello's standard-bearer Iago, or their wealth as in the case of the Griffin farming brothers – malicious envy can rear its ugly head. Sometimes when the envy in a person's mind has brewed and fermented over many years, elaborate fantasies about malevolent methods of levelling the playing field by bringing about the downfall of their rivals can start to emerge. The desire to feel the satisfaction associated with schadenfreude may even inspire dreadful acts of violence like those committed by Elliot Rodger in the US and Mary Konye in the UK.

The envy Mary Konye felt for Naomi Oni festered for many years, eventually manifesting as what the chief prosecutor in her trial described as an 'obsession'. But the final straw that triggered her deplorable act of violence seems to have been an insult that deeply wounded Mary Konye's self-esteem. A piece of evidence presented during the court case, and which helped to convince the jurors that this crime was worthy of a 12-year prison sentence, is instrumental here. It turns out that, shortly after she threw acid at her friend's face, Mary Konye uploaded a photo of Freddy Krueger[*] on her WhatsApp account, accompanied by the words: 'Who looks like *Wrong Turn* now?' *Wrong Turn* is the name of a horror movie that features a variety of disfigured characters. Naomi Oni had allegedly likened Mary Konye's appearance to these characters during an earlier argument, bringing the motive behind her devestating plot into sharp relief. This brings us to our final and arguably most destructive deadly sin of them all: wrath.

---

[*] Freddy Krueger is the hideously scarred star of the horror movie, *Nightmare on Elm Street.*

CHAPTER EIGHT

Wrath

I was angry with my friend:
I told my wrath, my wrath did end.
I was angry with my foe:
I told it not, my wrath did grow.

William Blake, *Poison Tree*

Now we enter Satan's lair – the Prince of Hell assigned by Bishop Binsfeld to the sin of wrath. His is the realm of excessive anger, aggression and violence. When it comes to the potential to cause harm by tearing people apart rather than bringing people together, wrath is surely peerless. After all, death is the ultimate force for separating a person from their loved ones and, of all the deadly sins, wrath delivers people to their death most swiftly.

The desire to hurt others comes in hot-headed and cold-calculated varieties. The harm they cause can take the form of physical and/or psychological damage. And Satan rarely operates alone; the other deadly sins are always happy to chip in and lend a helping hand. Envy and lust conspire to trigger violent fantasies in the brains of jilted lovers. Envy and greed egg wrath on in battles over sought-after resources. Conflicts occur on both micro and macro scales: between individuals; between families in multi-generational blood feuds; between neighbours over the garden fence; and between nations in disputes over borders. The underlying motive in all this often boils down to nothing more than wounded pride. Even the religious wars that have been fought throughout history and right up to the present day amount to little more than different InGroups fighting over who has the best imaginary friend, to the mind of your average modern athiest.

The harms associated with death are not limited to loss of life. It is the friends and family members of the dearly departed who pay the greatest emotional toll, left behind to mourn their loss and cope without them. Nor are the harms imposed by wrath limited to death. They can manifest in ways that make people's whole lives a living nightmare. Domestic violence can leave partners and children living in a state of perpetual fear. Victims of bullying at school and in the local community, can be left feeling suicidal and end up with psychological scars lasting a lifetime.

On the basis of the familiar rhythm of logic that has run throughout this exploration of the cardinal vices, you may already have an inkling of what is coming next. There is always *something* positive to be said about these horrible, malevolent behaviours, an aspect that we can't quite do without; something that provided our ancestors with survival advantage over the course of many generations and continues to pay dividends to this day. Considering that wrathful urges compel us to move directly into the firing line of other people's aggression, despite the clear danger this might pose to our survival prospects; were there no benefit to be gained at all, it would surely have been deleted from the human gene pool long ago.

Humans are notoriously warlike. Given the propensity of our species to accumulate far more resources than we need in the short term (Chapter 6), it turns out that there is a particularly high cost-benefit ratio for inter-human violence, compared to other mammals. The potential costs might be devastatingly high, but the potential benefits are extraordinary. If slaying a human rival yields control of a surplus of food, tools, clothing, weaponry and therefore power, not to mention shelter, land and the possibility of creating offspring with the female contingent of the invaded homestead, the potential benefits may outweigh even huge risks. Serious injury and quite possibly death are steep prices to pay for failure, but when the windfall arising from a triumphant conquest has the potential to yield sufficient power and resources to confer a survival advantage across many succeeding generations, it can still be worth it in the long run. When the InGroup's wealth and power stands to be boosted sufficiently to enhance even their great-great-great-grandchildren's chances of successfully passing on their own genes, the advantages of such a risky strategy are clear. If you doubt this, just consider what it did for the survival prospects of Genghis Kahn's DNA (see Chapter 4, p. 99).

As it paid such huge dividends through much of 'pre-civilised' human history, the propensity for aggressive confrontation to spill over into violence, so evident throughout the whole animal kingdom, has been retained as a core part of human nature. This doesn't mean we have to act on our aggressive impulses to thrive. Modern society has used various tricks to reduce aggressive confrontation more successfully than ever before in the history of our species. But we still retain these urges in our behavioural repertoire and they still have a significant impact on people's behaviour from day to day.

This is a dizzyingly vast subject area and so there is a need to be disciplined in terms of focusing on the aspects of wrath that are most relevant to the question at hand. In our exploration of why we do the aggressive things we know we shouldn't, we will grapple with those instances of when expressions of anger are socially appropriate and when they are not. We will try to understand the role aggressive behaviour plays in helping us to define boundaries of acceptable behaviour and in summoning the courage to face up to our fears. Of particular interest is where in the brain anger comes from and any consistent differences in the structure and the function of the brains of those who can keep a lid on their aggression compared to others who can't.

Train rage

When was the last time you got angry? This morning? Yesterday? Last month? Don't recall? For me, it was the day before yesterday.

I was heading down on the train to Brighton on England's south coast to do some filming for *Secrets of the Brain*.* I

---

* A science series I present on Insight TV.

happened to have been working on this chapter on the journey down, so when we arrived at the terminus, the table I was at was covered in science papers and books which took me a little while to pack away. I ended up being the very last passenger to disembark. As I'd arrived with plenty of time to spare I was dawdling, I'll admit to that right from the outset.

The platform attendant came into the carriage, walked up the aisle towards me, glanced at me briefly as I was packing up my things, then promptly stepped back off the carriage and disappeared. A couple of minutes later I was ready to go and started making my way to the exit, but when I hit the button to open the doors, nothing happened. It soon occurred to me that the mechanism locking all the doors on the carriage might have been activated, but this seemed unlikely for two reasons: no announcement had been made to say the train was being taken out of service, and the platform attendant had looked directly at me and said nothing. So I had felt comfortable assuming that I'd have plenty of time before the train could fill back up with passengers and set off again on the return journey. I quickly shuffled down to the next carriage, feeling baffled but not alarmed. I hit the first 'open doors' button I came to, again to no avail. Having exhausted all the other possible explanations for my predicament and now feeling fairly convinced that the train probably *was* being taken out of service, I started running. Sprinting through to the third carriage, fear and indignation rising, I finally got ahead of the platform attendant and managed to hit the 'open doors' button before he could deactivate those ones too. As I was scurrying up the aisle I had started to feel increasingly foolish. By the time I finally managed to get off the train, I was absolutely incensed.

I couldn't think of a single reasonable explanation for why this man, a person I had never previously laid eyes on, seemed to have intentionally trapped me on the train. Why would anyone do that? How could he look me in the eye, offer no warning of what he was going to do a few moments later and then walk the length of the train, locking the doors of carriage after carriage, knowing full well it would leave me stranded? It was the idea that he might have done this on purpose that was stoking my fury. But I held back, reminding myself that, you never know, it could have been an innocent mistake. Accidents do happen.

Emerging from the train right next to him I described what had happened from my perspective and, as calmly as I could, asked him for an explanation. He mumbled words to the effect of: 'Well, sir, passengers have three minutes to disembark the train...' It quickly became clear that he *had* known exactly what he was doing. No apology, just a weak excuse. With no reasonable explanation to hold back my ire, I gave him a piece of my mind, in no uncertain terms.

Unleashing a verbal torrent of abuse on a complete stranger is not my usual mode of conduct. In fact, I hate confrontations and try to avoid them wherever possible. So why did I lose my cool so thoroughly on this particular occasion? Given that I happened to be writing this chapter at the time, I spent a lot of time afterwards mulling over what made me blow my top. But before we go into that, let's consider the biological origins of anger and the role it plays in delineating social boundaries.

The anger advantage

Anger has its place in the emotional repertoire of every healthy, well-balanced human. David Hume even went as far as to say that, 'Anger and hatred are passions inherent in our very frame and constitution. The want of them, on some occasions, may even be proof of weakness and imbecility.'

Anger is a typical emotional response to feeling threatened. In this regard it can be seen as a defence mechanism. Aggression can serve to help people overcome their fear and stand up for themselves when mistreated by others, rather than meekly tolerating hostile behaviour. Anger can also provide the motivation to take a stand against moral transgressions, provoking intervention even when the person in question is not directly involved. It can inspire people to hold others accountable for their antisocial conduct, to draw a line in the sand and discourage a repetition of such behaviour in the future. Anger can play a vital role in regulating conduct in society because when it does *not* provide an antidote to people's natural fear of confrontation, a spiral of silence can result. If nobody manages to find the courage to stand up to antisocial behaviour then victimisation and oppression can spread, despite widespread disapproval. So anger *can* be used for pro-social purposes at the individual and group level. It starts to play an important role early on in child development.

Anger is one of the seven universal basic emotions,* the first glimmers of which start to emerge in infants between the ages of four and six months. They are *universal* in the sense that they emerge at this age in all human infants, wherever in the world they happen to be born, as indicated by the distinct facial expression that accompanies each emotion. Anger is usually expressed under circumstances where an infant has encountered an obstacle preventing them from reaching a desired goal. It is thought to serve the purpose of providing extra energy to help the infant overcome, and sometimes acquire external assistance in overcoming, the obstacle. From six to twelve months of age, rather than being fleeting, these expressions of anger can be sustained for longer periods of time and triggered under a wider variety of circumstances.

Anger can be reliably induced by restraining a child's arms or by taking away an entertaining toy. In fact, the toy doesn't even have to be removed entirely. If a toy that previously made a noise when the child pressed a button unexpectedly stops working, an angry response if often elicited. In essence, anger is a typical response when control over the environment has been taken away. One purpose served by the expression of anger is to influence others in a way that might enable control to be re-established.

Anger also pays dividends in parenting, so long as it is used sparingly and in the appropriate context. Displays of aggression

---

* The others, in case you haven't yet memorised them, are: happiness, interest, surprise, fear, sadness and disgust.

have a role to play when used to deter children from dangerous situations. Should a toddler wander off in the direction of fast-moving traffic, a swift change in emotional tone from gentle coaxing to an angrily barked 'STOP!' may be just enough to avert disaster by making an errant child stop dead in their tracks. Expressions of anger can be an effective means of defining the boundary between behaviours that are and are not acceptable.

My uncle gets angry very infrequently, as far as I can tell. On the rare occasion that I have witnessed his anger over the past four decades, a distinctive 'tell' manifests itself on his face. His upper lip twitches, on one side of his face only, revealing a single canine tooth that warns of his approaching fury. On one particularly memorable occasion when he stepped in to protect a family member, I once witnessed him intimidate the aggressor, who was a head taller than him and built like a brick wall, into cowering submission using nothing more than what I affectionately think of as his 'rage face'. He didn't even have to raise his voice.

When this classic mammalian threat signal — the carnivore's snarl — flashed across his face, my siblings and I always knew that we'd overstepped the mark. We would invariably stop whatever it was that we were doing straight away. It was an excellent deterrent because seeing this expression of primal anger flash across the face of a man typically so calm, easy-going and patient, created a powerful and effective contrast. He never needed to resort to aggressive behaviour because the threat alone, painted so starkly across his face, was sufficient to get the desired response when we were being particularly unruly and disobedient.

In light of all this, my own angry outburst in Brighton station makes more sense. When I hit the button to open the doors in carriage after carriage, control had been taken away from me. I felt trapped, helpless and vulnerable. Once I had confirmed that, as opposed to it being an unfortunate accident, I had probably been placed in that predicament intentionally, I was almost certainly motivated by a desire to punish the station attendant for what I felt was poor conduct on his behalf. I wanted him to know he had overstepped the mark. I felt that I'd been on the receiving end of an injustice. Scolding him seemed both warranted and appropriate. I wanted him to regret his actions so that he might take pause for thought before doing the same thing to someone else in the future.

To be brutally honest, the fact that he had made me feel stupid was probably an important factor too. My pride had been wounded by what I perceived to be his intention to make a fool of me for no apparent reason. I wanted to hurt his feelings as he had hurt mine: an eye for an eye. Childish, I know, but perhaps 'childish' for a good reason. Looking back, as I ran through the carriage with my panic levels steadily rising, I distinctly remember thinking: 'I haven't felt like this since primary school.' As this thought crossed my mind, I had a flashback to my old school playground where, for a few weeks one particular winter, the mean kids from the year above targeted me for their daily abuse. Nothing too serious, just half a dozen or so of them pelting me with snowballs with hard lumps of ice embedded in their core. This happened every break time for about a week, during a cold snap. Admittedly this is pretty tame by the standards of many people's experiences of bullying, but it was scary for me all the same. Tendrils of these distant memories of intentional victimisation had wrapped themselves suffocatingly around my throat and chest that day on the train in Brighton.

Giving that man a piece of my mind was undeniably satisfying. It provided a release for pent-up emotion and made me feel as if I had drawn a line in the sand that might benefit others in the future. It gave me a sense that the minor injustice I had suffered had been neutralised. The desire to punish a perceived injustice, however, can result in much graver consequences than merely verbally berating someone. The desire to get even can inspire genuinely horrifying acts of physical violence, as we saw in the last chapter with Mary Konye. And, as we all know only too well, wrath can sometimes go even further, motivating people to commit murder.

Picture a murderer

What comes to mind when you think of a stereotypical murderer? A man? Shifty eyes? Poorly groomed? Stubble, perhaps? Dishevelled hair? Scruffy attire. Maybe some tattoos, a facial scar or two, unusual piercings... that kind of thing. In terms of brain power you're probably thinking of someone whose intelligence is below average. Someone who may well have struggled through school due to a constellation of learning difficulties, troubled home life, discipline problems, bunking off school and inevitably falling in with the wrong crowd. Whatever sprang to mind, it's a fair bet that a university professor is not the kind of person you were thinking of.

In 2016, Hengjun Chao, former assistant professor at the Icahn School of Medicine at Mount Sinai, set out in his car from home in Tuckahoe and headed for downtown Chappaqua, both of which are in New York state. He pulled up outside Lange's Little Store and Delicatessen, took out a shotgun, pointed it at the entrance and pulled the trigger. He hit both an innocent bystander and his target, Professor Dennis Charney, Dean of the Mount Sinai School of Medicine, a world-renowned neurobiologist whose publication record includes many papers detailing his research into mood and anxiety disorders. The motive? Chao had been dismissed from a research post under Professor Charney seven years previously, for falsifying scientific data. Fortunately, Charney made a good recovery. The victims of another US academic, Dr Amy Bishop of the University of Alabama, were not so lucky.

In 2010, 50 minutes into a biology department faculty meeting that Dr Bishop regularly attended, she calmly took out a handgun and shot dead three of her colleagues. The dean of graduate studies, Debra Moriarity, having dived under the table for cover, realised she was close enough to try and grab Bishop's legs to wrestle her to the floor. Bishop stepped away and, pointing the gun straight at Moriarity's head, pulled the trigger three times. Fortunately for Dr Moriarity, the gun jammed and that is the only reason she lived to tell the tale. As well as those she killed, which included her boss Gopi Podila, three other colleagues were also wounded before the gun jammed. On 24 September 2012, Dr Bishop was sentenced to life imprisonment, with no chance of parole.

Why would an intelligent person, with a degree from Harvard Medical School, no less, commit a clearly premeditated triple murder, in front of many witnesses who knew her personally? The motive was crystal clear: she'd been rejected for tenure a few months before and was working out her one-year notice period. Tenure describes a much-desired job for life in academia and the decision regarding who should be offered one of these rare and coveted positions is made by other members of the faculty staff. It is the ultimate reward bestowed on the lucky few after many years of punishingly hard work and perpetual uncertainty. A *Psychology Today* blogger, who'd been through the same crushing experience of being rejected for tenure, described it as effectively being 'fired by your colleagues'.

The world's prisons are chock full of men who have committed spontaneous acts of violence in a moment of madness, with no apparent concern for the consequences. We are all familiar with the concept of people lashing out in anger, on the spur of the moment, without stopping to think about the long-term outcome. But when an ostensibly intelligent person puts together a carefully thought out plan that involves committing cold-blooded murder in plain view of many witnesses, this is somehow more shocking. The part of these tragic tales that often surprises people the most is why someone would commit a crime they have absolutely no chance of getting away with. What would drive someone to do something so stupid? In Bishop's case, it's less that we wouldn't expect a woman to be prone to feelings of aggression and more that female rage is usually expressed in a manner more subtle than brute physical violence. Research investigating gender differences in aggression indicates that men have a strong tendency towards being direct and violent, while women tend towards indirect and non-violent expressions. When intoxicated by the sin of wrath, however, anyone can be inspired to terrible violence, regardless of their gender or intelligence.

Origins of anger

Men commit acts of violence much more frequently than women. In fact, 90 per cent of all murders are committed by men. Given the clear difference between male and female tendencies towards violence, the first thing that usually springs to mind when looking for a likely biological culprit is testosterone. Halfway through gestation the testes of the male foetus produce a surge of testosterone and this directs brain development along a trajectory favouring more aggressive behaviour. Indeed, a surge of testosterone from a different source can also take place in the female foetus, with similar outcomes. A condition known as 'congenital adrenal hyperplasia' involves the adrenal glands producing a surge of testosterone, nudging female neurodevelopment along the path of masculinisation. Such women tend to be considerably more aggressive than their female peers when they reach adulthood. Then there is the surge in male sex hormones that occur during adolescence, which tends to run in parallel with rising aggression levels. But while it does play a key role in increasing men's height, weight and musculature, its participation in triggering aggression in adulthood is not so clear-cut.

Interventions that attempt to reduce testosterone levels in adult men who are prone to violence never seem to pan out as expected. The most likely explanation is that the main impact of testosterone on aggression levels takes place earlier in the course of brain development. Once an aggressive brain has been built, reducing testosterone levels usually has little impact on the person's tendency towards violence. By the time a person reaches full adulthood the role testosterone plays in forming an aggressive temperament has reached completion and so reducing it at that point seems to makes little difference.

While attempts to reduce violent behaviour with anti-testosterone agents tend to be ineffective, the reverse is not true. A study carried out by Harrison Pope and colleagues at the Harvard Medical School administered testosterone-boosting agents, or a placebo, to 100 men to establish whether it would increase their aggression levels. The concern was that the abuse of steroids leading to very high levels of testosterone might be responsible for inducing uncontrolled aggression in bodybuilders and athletes. Although the impact of the elevated testosterone was a bit hit and miss, in 8 of the 50 men given the real hormone there was a marked or moderate increase in aggression levels.

Moving on to the brain areas involved in aggression, the integrity of certain sub-compartments of the amygdala seems to be critical. This structure is famed for its role in generating feelings of fear and anxiety in response to threats. There are two human cases where a tumour pressing up against the amygdala was implicated in extremely violent conduct. The first was Ulrike Meinhof, a woman responsible for several armed robberies and bombings during the late 1960s and early 1970s in her role as co-founder of West German terrorist gang the Baader-Meinhof Group. The other was Charles Whitman, who in 1966 opened fire on the campus of the University of Texas in Austin, killing 16 people, having already killed both his wife and his mother earlier in the day. As we'll see later when we explore some of the psychiatric illnesses that are usually associated with disproportional levels of aggression and violent behaviour, the amygdala is often implicated, but rarely in isolation.

Another brain area crucial for feelings of anger and expressions of aggression is the anterior cingulate cortex (ACC). Since the 1970s it has been known that electrical stimulation of either the amygdala or the ACC can trigger angry vocalisations in experimental animals. Conversely, ablating these structures – intentionally damaging them through surgery – usually results in reduced expressions of anger. In more recent times, these rather crude investigations have been complemented by many non-invasive brain imaging experiments.

To study aggression in the lab, researchers have invented several ingenious approaches to winding up their volunteers.

These invariably take advantage of the fact that cranking up a person's frustration levels eventually pushes them over into feelings of intense anger. Methods range from directly insulting them, to frustrating them with an impossible task, to getting them to electrocute each other. The maddening 'point subtraction task' is very popular. Asking volunteers to solve impossible anagrams for which there are no correct solutions seems to be a particular favourite too. But the Taylor Aggression Paradigm (TAP) surely takes the biscuit for its capacity to elicit feelings that are most akin to wrath.

The TAP task involves a pair of volunteers giving each other painful electric shocks of variable strength. Whenever one person feels that the shock they just received was more severe than the one they gave to their partner previously, levels of indignation increase accordingly. The difference in the shock strength each person chooses to inflict on their partner, compared to that received in the previous round, is used as a proxy for their current desire for revenge.*

Studies using MRI to monitor activity levels across the entire brain while participating in the TAP task reliably yield activations in the ACC when participants were feeling aggressive. Best of all, the magnitude of the activation in the ACC seemed to mirror the degree to which the person was motivated to increase the strength of their next punishment. This is particularly interesting given that, as we are about to see, religious perspectives on what makes wrath so very devilish take the issue of vengeance very seriously. The ACC seems to be a prime candidate for the source of these very

---

* This scenario reminds me of a favourite childhood game I used to play with my best mate during the school holidays. We only had one pair of boxing gloves so we'd have one boxing glove each and use it to take turns punching each other gently in the face. It was a trust game really. You don't hit me too hard, I won't hit you too hard. Invariably it would escalate. Each of us always seemed to feel the other had used more force. It seems we chanced upon our very own version of the Taylor Aggression Paradigm! No wonder it pretty much always ended in tears.

urges. Please note that these particular activations are not in the dACC that repeatedly cropped up in previous chapters, but just beneath it.

Historical perspectives on wrath

Gods, on the whole, have not always set the best example when it comes to wrath. If anything they seem distinctly prone to displays of aggression. The Judeo-Christian God was certainly not averse to expressing discontent through merciless acts of violence. The Greek gods, Apollo worst among them, seemed to be forever inflicting violent punishment on anyone who opposed or simply displeased them. In the Hindu holy book, the Bhagavad-gita, we find Vishnu in his incarnation as Lord Krishna explaining to Prince Arjuna that it is his religious duty no less, as warrior and king, to kill his enemies. Aggression is clearly not always frowned upon in religion.

The concept of 'an eye for an eye'; mentioned in the Old Testament, may at first glance seem to sanction violence. In fact, modern Judaism interprets these verses as guidance on how people should be compensated for a loss. It is about limiting the extent of compensation to the value of the loss and ensuring that the compensation sought does not exceed it. Jesus himself went a step further, proclaiming that rather than seeking recompense at all, good Christian should instead turn the other cheek. This approach would certainly help to avoid the escalation in tit-for-tat retaliations that are typically observed in the TAP task.

St Gregory the Great delivered his judgement on the critical difference between good and bad anger as follows: 'There is an anger which is engendered of evil, and there is an anger engendered of good. Hastiness is the cause of the evil, divine principle is the cause of the good.' This definition of virtuous anger is evidently self-serving. On that basis alone it is tempting to discount it entirely. That said, the suggestion that haste might help to account for the dark side of anger is of greater interest. The implication that the threshold beyond which anger becomes a sin is partly to do with how well thought through an act of aggression is could be worth contemplating.

It would suggest that the short-term, impulsive, hasty decision to lash out is vicious, but less so if it is carefully considered.

Aristotle described anger as 'a burning desire to pay back pain'. A few centuries later, Seneca defined anger as 'the most hideous and frenzied of all the emotions', and accounted for the irrational choices made by those in the grip of an uncontrollable rage as a form of 'brief insanity'. Again this would seem to suggest that the vice in anger is to be found in its impulsive manifestations. He went on to list the many ways anger can cloud our judgement, making us 'oblivious to decency, heedless of personal bonds, obstinate and intent on anything once started, closed to reasoning or advice, agitated on pretexts without foundation, incapable of discerning fairness or truth.'

Rather than persuing Seneca and St Gregory the Great's line of reasoning, let's think more about the implications of Aristotle's notion of the irresistible impulse to settle a score. St Thomas Aquinas was unequivocal when he pointed an accusatory finger at the urge for revenge in his account of the sin of wrath: 'if one desires the taking of vengeance in any way whatever contrary to reason, for instance to desire the punishment of one who has not deserved it, or beyond his deserts, or again contrary to the order prescribed by law, or not for the due end, namely the maintaining of justice and the correction of defaults, then the desire of anger will be sinful, and this is called sinful anger.'

This would make the sin of wrath a desire to seek revenge that is disproportionate to the act that provoked it. While 'an eye for an eye' might be deemed reasonable, going beyond that would be to trespass into the realms of sinful behaviour. Let us apply this thinking to the examples of aggression we considered earlier. My outburst at the station attendant was, by my own admission, motivated by a desire to 'pay back pain' – so it satisfies Aristotle's definition. My conduct may well have been labelled by onlookers as a 'brief insanity, oblivious to decency' given that they would probably have had no idea what perceived injustice had provoked my hot-headed, emotional response. I certainly got some funny looks. I was guilty of anger, of that there is no doubt. On the question of whether I fell foul of the sin of wrath, I think St Thomas would have let me off the hook. My response was arguably neither 'beyond his deserts' nor 'contrary to the order prescribed by law'. Our assistant professors over in the US, on the other hand, could be in trouble. Considering whether or not their desired revenge was proportional to the perceived injustice, clearly it was not. If there *was* such a demon as Satan waiting in hell to punish transgressions of the sin of wrath according to Dante's specifications, Amy Bishop and Hengjun Chao could well find themselves being savagely attacked by their fellow sinners for all eternity.

Given the mixed messages we've been getting from religious and philosophical sources, on this occasion we will have to look further afield for insight on the question of where perfectly acceptable expressions of anger spill over into vice. The question of whether a certain aggressive response to a perceived injustice is morally right or wrong is not just a matter of concern for these two disciplines. The criminal justice system has to make such calls on a daily basis. So we will now take a brief look at what the world of jurisprudence has to say about wrath.

How much is too much?

In 1999, British farmer Tony Martin inadvertently started a huge debate over the right to defend property in the UK when he shot dead a 16-year-old boy who had broken into his home in Norfolk with the intent to commit burglary. When the case was tried in court, he was initially* deemed to have responded with excessive force and sent to prison to serve a life sentence for murder. Three years later, in a separate case, a man called Fred Hemstock shot at a car lurking suspiciously on his land on an isolated farm in Lincolnshire,

---

* On appeal the charge was reduced to manslaughter and his prison sentence was adjusted accordingly. He actually only ended up serving three years at Her Majesty's pleasure in total.

filling the belly of one of the men sitting inside the car with shotgun pellets, which required many hours of surgery to remove. When Mr Hemstock's case was tried he was found not guilty; the jury found him innocent of all charges. In both cases a gun was fired, resulting in a person's body being filled with lumps of metal. In one case somebody died, in the other they were merely wounded. Is that what made the critical difference when each aggressor came to be tried in court?

The law allows us to commit acts of potentially deadly violence in the context of protecting ourselves, our loved ones and our property. A certain degree of violence is sanctioned, but it must be proportional to the crime being committed against us. In the case of Tony Martin, he shot a kid at point-blank range and so it was deemed that his *intent* was to kill, a disproportionate response to an attempted burglary. In the case of Fred Hemstock, the shot was fired at a stationary car, the interior of which was dark, so he could not tell for sure whether or not it was occupied. His actions were *not* deemed to convey an *intent* to kill and were considered proportionate to the situation he was confronted with. He was acquitted.

The law treats similar violent actions differently according to the exact circumstances in which they occurred. One key consideration when a judge deliberates on an appropriate sentence is intent. The crime is considered to be worse if a person intends to shoot to kill, with the target standing right in front of them, as opposed to shooting blindly at a car where the specific intention is less clear cut. Another consideration, as discussed above, is whether the response to a situation is proportional or way over the top. Yet another consideration relates to the state of mind of the perpetrator at the time of the crime. The law differentiates between acts of violence that are hot-headed and committed on the spur of the moment, versus cold-blooded and pre-planned. Contrary to St Gregory's view, the hot-headed version is viewed less harshly, not more.

The logic of this revolves around whether or not the person being sentenced is likely to pose a threat in the future. Anybody is capable of violent behaviour when out of their mind with anger or fear. If a crime is committed under unusual circumstances that induce a moment of 'brief insanity', otherwise completely out of character, the person is often deemed unlikely to do that again and will usually be given a lighter sentence than one with a long history of violent conduct. If however the same crime was committed under similar circumstances, but in the context of a calmly planned and carefully plotted act of violence, the sentence will be *much* heavier, hence Amy Bishop getting life without parole.

Another major factor in evaluating the severity of a crime is the long-term mental health of the accused. Some adults are deemed more responsible for their actions than others. Several psychiatric conditions are associated with excessive aggression and so it is to these that we turn next in search of clues to the neurological causes of problematic aggression.

MRI on a lorry

Amy Bishop didn't take out her gun on the spur of the moment and start shooting her colleagues in a hot-headed rage. Evidence was presented during her court case to demonstrate that she had been practising at the shooting range over several weeks before she exacted her revenge. Similarly, Hengjun Chao didn't just happen to have his shotgun in the car when he took a drive down to Chappaqua that fateful day. He'd had years to ruminate over the injustice he felt he had suffered when he was sacked for falsifying data. He didn't pull out the gun in a moment of 'brief insanity' on the day that Dennis Charney sacked him; the shot was fired *seven years* after he had been dismissed. In both cases the acts of violence were committed in a cold, calculated fashion. In this regard they share superficial similarities with psychopathic violence, as opposed to the impulsive, explosive fury common to pub brawls, football hooliganism and street fights. Although there is no hard evidence, to my knowledge, that either Bishop or Chao are psychopaths, peering into the workings of the psychopathic brain may nonetheless provide some useful insight into a state of mind that is conducive to cold-blooded and premeditated crime.

A very high proportion of criminals serving prison sentences for acts of violence have a diagnosis of psychopathy.* In the US prison system, estimates of the rates of psychopathy range from 25 to 45 per cent. This has provided some fantastic subject matter for an extremely ambitious series of imaging studies to understand what's different about the brains of violent psychopaths. Kent Kiehl trained under Robert Hare – the man who invented the official system for measuring psychopathy currently in use all over the world – and went on to accept a position at the University of New Mexico, which had agreed to fund an ambitious research project to scan the brains of violent psychopaths. Professor Kiehl commissioned Siemens to build an MRI scanner to his specifications in Germany, shipped it to the USA and hauled it into the Western New Mexico Correctional Facility on the back of a lorry. Before we get to what they found in the psychopaths' brains, it's important to clear up a common misconception: not every psychopath is destined to commit violent crimes.

Psychopathy is not always associated with uncontrolled aggression. Despite the popularity of the murderous psychopath in films, crime dramas and high-profile news stories, many are in fact perfectly law-abiding citizens. A high proportion of people who rise to the very top of careers in the police, military, law and even surgery show the distinctive hallmarks of psychopathy, without ever committing the criminal acts for which psychopaths are notorious. With rates of psychopathy in the general public hovering around the 1 per cent mark, they are all around us, yet many are responsible and productive members of society. Psychopaths, whether violent or otherwise, all share the characteristic of profound emotional detachment. The lack of self-conscious emotions

---

* This is not to be confused with psychosis, which involves paranoid delusion and auditory hallucinations. Psychotic people (with psychosis) have difficulties accurately comprehending reality. Psychopathic people (with psychopathy) have a perfectly good grasp of reality, but they have great difficulty understanding other people's feelings.

210 THE SCIENCE OF SIN

leaves them unaffected by horrifying scenes of violence and suffering that would leave the rest of us reeling. Whether the psychopath commits the crimes or fights them, they can remain emotionally unaffected by even the goriest experiences.

In an ideal world, an experiment to find the critical brain areas that generate a propensity to psychopathic violence would compare violent psychopaths to non-violent psychopaths. Unfortunately only the violent ones are usually identified, by virtue of their getting caught up in the criminal justice system. As they are not causing anyone any harm, or at least not getting caught committing any crimes, the non-violent ones tend not to come under scientific scrutiny. Sadly it's not a perfect world, so we'll have to work with what we're given.

Over the past decade Professor Kiehl and his colleagues have used their portable MRI scanner to identify several important differences in the brains of violent psychopaths as compared to the non-psychopathic control subjects. They found functional differences in the responses of the anterior cingulate cortex (ACC) and amygdalae to emotionally disturbing sights and sounds. Both structures produced a weaker response in the psychopaths than their non-psychopathic counterparts. A separate study determined that the amygdalae in psychopathic brains are physically smaller and seem to be dysfunctional in terms of their capacity to trigger the usual physiological cascade that prepares a person to deal with aversive stimuli. No wonder psychopaths seem to be fearless. The very brain system that orchestrates the fear response is both physically and functionally deficient. It's interesting to speculate on what might have been going on in Chao and Bishop's amygdalae at the moment they pulled the trigger. As they dished out their retribution, were they cool and calm like a psychopath? Or were their amygdalae producing the usual responses to such circumstances, making their palms sweaty and their hearts pump furiously like anyone else who found themselves in such a dire situation?

In terms of structural differences, the psychopaths are usually found to have reduced tissue volume in various orbitofrontal cortex (OFC) regions. This is particularly interesting because it could explain some of the dysfunction in their capacity to make well-reasoned decisions. The latest thinking, deriving from human and animal studies, is that lateral parts of the OFC – closer to the side rather than the midline of the brain – contain networks of neurons that represent the predicted value of each possible course of action. And, as discussed in a previous chapter (see Chapter 5, p. 115), the medial orbitofrontal cortex (mOFC) integrates this with other important contextual considerations such as the recent outcomes of similar decisions, current emotional state and likely long-term consequences to enable a final choice to be made. The reduced tissue volume, and therefore computational power, in the OFC of psychopathic brains might explain why their decisions don't seem to take into consideration important factors like the long-term consequences of their choices.

Of the many problems involved in the psychopathic brain, two are of particular interest here. First, psychopaths are severely disabled in terms of their capacity for emotional empathy and so they feel no emotional discouragement when contemplating actions that might cause others harm. Second, they do not seem to care about the future consequences of their actions. My pet theory is that these deficits are fundamentally intertwined: they have zero empathy for their future selves.

We think of empathy as our ability to feel what other people are feeling. In many ways our future self is almost as different from our current self as another person. We all struggle to care as much about our future selves as we do about our current selves. That is why we eat unhealthy food to excess now, even though we know it will mean getting fat further down the line. This is why we have sex with people that aren't our spouse, even though we know betrayals of trust are often insurmountable in the long run. This is why we don't bother taking exercise, even though we know it makes a heart attack much more likely later in life. While we non-psychopaths might live to regret the actions of our past selves once we find ourselves fat, divorced or fitted with a pacemaker, this is not the case for the psychopath. Not only does their profound lack of empathy seem to apply to their future selves as much as to other people, but they don't even care about their fate when they come to pay the penalty for their past actions. Lack of remorse is a key feature of psychopathy, after all.

Similar to your average criminal psychopaths, Chao and Bishop clearly had no concern for the consequences of their planned acts of violence. They were both highly educated people who had plenty of time to think about the likely repercussions of what they intended to do. They must have known it would land them in prison, but they simply couldn't care less about their future selves. Could the collapse of their dream of a career in academia have been manifested in a misfiring mOFC? Could it have become so perturbed that their 'burning desire to pay back pain' became so powerful that the predicted reward associated with exacting their revenge seemed worth paying the penalty of spending the rest of their lives in prison? We have no way of knowing for sure, but it's a fascinating possibility.

From Cold-hearted to Hot-tempered

Our search for the neurological weak links that might help to account for wrathful behaviour takes us from the realms of psychiatric illness that is characterised by cold, calculated violence to those involving hot, impulsive and explosive anger. In our hunt for clues as to how the tendency towards excessive aggression arises, we'll consider how the capacity to accurately detect other people's emotions impacts on anger levels, a condition where aggression is forever on a hair trigger and search for brain areas that might be involved in helping us regulate our anger on a daily basis.

In psychiatry the 'cold and calculated' style of aggression typically seen in psychopaths is described as 'proactive' or 'instrumental' aggression, because the violence is used as a means to an end. The 'hot-headed' version is termed 'reactive' aggression, because the violent conduct usually achieves no discernible goal.

Children regularly exposed to physical, psychological or sexual abuse are often pushed down a neurodevelopmental path towards reactive aggression. The repeated exposure to real-life threatening situations in their daily experience gradually re-wires their brains in an effort to adapt to the demands of that environment. This results in them becoming hypervigilant to threats, in other words, constantly on guard. This is the exact opposite to the under-responsive amygdala responses in the psychopathic brain, which tends to leave them unruffled even by horrific scenes.

Once the amygdala adaptations have occurred, the person in question ends up having great difficulties in accurately perceiving other people's emotional states. Under normal circumstances the amygdalae would produce a reliable response to angry or scared-looking faces. This is useful because anger on a person's face indicates that they might be a direct threat and fear on a person's face suggests that they might have spotted some kind of danger nearby. Either way it is helpful for the amygdalae to trigger the fight-or-flight response to prepare you for action. The trouble is, in those with hyper-responsive amygdalae, even neutral facial expressions trigger a strong response, switching the body and brain into action stations. When that person feels the physiological changes in their body readying them for confrontation – their elevated heart rate, faster breathing, high state of alertness and so on – they often conclude that they must be under threat and so their aggression levels start to rise. This could explain why so many unprovoked acts of violence start with comments like: 'What do you think you're looking at?'

A condition called Intermittent Explosive Disorder (IED) involves repeated episodes of sudden, impulsive aggression and violence, in response to minimal provocation, which tend to be completely disproportionate to the situation at hand. IED people regularly throw temper tantrums for no apparent reason and are prone to incidents of road rage and domestic abuse. This condition is associated with high emotional arousal – IED people also often misinterpret facial expressions and body language as described above – in combination with difficulties in inhibiting their aggression as it starts to rise.

A recent brain imaging study investigated impulse control in three different groups of young men: one group were diagnosed with IED, another group were cocaine addicts and the third group were healthy control subjects. Two sub-regions of the dlPFC (dorsolateral prefrontal cortex) were found to be more active in IED people when they failed to control their impulsive responses compared to the other two groups. Most interestingly, the responses in one of these two sub-regions were positively correlated with a person's propensity to react aggressively across all groups.* In other words, this 'hot-headedness-related' sub-region of the dlPFC was more active the more aggressive the person was in their day-to-day life, irrespective of whether they were an IED patient, a cocaine addict or a control subject. This suggests that this same area probably plays an important role when *anybody* loses their cool, whether they have a psychiatric condition, an addiction, or neither of the above.

Another group of people infamous in the world of psychiatry for having great difficulty controlling their aggressive outbursts are elderly people dealing with the effects of frontotemporal lobar dementia (FTLD). However not all FTLD people are prone to this particular symptom, just a sub-set of them. Studies that have scanned the brains of a large number of FTLD people, some prone to aggression and some not, revealed that only when certain parts of the dorsomedial prefrontal cortex (dmPFC)† are compromised do these explosive bouts of anger seem to occur. This suggests that the dmPFC may contain neural circuitry that enables anyone in whom these regions are functioning normally to successfully regulate their aggression. This would be an interesting region to evaluate in people trying to improve their capacity for anger management.

---

* According to a standardised measure of aggression.
† The medial prefrontal cortex (mPFC) is on the inner surface of the brain, where the left and right hemispheres rub up against each other just behind the forehead. The dorsal part of the mPFC (dmPFC) is simply the strip of the mPFC close to the top of the head.

Anger management

Maintaining our place in the pecking order requires that we have the capacity to express anger to assert ourselves. But to remain a welcome member of the InGroup we also need to be able to control our aggression unless it is absolutely necessary. This particular skill is as important, if not more so, than having the capacity to express anger in the first place. Bearing in mind the potentially lethal consequences of expulsion from the InGroup in the era of our ancient ancestors, the evolutionary selection pressures that incentivised the development of brain areas enabling us to 'bite our tongue' unless an outburst was strategically advisable, was clearly essential.

Anyone who picks a fight with a bigger, more aggressive, better-resourced person could well find themselves being wiped out of the gene pool. Even if they don't end up getting involved in an act of violence, giving in to the temptation to engage in an angry confrontation also runs the risk of ruining their reputation. While reputations can take a lifetime to build, it takes just one ill-judged outburst to leave them in tatters. As aggressive encounters are threatening, they tend to activate the amygdala. This makes aggressive outbursts more memorable than other social interactions, so people don't forget them quickly. In other words, they are prone to hold a grudge against the aggressor. The ability to manage aggression appropriately is critical to bringing people together rather than pushing them apart.

Areas of the prefrontal cortex that seem to play an important role in our anger management skills – including but not limited to the dmPFC/dlPFC – are among the very last parts of the brain to reach full maturation. In many cases this process is not actually completed until a person reaches their mid-twenties. In some people adverse life experiences prevent these brain areas from ever developing fully. Poor regulation of aggression is potentially lethal, yet the threat of an inadvisable violent confrontation is not limited to the hot-headed or cold-calculating individual themselves, sometimes it can have ramifications for their whole InGroup and even as yet unborn generations.

History is littered with examples of blood feuds where
family members have had to pay the price for an ill-advised,
spontaneous confrontation that took place between ancestors
way back in the mists of time. All it takes is a hypersensitive
amygdala misinterpreting a neutral facial expression as
threatening, in combination with a compromised dmPFC/
dlPFC circuitry rendering a person unable to control their
temper, and you can have a vendetta on your hands that could
potentially last for a very long time. In the thirteenth century
bloody rivalries raged for years between Italian noble families,
in the fourteenth century Scottish clans were at it, as were
rival factions of Japanese samurai in the seventeenth century
and as recently as the late nineteenth century the US had
warring families like the Hatfields and McCoys. Rather than
the tit-for-tat electrocutions we saw in the TAP experiments,
these feuds involved members of one family, clan or samurai
sect committing murders to avenge earlier murders that were
themselves acts of revenge.

Even in the relatively peaceful times of today's Western
world, these tribal instincts still manifest themselves through
football fanaticism. English football became synonymous with
hooliganism in the late twentieth century, when fans of rival
teams would meet up at pre-arranged locations to do battle
on the streets and on the terraces. From a neuroscience
perspective, it could be argued that these people had effectively
trained their amygdalae to become hyper-responsive to enemy
colours. The sight of a rival team's football strip was sufficient
to trigger a powerful fight-or-flight response resulting in
violence week after week. Although problems associated with
hooliganism have subsided in recent times, these instincts
remain in die-hard fans.

In the recent terrorist attack on London Bridge in June 2017,
a man called Roy Larner stood up to four armed men who had
stormed Borough Market to stab innocent members of the
public more or less at random with huge knives taped to their
wrists. Taking on all four at the same time, with his bare hands,
he saved many lives that evening by distracting the attackers'
attention away from other people and buying the armed police

precious time to arrive.* What triggered Roy Larner's aggression, allowing him to conquer his fear and provide the incredible courage to take on four angry men armed with giant hunting knives, despite being completely unarmed himself? One of the terrorists was wearing an Arsenal football shirt, prompting Roy to stand up and shout 'F*** you, I'm Millwall!' as he waded in headfirst to battle with the old enemy.

There are good and bad sides to anger and aggression. When used sparingly it can be used to signal transgression of the boundaries of acceptable behaviour, without necessarily needing to resort to physical aggression. Even acts of violence can be socially and legally acceptable, but only in the context of defence against a criminal act and only when proportionate to the prevailing circumstances. This can be something of a grey area at times, and making judgements on where these conditions have and haven't been met are a challenge for the law courts on a daily basis.

Where aggression *can* be unequivocally labelled as diabolical is when it constitutes a desire for disproportionate levels of revenge. As we saw in the TAP study, the best candidate we have for a brain area that generates the urge to take revenge resides within the ACC: the stronger the activation, the greater the degree of retaliation. We've all felt what it's like when the activity levels in this area ramp up and start to dominate our overall state of mind. Furious rumination over a perceived injustice can simmer for long periods of time until it finally spills over into acts of vengeance that are often quite outrageous. As the proverbial pot boils over, we find ourselves highly motivated to get our own back and make them regret what they've done. When people are under the influence of wrath the desire for vengeance is extremely myopic; it takes little heed of the likely long-term consequences. Satan's grip leaves people caring little for the fate of their future self. All they care about is dishing out retribution for the injustice they

---

* The attackers were all shot dead in less than 10 minutes after the attacks began.

have suffered. In this regard, such instrumental aggression seems to have similarities with psychopathic violence. Yet with their difficulties with empathy and their compromised amygdalae, psychopaths can calmly cause harm to others *because* they don't have the usual repertoire of emotions that naturally discourage the rest of us from doing terrible things to other people. Their dysfunctional decision-making circuitry also leaves the psychopath unlikely to take into consideration the inevitable future punishments they will eventually have to endure. The scariest thing about those who fall foul of the sin of wrath, on the other hand, people like Amy Bishop and Hengjun Chao, is that they are capable of the same short-sighted decisions and cold-hearted acts of violence, despite having ostensibly normal brains.

CHAPTER NINE

Save Our Souls

The mind is its own place, and in itself
Can make a Heaven of Hell, a Hell of Heaven.

John Milton, *Paradise Lost*

In this chapter we are going to consider some ideas and techniques that might help to reduce the harms caused by the seven deadly sins in our own lives and in society at large. Sadly, there are no miracle cures. Sorry about that. Not in the sense of permanent solutions that work overnight, anyway. However, there *are* ways to train brains to resist temptation more effectively, assuming the person in question has sufficient determination to apply it in their daily life. A full and permanent fix would take months if not years to master. For the impatient, there are some tricks at our disposal to gently nudge us away from selfish decisions and towards the pro-social options. Together these can help to reinforce our sense of being an accepted part of a community and give us access to all the benefits of stable InGroup membership.

Successfully navigating the fine line between vice and virtue is more an art than a science. Science *is* starting to catch up, slowly, and in the final chapter we'll take a peek at some of the more sophisticated futuristic interventions on the horizon that might one day help us better control our anti-social impulses.

For now, we are going to take each deadly sin in turn and consider strategies available to us right now to facilitate the better management of temptation. Applying these strategies in our daily lives might even help to save our souls – though not from an eternity of suffering at the hands of the Princes of Hell. Rather, by helping to make us feel more meaningfully connected to others, as opposed to driven apart into social isolation, we may be able to improve our quality of life while still drawing breath here on Earth.

The primary aim of the previous chapters is to use science to throw some light on why we do the things we know we shouldn't. The hope is that simply by understanding what happens in our brains when we struggle to effectively manage our most unpleasant impulses, that knowledge alone might help us to make better life choices. Following the trail of breadcrumbs through the dizzyingly vast labyrinth of interconnected areas of research has yielded some surprises along the way. From the overdeveloped sense of self-importance, via struggles with irresistible appetites for food and sex respectively, the insatiable desire for more, the tendency to covet what others have and dearly wish that they would lose their advantage, all the way through to the intoxicating urge for revenge – we've found that certain brain areas have cropped up again and again.

Could these be the neural epicentres at the root of the anti-social behaviours that St Gregory the Great clustered into the seven deadly sins? Or would that constitute a vast over-simplification? If wrestling with our demons *was* underpinned by the same set of cognitive shortcomings, might addressing the underlying brain problem help across the board? If St Gregory was right about Pride being the queen of all the deadly sins, approaches that reduce narcissistic tendencies might yield benefits across all our antisocial impulses.

Before we continue, a quick disclaimer. Please bear in mind that, as a neuroscientist, I have no medical training whatsoever. Those concerned about full-blown mental illnesses should seek the advice of a GP, psychiatrist or clinical psychotherapist and prioritise that advice over anything you read here. Psychological counselling has at its disposal a variety of approaches supported by plenty of data to indicate where it yields benefits. By comparison, in this chapter you'll find some scientifically informed hunches regarding strategies that we might consider using to help rein in some of our more unpleasant urges. These approaches might be useful in helping us regain control in situations where we know exactly what we shouldn't do, yet do it anyway. To know for sure, they would need to be tested in large-scale, double-blind, clinical trials designed to study the efficacy of these ideas in controlling symptoms of each capital vice.

With this in mind let us consider seven categories of strategies that might help us to make more pro-social choices and fewer antisocial ones.

Lancing Lucifer

Given the current epidemic of narcissism that appears to be running rife in the Western world, it is vital that we try to identify and neutralise the key factors responsible for killing off our humility. What is it about the modern world that produces such fertile conditions for Lucifer to expand his fanbase year on year? The US researchers who brought the narcissism epidemic[*] to the world's attention have suggested the following hit list of potential culprits:

- Celebrity idols taking over as the most influential role models.
- Online social networking as a narcissists' playground.
- Parenting practices that lead to a damaged sense of self-worth.
- Misguided approaches to building self-esteem in education.

Trying to change parenting, teaching and how the broadcast/online media are regulated is no easy task. There are so many moving parts that getting all parties to see the light and progress in a coordinated fashion towards making an environment that reduces rather than promotes narcissism presents a huge challenge but one that is not insurmountable.

As we saw in the Pride chapter (see Chapter 2, p. 49), when it comes to parenting, pitfalls lie at both extremes: neglectful and over-attentive approaches can both be problematic. Raising awareness of this, perhaps by including this in the

---

[*] e.g. *The Narcissism Epidemic* by Jean M Twenge and W. Keith Campbell

National Parenting Trust syllabus, would be a good first step. The importance of providing love and support unconditionally, in combination with giving consistent instructions about acceptable behaviour and accurate feedback when these expectations have and have not been met, could be drilled into parents right from the outset.

One major factor implicated in the narcissism epidemic involved late-twentieth-century schemes that aimed to boost self-esteem in children. These backfired because the children received praise in an effort to make them feel good about themselves, but regardless of whether they had put in much effort or not, and whether their behaviour had been good or bad. The aim was to make them feel valued, but it just left children expecting praise regardless of their conduct. No wonder rates of entitlement and self-importance rocketed.

The brave new world of multimedia technology has developed at such a breakneck pace that those with the power and responsibility to legislate simply cannot keep up. On the one hand, it is exciting and liberating, but on the other it leaves a regulation-free vacuum in which anything goes. When Endemol created *Big Brother* in 1999 and went on to sell the format all over the world, John de Mol couldn't possibly have known that reality TV would go on to proliferate at such a rate that it ended up warping cultural perspectives on what behaviours are socially acceptable in a few short years. When Facebook was launched in 2004, Mark Zuckerberg and co-founders couldn't possibly have known it would end up being an environment in which narcissistic behaviours would be amplified so effectively. In less than a couple of decades, boasting about and exaggerating every positive experience and achievement has gone from being frowned upon and actively discouraged, to being accepted as a welcome and sometimes even necessary part of daily life on social media. Now that we are starting to glimpse how social media and reality TV might be influencing real-world behaviour and aspirations, the time may have come to think seriously about whether we should just let these phenomena run their course, or intervene to fight back against the rising tide of narcissism.

But before we start lobbying Ofcom to formulate new regulations, or try to convince schools to introduce Narcissism Prevention Initiatives into their Personal, Social, Health and Economics lessons, we are going to need to work out the fine details of cause and effect. In the meantime it might make sense to start focusing on how we might each reduce our own narcissistic tendencies.

Get over yourself

Mindfulness meditation has been intensively studied in recent years and its positive impact on mental health is now broadly supported by an extensive body of scientific research, so much so that it's now available on the NHS. A recent review paper in *Nature Reviews Neuroscience* summarising the findings of more than 20 brain imaging studies that investigated the impacts of various forms of meditation concluded that, not only is the practice of mindfulness beneficial to physical and mental health, but it also improves cognitive function. A key principle of many forms of meditation is essentially to let go of the subjective perspective, which places the *self* at the very centre of every thought, emotion and sensory experience, and instead regularly practise the habit of taking a more objective perspective. The evidence indicates that the longer a person practises mindfulness meditation, the lower their baseline cortisol levels become. Given that the higher a person scores on the Narcissistic Personality Inventory, the higher their cortisol levels tend to be, this effect alone could pay dividends for the average narcissist and perhaps even mitigate against the damaging influence they have on the people around them. Practising meditation regularly and on a long-term basis (both prerequisites for neuroplastic change) impacts on the structure and function of several brain areas that could be very relevant to managing the sin of pride.

Several mindfulness meditation brain imaging studies have found changes in parts of the frontopolar cortex implicated in meta-awareness. Meta-awareness is the very human capacity of reflecting on the feelings and thoughts that pop into our heads. A key strategy in many meditational practices involves encouraging people to nurture a non-judgemental frame of mind, whereby whatever thoughts and feelings pop into their heads unbidden should simply be acknowledged (as opposed to blocked out), and then allowed to pass out of mind again. Regularly practising such habits of thought can be extremely helpful in promoting wellbeing because it gradually eradicates the unhelpful, negative commentary that accompanies many people throughout their lives.

'Rumination' describes dwelling on negative thoughts about life events, both recent and historic, often for prolonged periods of time. Such thought patterns tend to be self-critical and are well known to be a core feature in many unhealthy mental states. People tend to beat themselves up with regret over their own past conduct, or focus intensely on other people's perceived indiscretions, for instance thinking 'I wish I hadn't done that, what will they think of me now' or 'How dare they say that...' By subtly tweaking how we use our skills of meta-awareness we can all learn to use it to reduce, rather than exacerbate, our social pain. As narcissists are particularly prone to feelings of social pain, mindfulness may be a very effective way of tackling the sin of pride.

Profound feelings of loneliness and isolation – often stemming from a conviction, learned in childhood, that the narcissistic person has no intrinsic worth – can lead to a strategy of mitigating against the distress this causes by perpetually seeking admiration from others. Fleeting feelings of satisfaction triggered when they do receive flattery, endorsement or other forms of social support provide temporary relief from the social pain, but do nothing to deal with the underlying cause. It would arguably be better to eliminate the excessive social pain generated in the narcissists' dACC (dorsal anterior cingulate cortex) in the first place. Several brain imaging studies of meditation have concluded that it has the potential to induce physical changes throughout the ACC *and* the white matter tracts that enable ACC activation to be modulated by the PFC (prefrontal cortex). The implication is that practising meditation improves the practitioner's capacity for emotional self-regulation. If somebody who has a high Narcissistic Personality Inventory score wanted to take steps to reduce their experience of social pain, mindfulness meditation should (after weeks or months of daily practice) help them to develop the brain pathways for better emotional management, to reduce rumination and to become less reliant on positive feedback from others. That would be great for them and should make them less of a burden on friends, families and co-workers. As a consequence, their relationships might improve, allowing them to benefit from the security that comes from feeling like a genuinely accepted member of an InGroup.

While mindfulness meditation takes much practice before inducing such beneficial brain changes, there is a relatively quick fix that could pay dividends in the meantime. Social pain can actually be abolished with a drug usually used to reduce physical pain. As mentioned in chapter 2 (p. 45), the core brain areas activated when people experience physical pain show considerable overlap with those involved when they feel social pain. The drug in question reduces activity in these brain hubs and has long been known to have a beneficial impact on physical pain. While the various opiate-based pain-killing drugs such as opium, morphine and heroin induce a potentially addictive chemical high as well as numbing the pain, this particular class of drug does not. It's not just a matter of masking the emotional pain with feelings of pleasure; it actually reduces the brain activations creating the feelings of pain in the first place. So it is broadly safe for general consumption.

A surprising body of research demonstrates that this drug, acetaminophen, a commonly used over-the-counter pain reliever, can reduce the perception of social pain. This effect was demonstrated whether the pain perception was measured subjectively by means of self-reporting, or objectively using MRI. Participants prescribed a three-week regimen of acetaminophen reported experiencing fewer hurt feelings in response to social exclusion, and in a separate experiment reduced activity was observed in brain areas associated with social pain (the dACC and AI). If the social pain that is a daily part of a narcissist's life experience could be reduced through prophylactic use of a conventional painkiller,* then their anti-social tendencies might also be diminished. Acetaminophen, by the way, is also traded under another name: paracetamol.

Positive correlations have been observed between narcissism` and addictions to exercise, social media, alcohol, gambling and compulsive shopping – all of which are impulse control problems. Such behaviours may reflect attempts to reduce, or distract from, the narcissist's amplified feelings of social pain. It would be interesting to see whether acetaminophen had any impact on these behaviours. If narcissists didn't feel their social pain so intensely, perhaps the desire to compulsively exercise, tweet, drink, gamble or shop might evaporate.

A more extreme approach to dealing with excessive narcissism could involve the use of Deep Brain Stimulation (DBS), but of course this would only be appropriate for those in whom it was causing major problems. That is because DBS involves surgically implanting electrodes into dysfunctional brain areas in order to apply weak electrical currents at very specific locations. Thousands of these procedures have been carried out around the world, bringing long-lasting symptom relief to people with advanced Parkinson's Disease, severe obsessive compulsive disorder and a range of other neurological problems. A certain degree of success has also been achieved when electrodes have been implanted into the dACC of people suffering with a variety of problems involving chronic pain. If acetaminophen therapy is someday proven useful in controlling the symptoms of narcissism, via reductions in feelings of social pain, DBS might be the logical next step in the search for an effective therapy to deal with severe cases.

Therapeutic use of psychedelic drugs could arguaby one day play a role in expediting the process of reducing a person's

---

* That is, if the drug is used in advance to diminish the activity of brain areas that create social pain before it is actually induced.

overactive ego. Controversial as it may sound, several serious scientific studies have investigated the use of hallucinogenic substances like psilocybin – the active ingredient of magic mushrooms – administered in the company of specially trained counsellors, to help alleviate the symptoms of people suffering with major depression. While you might think that a mushroom trip would be the last thing you'd want to give to a mentally ill person, many patients have experienced relief from their debilitating depressive symptoms, sometimes for the first time in decades. Better still, the relief is often fairly long-lasting, six to eight weeks in some cases, and that is after a single session. Despite the drug only being in their system at psychoactive levels for a few hours, it can induce a fundamental shift in their perspective and outlook on life that is maintained long after the psychedelic effects wear off.

The reason such an unusual form of therapy could prove helpful for narcissism is because psychedelic drugs are well known to induce experiences that make it feel like the boundaries between the self and the outside world are melting away. Far from being frightening, people often describe this experience as a deep and profound connection, not just with other people, but with the universe as a whole. Admittedly this may all sound a bit strange, but these are not just the testimonies of recreational drug enthusiasts out of their heads at a music festival; they are everyday people, most of whom wouldn't dream of taking psychedelic drugs under any other circumstances. Ego dissolution is a scientifically recognised effect of psychedelic drugs. And as narcissism is a particularly ego-centric state of mind there is every reason to believe that, when administered under the right circumstances, that is with the support of a specially trained psychological counsellor as in the depression studies, those suffering the consequences of high levels of narcissism may benefit from the experience of feeling intimately connected with others. Before you go rushing off to the countryside to go mushroom-picking (which, by the way, can be deadly since many mushrooms easily mistaken for the 'magic' ones are highly toxic) it would make sense to first wait for the relevant studies to be conducted and published in peer-review journals. Once the protocols for depression psilocybin therapy have been refined and adapted for narcissism research, there's every chance it could prove useful. Watch this space.

Beating Beelzebub

Regularly overeating leads directly to several pretty nasty diseases. Conversely, calorie restriction protects the brain and slows the ageing process by reducing levels of inflammation that would otherwise start to interfere with cognitive functions. Limiting daily food intake yields huge benefits, but this is easier said than done. The task is made much harder by powerful marketing forces dead set on profiting from our easily exploited weakness for overindulgence.

Once the habit of overeating has been established it's very hard to change, so it is best to entrain healthier habits as early as possible. Adolescence is a period of heightened self-obsession, but also a period during which teens start to become angry about social injustice. During these years adolescents often start to feel strongly about 'big issues', expressing sentiments against global warming, animal testing, nuclear weapons, ecological destruction and species extinction, to name but a few. The reason this occurs in the teen years is because this is when the stage of neurodevelopment is reached where they can start taking a perspective that goes beyond their own interests, those of their family and of the culture to which they belong. This is also the stage at which young people become hypersensitive to all sorts of perceived unfairness and develop a yearning to find a deeper meaning in life.

It turns out that all that teenage angst can be harnessed to alter their attitudes to junk food. When presented with evidence of cynical strategies used by multinational food companies, they will typically feel outraged. By demonstrating that corporations profit from our ever-expanding waistlines and understand the relevant health consequences only too well, junk food can switch from being viewed as a source of innocent temptation, to a vile scandal. Amazingly this can ultimately induce them to reduce their daily consumption of unhealthy high-fat/high-sugar foods. Given that teenagers are notorious for struggling to resist their impulses, this seems nothing short of a miracle!

Dietary fibre could be the as-yet-unrecognised champion in the fight against our gluttonous yearnings. For many years, the importance of eating fibre focused entirely on its role in promoting bowel movements. Recent evidence points to a much more important benefit of this basic component of nutrient-laden fruits, vegetables and wholegrains. It turns out that, although we cannot absorb any nutrients from fibre (because human gut enzymes cannot break it down), it's nonetheless very good for us. It feeds the so-called good gut bacteria, which produce various chemical waste products, some of which travel up to our brains to make us feel fuller sooner.

Getting off the sugar roller coaster is something we all need to do if we want to live to a ripe old age and keep our brains in good condition while we're at it. There's good evidence to indicate a high-sugar diet is very bad for body and brain health. So consider ditching your morning bowl of high-carbohydrate processed cereal, Danish pastry, fry-up or toast with jam, opting instead for unprocessed wholegrain cereals like porridge, muesli or granola. This provides not only a hearty dose of hunger-relieving fibre, but also plenty of slow-release carbohydrates that release their sugar molecules into the bloodstream gradually, rather than all in one go. Those fast-release carbohydrate options induce a large squirt of insulin from the pancreas in order to deal with the flood of sugars into the bloodstream. But this means so much glucose is removed from the bloodstream that you end up running low on sugars (and energy, patience and so on) an hour or so later. By comparison, slow-release options don't cause such a large release of insulin, which allows you to maintain a moderate level of blood glucose to supply body and brain throughout the morning. This helps to avoid the habit of seeking out delicious yet unhealthy snacks to top up your blood sugar levels throughout the day.

Consuming nutritious, slow-release carbohydrate, high-fibre content foods habitually, to keep your energy and hunger levels on a more even keel throughout the day, is only half the battle. Reducing exposure to the marketing tactics that are specifically designed to make eating processed foods on a daily basis seem desirable and affordable plays a huge role in the battle to keep Beelzebub, Bishop Binsfeld's chosen demon for gluttony, at bay. Eating take-aways or cheap supermarket ready meals on a daily basis is not normal for people with a healthy BMI and it is not harmless. So when adverts for fast food come up on your TV screen, change the channel. When they pop up on your computer screen, switch to a different website. When your route home takes you past your favourite fast-food restaurant, go the long way round to avoid it. When you're in the supermarket, don't go down the aisle with the desserts, sweets and cakes. It may all sound a bit over the top, but averting your eyes, ears and nose from the influences that are designed to gradually wear down your resolve is vital. Each exposure brings you a step closer to giving in to the urge to eat something sweet and fatty – the very flavours our brains evolved to favour. If you allow those foods into your house you *will* eat it at some point. The only way to resist gluttony is to not buy irresistible foods in the first place.

Embracing a friend, lover, family member or even pet causes release of the neurohormone oxytocin. This creates feelings of comfort and helps to build trust between InGroup members. When oxytocin is injected directly into the brain it is powerfully anorexigenic: it stops us feeling hungry. It does this by binding receptors in the ventromedial hypothalamus, temporarily reducing the reward value of food and making us feel less ravenous. So we should all consider the option of seeking out physical affection, rather than snacks, when trying to resist the temptation to overeat. Often when we eat, comfort is what we are really after and so alternative sources of oxytocin – a hug or just a good chat with a friend to give us the sense of human connection – could supply the feelings of security we really crave.

If you sleep poorly, you will make poor eating decisions the following day. If you often sleep badly, then this could be making you fat. Bizarre as it may sound, to improve eating habits, taking immediate steps to improve 'sleep hygiene' is one of the best possible things you could do. If your bedroom is a place where the only things you ever do are sleep, read or have sex then, after a couple of weeks, your brain will adjust its expectations of what happens in that particular space. But if you spend 10 to 30 minutes fiddling with your smartphone in bed just before you drift off to sleep each night, then your brain will subconsciously prepare for stimulation when you go to bed, rather than getting ready to switch off and sleep. Not only that, but each text, email, internet search, Facebook post, tweet, Instagram photo and app you dip into causes a tiny dose of cortisol to be squirted from your adrenal gland. The cumulative effect of all these little surges of cortisol is that they raise your vigilance levels at precisely the moment you really want the opposite, to get off to sleep and then stay asleep until morning. More on this shortly...

If you regularly wake up in the middle of the night then you would be well advised to start eliminating each potential cause of the disturbance that is preventing you from maintaining unconsciousness for seven or eight hours each night.

- Vision – if there is light seeping into your room you might need blackout blinds.
- Hearing – wear earplugs.
- Touch – make sure you are comfortable and have a smooth mattress and sheets.
- Smell – try adding calming scents such as lavender oil.

By the time we wake up in the middle of the night, we usually have no memory of what it was that actually woke us, so a little bit of detective work may be in order. If none of these things make any difference after a couple of weeks' dedicated experimentation, then in all likelihood it is your smartphone that's to blame.

Here's why. Consider this. You wake up in the middle of the night. You have no idea why. Maybe you've tossed and turned to the point that you've ended up in a position that is cutting off the blood supply to a limb. Perhaps there was a loud noise outside that roused you into semi-awareness, but not quite loud enough for you to have any recollection of what happened. Whatever the cause of the rude awakening, you're awake now, so what do you do? Most people in this situation look at their smartphone. Bad idea.

The reason smartphones are the primary enemy of sleep, and therefore our waistlines, goes way beyond the fiddling before bedtime and delaying our descent into sleep (although these are factors). When we wake up in the middle of the night to check the time on a smartphone, it's impossible not to glance at the icons signalling the presence of an unread message or ten. Of all the unanswered emails, text messages, social networking notifications and missed calls, some could potentially be important, but in reality they can all wait until the morning. The very possibility that there might be something urgent among the spam sends a shot of cortisol into the bloodstream and up into the brain, nudging the brain out of sleep mode.

Cortisol levels naturally rise, slowly but surely, over the course of the night so that, come morning, we are mildly stressed. This prepares us to get up and go. It actually helps to release the energy we need to get out of bed and take on whatever challenges we might have in store. When a spike of cortisol is triggered part-way through the night, however, it can be tough to get back to sleep, which means we end up feeling a bit frazzled come morning time. This may have been happening for so long now that you have no recollection of what it feels like to wake up refreshed. It doesn't have to be that way.

As far as the untimely secretion of cortisol is concerned, there's nothing quite like a smartphone for making us worry unnecessarily over nothing in the middle of the night. As for the notion that you might somehow be able to ignore the waiting messages – forget about it. Not knowing sends the mind spinning over all the possibilities regarding what might be waiting. If you want to sleep better, you really must be brave and leave your smartphone beyond the threshold of your bedroom door. If not, your sleep will continue to be disturbed and your daytime efforts to eat healthily will be perpetually thwarted by the fatigue that you have forgotten is *not* a normal part of daily life.

We've all heard the advice that when you're heading out to the supermarket: 'never shop hungry'. The reason for this is that hunger hormones like ghrelin send the predicted reward value for any high-calorie foods through the roof. When blood glucose levels are running low, our ability to resist the temptation of high-calorie foods is severely reduced. This is partly due to ghrelin, but also because regions of the dlPFC (dorsolateral prefrontal cortex) involved in exerting our capacity for self-control are less able to exert an influence on the OFC (orbitofrontal cortex) brain areas that weigh up the predicted reward values of various food items. The functional disconnection between these brain areas makes people more likely to overvalue sweet or fatty stuff and act on the impulse to satisfy immediate gratification over more sensible long-term choices. Eating slow-release carbohydrate snacks 20 to 30 minutes before going shopping or choosing what we are going to eat at mealtimes can change all this by taking on a little extra sugar at just the right time, reducing levels of hunger hormones just prior to decision time and helping to top up blood glucose so the brain has adequate resources to fuel the areas that support disciplined food choices. Specifically, by boosting the availability of glucose in the dlPFC, it can exert a greater influence over the OFC, so you can make smarter food choices. Ensuring that we're only *moderately* hungry at the time we choose the food that goes into our meals means we stand a better chance of making the selection in favour of long-term healthy goals as opposed to the lure of immediate gratification.

Finally, people tend to make better decisions towards the start of the day and worse ones later on. So choose what you're going to eat for dinner sooner rather than later. What's more, this 'decision fatigue' occurs more quickly the more decisions a person has to make. Whether the choices are straightforward or complex seems to make no difference. This is why after a hard day of decision-making we are considerably more likely to find ourselves chomping through a whole family-sized bar of chocolate when the original idea we had in mind was just to have the odd chunk or two. Forewarned is forearmed!

Avoiding Asmodeus

Lust is the deadly sin that has probably changed the most since it was first flagged as a cause of social strife. For much of human history, sexually transmitted diseases and unplanned pregnancies were the source of much human suffering, not least for the unwanted babies. Since the invention of efficient methods of contraception, especially barrier methods like the condom, such negative outcomes have been drastically reduced (assuming they are used properly). The harms induced by the sin of lust that we are going to consider include sexual crimes, adultery and the disruptive influences of excessive use of pornography. We'll examine what lies in the armoury to help protect us against each of these libidinous evils in turn.

To reiterate the overarching theme of the lust chapter, people have no conscious control over what makes them feel sexually excited, whereas acting on those feelings of sexual arousal is a completely different matter altogether. When acting on these urges has a strong likelihood of placing others at risk of harm, there are pharmaceutical compounds available to quench the libido. As for sexual urges that are not criminal, but could still cause serious damage to relationships, we can but emphasise the importance of taking a long-term perspective, to frame the temptation to cheat in a way that makes acting on such impulses seem plain stupid and so easier to resist.

We are a long way off a miracle cure to help eliminate the threat posed by sexual predators. The drugs typically given to sex offenders to reduce their libido are far from ideal and the scientific data to support their use is not always terribly strong. They comprise three different classes of drug. The first are man-made versions of female hormones, such as medroxyprogesterone. This is what was prescribed to the 40-year-old teacher whose brain tumour left him with uncontrollable sexual urges, after being charged with child molestation. Such drugs are usually prescribed to women as a form of oral contraception or as hormone replacement therapy for those going through the menopause. The evidence of the impact of such drugs in men suggests it leads to the abolition of deviant sexual behaviours within one to two months of treatment. This comes at a price though, as it's associated with side effects in a significant proportion of men, most commonly weight gain and headaches. The main problem with these side effects in this context is that it can interfere with compliance, the person's willingness to take the drug.

The second class of drugs routinely given to sex offenders are selective serotonin-reuptake inhibitors, a type of antidepressant where suppression of libido is a well-known side effect. It is recommended for adolescents showing early signs of sexual deviancy because the effects are relatively mild. Such medication is given in the hope that it will help to avoid the development of greater problems regulating sexual behaviour in adult life.

A third drug type, the gonadotropin-releasing hormone analogues, target the hypothalamus to suppress release of a hormone that travels in the bloodstream down to the testes to increase production of the male sex hormone testosterone. Originally, such drugs were manufactured to help treat prostate cancer, a disease aggravated by the presence of testosterone. Within one month of treatment, circulating testosterone is reduced to a level only usually attainable through castration. The incidence of deviant sexual fantasies plummets, as does sexual behaviour in general, and the side-effect profile is better than the alternatives.

It has been predicted that, over the next few years, it will become possible to detect those whose sexual inclinations place children at risk, on the basis of their brain's responses to a standardised battery of pornographic images. Then what? Do we lock them up as a precautionary measure? Force them to take drugs to chemically castrate them? Or require that they undergo brain surgery to make them permanently incapable of producing the male sex hormones? There are major ethical hurdles to overcome before we can take steps to protect the public from paedophiles who have yet to act upon their libidinous urges. If no crime has been committed, yet their brain produces a sexual response to child but not adult pornography, what should we do? These are very tough questions and there are no simple answers. But one thing seems clear. Society's feelings of disgust towards people with paedophilic impulses, whether these urges have been acted upon or not, is currently driving these people into hiding and onto the dark web, rather than into clinics that might help them manage the impulses. That seems very dangerous.

Now we will move on to adultery. Sleeping with your friend's partner is never advisable. A long-sighted perspective on the consequences of such a decision is instrumental to summoning the power to resist the lure of Asmodeus's temptation. Betrayal destroys trust – plain and simple. Yes, there are examples of people forgiving partners for an indiscretion, but trust, once betrayed, can never be fully recovered. And trust is at the heart of every successful long-term relationship.

Everyone has the potential to cheat on their partner. Until it actually happens this is just a theoretical possibility. It *could* happen, but it never has. At this point there is every reason to feel optimistic and to presume it is likely to stay that way. The moment someone cheats on their partner, on the other hand, everything changes because they actually have a track record. From that point on it is no longer merely theoretically possible, it has actually happened. The odds of something happening again are very different from those associated with something happening for the first time*. This may seem like a subtle

---

* If you think back to the wrath chapter, this follows a similar logic to that followed in law, where the prison sentences handed down to those with a track record of violent crime are harsher than those for whom it is out of character.

distinction, but it is huge. When an act of unsanctioned infidelity has happened once, the chances of it happening again seem much higher. From the perspective of the person whose trust has been betrayed, they will likely feel stupid and quite possibly regret having been naïve enough to believe it would never happen. That is where the permanent damage is done. Once a person experiences the crushing blow of betrayal, it is difficult to fully recover from it.

When we are tempted by forbidden sexual fruits, Asmodeus plays all sorts of mind-games with us in an effort to reason away objections: 'It won't mean anything.' 'It's just sex.' 'I've got an insatiable sex drive and I need this.' Or the classic: 'What they don't know can't hurt them.' Relationships *do* survive infidelity, but once deception has been revealed, they are damaged. And that is the thing to focus on when Asmodeus presents opportunities to cheat on someone. The thought you can beat Asmodeus away with is: 'go there and the trust dies'. Without trust there can be no real intimacy, so infidelity robs relationships of intimacy, even when they do manage to persist.

In the rare cases where the deception does remain hidden for many years, the lies involved in creating the deception cause damage anyway. People always think they'll be able to hide the truth from their partner, but something always gives the game away eventually. It might be the person's own festering guilt, or inconsistencies in their cover story, or the intervention of a third party to reveal the lie; nobody gets away with it for ever. That's the other stick you can hit Asmodeus with. When the intoxicating lure of adultery arises, the most effective way to resist temptation is to remember that trust takes years to build, but a single act of lust to destroy, because betrayal rarely stays secret for ever.

Excessive consumption of pornography leads to destructive influences in terms of promoting negative attitudes to condom use and warped perspectives on what constitutes best practice in real life sexual intimacy. It's clearly impractical to try and change a broadly unregulated industry. The most effective approach would probably be to think about better ways to restrict access and advise people on how to use it in a way that reduces harm. In terms of access, the most effective way to deal with it would be to penalise internet providers. Ultimately they control the flow of data. If they wanted to restrict access to free online pornography, it is entirely within their power. The problem is if one company did this then everyone would run to the competition, so it would require coordination to be effective.

The gradual entrainment of an addictive compulsion to use porn can render real-life sexual partners inadequate to satisfy sexual desires. Given the huge benefits of a healthy sex life to human wellbeing, this is a truly terrible state of affairs. If a person consumes pornography on a daily basis and their sexual performance in real life is suffering as a result, it may cheer them to hear that after just a few weeks of porn abstinence their libido will return. Given how deeply engrained many people's porn habit is, this is much easier said than done. Many will really struggle to resist the temptation in the early days. Knowing that it *is* possible to re-establish normal sexual behaviour by not looking at porn for a few weeks may inspire people to give it a try. The impact of pornography on culture as a whole is much more problematic.

Pornography depicts a wide variety of acts that do little to promote long-term bonding, which is arguably the most valuable aspect of the sex act beyond procreation. Porn cameras are obsessed with capturing penetration, because that's what the market demands. When aspects of love-making that *do* have a positive impact on long-term bonding – embracing, kissing and caressing – are featured, they are usually fast-forwarded through. So the aspects of sexual congress that yield the most important dividends in a real-life relationship are being systematically overlooked by both porn directors and the consumer. When young people slavishly reproduce what they see on the screen in their own bedrooms, they don't know any different and accept it as the norm. The solution? Anyone who wants to boost their vasopressin and oxytocin levels to harness the power of sex in long-term bonding, as opposed to focusing entirely on the dopamine buzz of orgasm, would be well advised to take their sex tips from Tantra rather than YouPorn.

Berating Belphegor

Now we turn to sloth, the insidious form that is cunningly disguised as industriousness. For those legions of digital slaves, entranced by beautifully designed algorithms luring them into investing endless hours of their free time squinting into screens, yet resulting in the fulfilment of no meaningful goals, the first step is to put it down. Better still, put the smartphone, tablet and laptop in a completely different room, on silent. There is evidence to suggest that just having a smartphone within arm's reach reduces working memory by 10 per cent and fluid intelligence by 5 per cent.

If you do try to put your technology away, only to find it miraculously reappearing in your hand, then you might consider investing in something like a K-Safe. These are sturdy, plastic boxes that have a lockable lid, controlled by a countdown timer. You spin the dial on the top of the lid to set the timer to count down anything from one minute to 10 days and it will keep any temptation safely locked away until the timer reaches zero. The most impressive thing about this, if my experience is anything to go by, is that once you *know* that you can't get into that box for a set period of time, you soon end up putting it completely out of mind. If the thought occurs to you to retrieve the contents, just knowing that it will still be locked away allows you to quickly forget about it and get on with something else instead. You also find yourself thinking very carefully about how long you lock it away for each time.

This scenario bears an uncanny resemblance to the ancient Greek myth of Odysseus. Knowing that hearing the irresistible song of the sirens had lured many captains before him to dash their ships on the rocks, he ordered his crew to lash him to the mast before they sailed past so that he could listen to their enchanting music, yet remain powerless to act

on the temptation to steer closer to get a better look.*
Sticking the source of your compulsive desires in a time-
locked box has a similar effect, by rendering you powerless to
act on the temptation you know full well you'll be assailed by
at a later point in time. When it comes to managing all our
temptations, it really does pay to think like Odysseus wherever
possible.

We all battle with the temptation to slack off from time to
time, but there's considerable variation in how we each
respond when the urge to shun our duties arises. Poor digital
hygiene, affecting those who are slaves rather than masters to
their technology, diverts valuable time away from useful work
in dribs and drabs throughout the day. All anyone has to do
before they start to drown in a limitless ocean of procrastination
is to simply unlock their smartphone or tablet and they're off.
If you can employ a strategy of keeping yourself physically
separated from your phone for an hour at a time, keeping the
temptation to compulsively check it beyond arm's reach, you
will find yourself able to continue work after each short break
more easily. You'll have retrained your brain to be capable of
sustained attention once more, having previously derailed
these capacities through your incessant media multitasking.
While surfing the internet and checking social media feeds is
usually more interesting than doing work, staring into space is
not. So if the only thing between you and boredom is more
work, then it will seem a more appealing option than when
you have your smartphone constantly to hand. The more
people engage in daydreaming the more they unleash their
inherent creativity, so even if you *do* spend more time staring
into space, that could well turn out to be a good thing. Nature
abhors a vacuum.

You might also consider buying a skipping rope. If each
time you lost the will to continue working, instead of fiddling

---

* Sirens were beautiful but dangerous women who lured sailors onto
the rocks with their beautiful music and singing. Odysseus cunningly
ordered the crew to fill their ears with wax so they wouldn't be able
to hear the sirens' song.

with your phone or messing around on the internet you got up and did some skipping instead, you could at least benefit from some exercise as you slack off. This is known as 'virtue bundling'. By doing something physically energising any time you feel tempted to ease off on the mentally taxing work you need to do, you'll have cunningly converted the temptation to commit the capital vice of sloth into something that's actually virtuous. Not only does this give you a time-limited break from the mental work (you can only skip for so long before you start tripping over your feet) but the physical stimulation also induces the release of energising hormones to wake up your weary brain, recharge your attentional resources and help you to focus when you get back to the real work.* A study published in early 2018 demonstrated that just 10 minutes of moderate exercise was sufficient to produce measurable improvements in cognition directly afterwards.

There is a passion out there for everyone – something that, deep down, they will find intrinsically rewarding. The problem is, not everyone knows what their passion is. In the meantime, such people usually spend their free time watching television, films and YouTube videos of cute animals doing silly things. The trouble with this is that it encourages yet more time to be spent sprawled out on the sofa, which as we now know is much more deadly than it seems.

Hobbies generally involve a sequence of actions to be followed that enable some kind of end goal to be achieved. But the main source of enjoyment in a hobby is the pleasure produced as a result of performing the sequence of actions rather than reaching the end product. Take a collector, for example. They invest huge amounts of time and effort hunting down new pieces for their collection. If they were ever to 'complete' their collection, their work would be done and

---

* If skipping does not strike you as a viable way of taking a break in *your* place of work, consider this: if it is acceptable for some of your colleagues to take a few minutes periodically to go outside and fill their lungs with smoke or vape, why shouldn't you spend a few minutes each hour whirling a skipping rope through the air?

their hobby would be dead. *Then* what would they do to feel satisfied with how they spend their spare time? The hobbies that bring the greatest joy never end. Those who love hiking will always be able to find another place to hike. Those who paint will always find something else to paint. Those who love sport will, for as long as their bodies permit, always be up for playing another game. Those who play a musical instrument will always find they can improve their skill, always find another piece of music to master. Hobbies are intrinsically rewarding because they involve *doing* something in pursuit of a goal, but do not focus entirely on the end result. Television and films are carefully constructed to deliver a sequence of specifically designed moments of reward, but they do all the work for us, robbing us of a huge source of potential satisfaction. Greater pleasure is derived from working for our rewards than just being given them.

There are several prescription drugs that can improve symptoms of apathy. These are not, as yet, dished out willy-nilly to people who are plain lazy – that would be unethical. But there are several classes of drugs that could, theoretically, be used to increase people's motivation levels. Amphetamines like methylphenidate are often prescribed to children with attention deficit hyperactivity disorder (ADHD) to help them focus. These substances are increasingly being bought on the black market for those who want to use them, not for medical purposes, but to gain the competitive edge over their rivals. Another so-called 'smart drug' called modafinil, originally created for military use to help soldiers, sailors and pilots reduce the cognitive sluggishness that arises when sleep-deprived towards the end of a long shift, has found its way into the civilian workplace. An anonymous survey conducted by the science journal *Nature* in 2012 indicated that 20 per cent of academics had used, or regularly use, such smart drugs in order to increase their productivity. This raises the possibility that, in the not-too-distant future, dropping a tab of methylphenidate or modafinil after lunch will seem no more contentious than having a cup of coffee. The trouble is that, unlike coffee, these other smart drugs were only invented in the past couple of decades so we have no way of knowing what the unwelcome side effects of using them over long periods of time might be. In the meantime, businesspeople, online poker players and academics are taking the gamble of keeping sloth at bay with these relatively new-fangled substances, which should give us the answers to the question of how long-term use might affect humans sooner rather than later. Depending on the results, we might consider giving them to the chronically lazy as well as the mentally ill.

There may be no need to resort to drugs. Many people who suffer from a drastic lack of get-up-and-go have simply never experienced what it is like to truly have no control over what happens in their life. They simply lack the perspective to realise how lucky they are to have any options at all. In the meantime they will often feel put out that life hasn't dealt them a better hand, complain about how bad their career prospects are and moan about everything that seems to conspire to make life so hard. People like this perceive the 'locus of control' as being external – the world controls their fate. What they need is to develop an internal locus of control – to take control of their fate. This is a vital ingredient of high motivation.

In the absence of a psychiatric illness, lack of motivation in society so often revolves around a lack of perspective, perceived opportunity and/or relevant experience. The children of Belphegor who fall into this category could be sent to war zones. Not to fight, but to volunteer. Experiencing first-hand the true horrors that people in refugee camps around the world have to suffer on a daily basis might give them some much needed perspective on the opportunities and basic comforts they take for granted. To many people in the world today, feeling absolutely sure that there will be clean water available to drink and food to eat tomorrow would be like a dream come true. Most people reading this book, on the other hand, will probably take the idea of turning on the tap and having unlimited quantities of drinking water come gushing out for granted. A life swap would do wonders for banishing Belphegor back into his dismal lair for many of these folk. To spend some time helping people who manage to remain optimistic and motivated, despite a complete lack choice in life, may be inspirational. At the very least, understanding how hard and short life can be elsewhere in the world might change their approach to life back home. Memories of such experiences may boost the ailing dopamine levels in their striatum sufficiently to start pursuing meaningful goals upon their return.

It is clearly impractical (not to mention dangerous) for the slothful to travel to war-torn parts of the world, just to understand how fortunate they really are. One of the great hopes of the forthcoming virtual reality revolution is that it will enable people to travel to far-flung places without even having to step out of their houses. Clearly this technology also has the potential to make sloth worse not better by discouraging people from ever leaving their homes. Used properly, however, it has a tremendous capacity* to enable everyday people to feel like they are right in the middle of a real life war zone, or to freely explore the favelas of Rio de Janeiro, the crack dens of Detroit or the slums of Calcutta; to experience the sights and sounds of real life poverty. Virtual reality technology is becoming increasingly available to the everyday consumer and at much more affordable prices than ever before, so the possibility of using it to make people realise how lucky they are and how many opportunities they have, is real.

In the meantime, people suffering from a chronic lack of motivation might be encouraged to lend a helping hand closer to home. Volunteering in a local soup kitchen, old folks' home or homeless shelter might broaden their horizons, or give them a taste of the deep satisfaction that can be derived from helping others and provide a more balanced perspective on their own situation. Who knows, it might just provide the impetus to get them up off the sofa and away from Netflix for long enough to

---

* To learn more about what virtual reality has in store, the *Voices of VR* podcast comes highly recommended

investigate their options further afield, rather than just sitting around waiting for opportunities to fall in their lap.

Muzzling Mammon

Applying short bursts of high-frequency magnetic stimulation across the skull to disrupt specific parts of the dlPFC brain circuitry that drive greedy decisions might not be everybody's cup of tea, but it really could help loosen Mammon's grip.* It is rare to be able to point to a specific study demonstrating the effectiveness of brain stimulation in influencing people's propensity to commit a deadly sin, but according to the work of Leonardo Christov-Moore and colleagues at UCLA such an intervention does indeed make people's economic decisions more pro-social and less pro-self. The best bit? It works by returning us to our default state, incapacitating brain areas that would otherwise step in to over-ride our intrinsically pro-social nature. A similar result could also be achieved simply by compelling people to make financial decisions quicker. As we know from the work of David Rand and colleagues, who showed that fast, spontaneous decisions tend to be more pro-social, while slow, deliberate ones seem to give people time to talk themselves out of the more altruistic options. If we could somehow prime people to trust their intuitions more, rather than over-think the decision to the point of screwing other people over, it might just result in more generosity and less selfishness. This observation may also explain why charitable events often take the form of auctions, which have a distinct propensity to encourage fast, spontaneous decisions.

During their ascent to the very peak of the capitalistic tree, the bosses at Microsoft were greedy for market share and merciless in their pursuit of it. They used every trick in the book. Some might even go as far as saying they *wrote* the book. But having crushed the competition with tactics not dissimilar

---

* This refers to the Theta Burst Stimulation approach to using Transcranial Magnetic Stimulation devices, which involves applying a 50 Hz magnetic field once every 200 milliseconds.

to acts of flagrant greed, once Bill Gates *et al.* had actually built their fortunes, a tremendous appetite for altruism started to emerge. Why? One factor is that ostentatious acts of generosity can boost a person's social standing. When you're already one of the richest and most powerful humans on the planet, what better way to differentiate yourself from all the other billionaires than to outcompete them in the munificence stakes. My charitable donation is bigger than yours!

Happily, this is probably more than simply one-upmanship. Giving is actually intrinsically rewarding. Doing something that helps others creates a pleasant feeling, as does thinking back to the act of selfless generosity. Several MRI studies demonstrate that winning money increases activity in the reward pathway and losing money decreases it. But when money is taken away from the person in the scanner and placed in the account of a worthy charity, instead of a decrease in activation of the ventral striatum, an increase is observed. This evidence that charitable giving is intrinsically rewarding, despite the net loss to the individual, is encouraging when we consider humanity's prospects for success in the battle with Mammon. To be naturally encouraged to help others makes sense for a socially dependent creature like the human being. If only more people could be introduced to the experience of giving as its own reward, rather than spending their entire life fighting tooth and claw for personal gain, it might reduce some of the collateral damage caused by greed.

We know that oxytocin is involved in reinforcing bonds between members of the InGroup, but there's also a pretty sturdy body of evidence to suggest that it increases aggression towards members of the OutGroup too. Other studies have found that it might even shift the boundary between InGroup and OutGroup. Increasing oxytocin levels in a person's brain, by squirting it up their nose, can gently nudge them towards more cooperative decisions. MRI scans of people's brains during engagement in neuroeconomic tasks that implicitly test how greedy they are, have shown that increasing oxytocin levels in the brain diminishes greedy behaviour by reducing activation in part of the frontal lobes that form a key part of the default mode network. The decreased activation in this area is thought to make people less greedy by virtue of reducing the sense of a distinction between self and other, bringing us to some interesting brain imaging research conducted with the help of Buddhist monks. More on this shortly.

Stick most people in an MRI scanner, get them to play an economic exchange game and whenever they are on the receiving end of another person's greedy behaviour their brains will light up in a way that reflects their acute feelings of discomfort. Under exactly the same circumstances, if the person in the scanner happens to be an experienced Buddhist monk, this does not happen. Their emotional pain networks stay remarkably quiet even when they are offered an extremely unfair split of the bounty. Unlike the rest of us, their choices throughout the rest of the game suggest that they continue to trust their trading partner, even in the face of blatant evidence to the contrary. Does all that meditation make them soft in the head? Are they simply gluttons for punishment? Or is something else going on?

Extensive practice of mindfulness meditation gradually breaks down the mental boundaries between the self and others in a manner not dissimilar to that experienced though the use of psychedelic drugs. While psilocybin (see p. 227) targets a very specific neurotransmitter receptor[*] throughout the brain, typically causing sensory hallucinations and other disorienting side effects, meditation achieves ego-dissolution by thought alone and so does not produce these potentially disturbing experiences. While it may take a lifetime to achieve enlightenment, there is every reason to believe that greedy behaviour may be reduced along the way. MRI research scanning the brains of experienced Buddhist monks has demonstrated that, through their many thousands of hours of

---

[*] A neurotransmitter receptor is the 'lock' that sits in the synapse (the gap between neurons) that a specific neurotransmitter 'key', released into the synapse, can fit into and activate. Psilocybin is unusual in that it fits only one of the dozens of different types of receptors in the brain through which serotonin exerts its effects

practice, they can actually rewire the brain areas that create our sense of a division between the 'self' and others. The brain areas known collectively as the Default Mode Network (DMN) – which many neuroscientists[*] now consider to be vital for generating our sense of 'self' – are usually very active when inexperienced mediators and those who don't meditate at all lie quietly in the scanner doing nothing. In the brains of experienced Buddhist monks however the DMN remains remarkably quiet when they are engaged in self-reflection.

If oxytocin makes people's decisions less greedy and more pro-social by reducing the activity of the DMN (see p. 246), and DMN activity can also be reduced through extensive mindfulness meditation, then perhaps meditation can diminish our tendency to make greedy decisions as well as reducing the suffering induced by other people's greed. If only we could find a way to compel the financial industry to make daily mindfulness meditation compulsory, we might just win the war on want. Given that health problems associated with chronic stress are rife in the banking sector, this may not be as fanciful as it seems. Goldman Sachs, JP Morgan and Barclays, to name but a few, have invested in providing mindfulness courses and retreats for their staff in an effort to reduce the rate of burnout and chronic illnesses. While the banks' motivation in providing these services is to increase productivity and reduce time taken off work due to stress-related illnesses, there is the hope that by incentivising bankers to embrace these opportunities, any progress they make in ego-dissolution might diminish their inordinate desire for more as a welcome side effect.

Reducing ego *could* banish the sin of greed, but even once you've convinced people to give meditation a go, it could take a long time for it to start paying dividends in terms of encouraging a more generous outlook on life. It might be

---

[*] I first came across this concept in an interview I did with neuropsychopharmacologist and all-round living legend Professor David Nutt, the former drug czar to the UK government who got sacked for equating the harms of MDMA to horse riding.

quicker and more practical to simply convince people that the endless pursuit of more money rarely leads to happiness. While many people make the common assumption that more money means greater happiness, the data simply doesn't support this widely held assumption. Beyond a certain threshold, there is simply no positive correlation between income and happiness levels. With excess wealth comes excess stress and there is good evidence to suggest that the rich find it harder to achieve peace of mind.

Perhaps telling our children bedtime stories detailing the miserable lives of the 'super-wealthy' – those with bank balances that surpass the $25 million mark – could start to counteract the broadly accepted wisdom that all our troubles magically evaporate if only we can find a way to make more money. That way when they grow up into adults who have reached moderate levels of wealth, they might start seeking more fertile grounds in which to sow the seeds of contentment, rather than perpetually aspiring to greater wealth.

If more people could take a closer look at the hyper-competitive bubbles in which the super-wealthy actually spend their daily lives, it might soon become apparent that they are often more socially disconnected than those with a more moderate income. For example, on the dating scene, a common complaint of the offspring of the super-rich is that they are always worrying over the motives of whoever they are with. 'Do they really love me, or are they just after my money?' is a typical cause of concern.

Never having to work again may sound great, but doing some form of meaningful work plays a critical role in producing feelings of contentment for the vast majority of people. Career advancement, or just the feeling of having got a good day's work in the bag, are both major yardsticks through which we get a sense of making progress day to day, year to year. Yet there are innumerable examples of the offspring of the super-rich taking a lacklustre approach to choosing and pursuing a career. After all, if you didn't actually need the money, it's easy to see how someone might be tempted to hit the ejector seat button as soon as the novelty of a new job wears off, after falling out with a co-worker, or the going gets tough in some way.

Nobody has a clearer perspective on how excessive wealth can erode rather than improve quality of life than self-made millionaires – those who came from nothing and achieved everything entirely by their own efforts. Seeing the evidence of what being born into money does to people in terms of increasing stress, cynicism about other people's motives and the acute sense of entitlement, often convinces the newly rich that to pass their wealth on to their children would only be doing them a disservice in the long run. As more and more millionaires follow in the footsteps of Sting and Anita Roddick, choosing to give their entire inheritance away rather than risk it corrupting their children's character and ambition, the next logical step is surely to kill off the aspiration to try and make those millions in the first place.

Evading envy

Envy, as we have seen, can inspire some truly horrific behaviours. It is the unfortunate habit of constantly comparing ourselves to others and coming out of that process feeling inferior that is the root cause of the suffering that makes those with high levels of dispositional envy do such terrible things to other people. The solution? Doing everything in your power to eliminate situations that encourage you to compare yourself with others is a good place to start.

The ancient Greeks accepted envy as an unavoidable fact of life. They developed social customs to avoid the incitement of envy and even put in place laws designed to eliminate its negative consequences in situations where envy was likely to get ugly. For example, after every victory in major athletics competitions the winners would routinely shower the crowd with generous gifts. The goal of such behaviour was to avoid the unpleasant repercussions that might arise if the audience became too envious of their Herculean prowess. Taking a leaf out of ancient Greece's book by using a combination of humility and generosity of spirit to evade potential acts of envy-fuelled retribution could be invaluable in helping to mitigate against the anti-social influence of this particular capital vice. Ostracism was another effective strategy. This law was designed to extinguish rising envy in the masses when a public figure was deemed to have become too big for their boots. People who fell foul of this law would be exiled for 10 years to allow the tension to subside, after which they could re-enter society with full honours and have all their possessions returned to them.

If you wanted to reduce feelings of envy in your life, who would your top five candidates for ostracism be? I can certainly think of a few people I wouldn't mind seeing banished into the wilderness for a decade or two. Sadly it is unlikely that the law of ostracism is likely to be re-introduced in Europe anytime soon, but there are several steps we can all take to reduce our exposure to influences that readily spark envy. Recent research has indicated that, for those prone to envy, quitting Facebook genuinely does improve wellbeing. Reducing exposure to reality TV and celebrity-centric tabloid media would probably also work wonders.

Another useful way of mitigating against envy is to spend more time thinking about what really goes on behind closed doors in the lives of those who seem to be doing better than ours. It is important to bear in mind that we are almost always comparing our lives to an airbrushed version of other people's, whether it's the things we see online or the things we hear on the grapevine. It can be tricky to uncover the truth about what life is really like for those in our everyday lives who make us feel envy most acutely, namely those from a similar background to ourselves, whose achievements are specifically relevant to our lives, but it may be possible to reverse our tendency to take other people's perceived advantages at face value.

The media love to create the illusion that we are being given a sneaky peek into the 'real' lives of our favourite celebrities. Journalistic mechanisms filter celebrity stories to ensure that we are exposed to those most likely to create the greatest sense of shock and awe. That's what sells newspapers.

Similarly, the gossip that circulates in our social circles, the stories we hear about rivals that make us feel envious, distort the truth in a similar way and for exactly the same reasons. The gossip that spreads the furthest is the most sensational and the very reason it is sensational is because the truth has been carefully filtered, exaggerated and embellished to make the biggest impact, increasing the likelihood of it being passed on to reach our ears. In other words the juiciest bits of gossip will almost always be not entirely true. Being mindful of how prevalent these distortions of reality are, not just in the media but in our everyday work and social lives too, is a great strategy for dodging envy.

The outrage we feel when we learn about the privileges enjoyed by those in the public eye and the unbelievable sums of money the stars earn is one of the major factors that makes celebrity stories newsworthy. But it is rarely the whole story. By actively investigating the traumatic childhoods, the drug addictions and the broken relationships documented by celebrity biographers, we can shatter the illusion that their lives are better than ours. Apply the same thinking to the people in our everyday life that make us feel inferior, imagining the huge pressures they may well be under, what keeps them up at night, their troubled relationships behind closed doors, their ongoing health problems, these may even enable us to convert our envy into sympathy.

Rather than wishing that we could have all the benefits that they enjoy, or fantasising that they might suffer some kind of horrible mishap, by focusing on the distorting influence of the media and gossip, we can cut through the smoke and mirrors that exaggerate other people's advantages. When done effectively we may soon find ourselves thinking that we wouldn't wish the curse of their apparent success on our worst enemy. Rather than looking up to celebrities and rivals, thinking that they are better, happier, superior to us, we can nurture the opposite perspective. Exciting as their life might seem from the outside, with more accurate knowledge about how screwed up their lives often are and less of the tabloid hype, we probably wouldn't swap places with them for all the money in the world.

How many times have you heard people say words to the effect of: 'If I won the lottery this week, all my troubles would be over'? The illusion, particularly common amongst low earners, is that more money equals greater happiness. The evidence, as discussed earlier, contradicts this view. Winning the lottery is, statistically speaking, more likely to make life worse not better in the long run. The type of problems lottery winners usually encounter involve falling out with friends and family, who suddenly start showing more interest in the person after their windfall than ever before. Even the suspicion that there *might* be an ulterior motive is perfectly sufficient to disrupt relationships. A loan here, a helping hand there, a free ticket to the match or show, another small donation to the ailing business. The knowledge that a person has won a large amount of cash can create envy and then resentment whenever that person does not act with great generosity. If you think about the factors that trigger envy it makes perfect sense. The person is similar to you in terms of background? Tick. The advantage they gain over you is undeserved? Well, they just got lucky, didn't they! Tick. With the lottery winner's creeping paranoia on one side of the equation and their friends and family's increasing resentment on the other, people soon start falling out and the size of their InGroup gradually diminishes.

As for those that we envy in the old-fashioned sense, those with whom we feel we share a similar background and yet their levels of attainment surpass our own, another approach is possible. It is possible to gradually convert envy from the malicious form into the benign. That way you can use their example to inspire you to greater things. By taking a forensic interest in how they achieved the advantages they have over you, this can direct motivation into finding ways to close the gap by emulating their example rather than plotting their downfall. By putting in the extra effort to invest in whatever training or resources you might need to elevate yourself to their level, rather than engineering their demise, you might even find yourself shooting right past them. It can also be helpful to remember that when people reach the top, the only way is down. People at the top of their game know this only too well and the stress involved in trying to maintain dominance over the competition can severely compromise their quality of life.

Learn from the example of those who make you feel envious. Analyse what they are doing that you are not and use this to improve yourself, rather than bitching about them behind their back. It's often so much better to be steadily making upward progress, rather than sitting on a pedestal vulnerable to other people's envious ill-will.

Slaying Satan

When it comes to dealing with wrath Botox can help. Yes – Botox. In your face. An MRI study conducted in Germany in 2009 revealed that when people have cosmetic Botox injections to paralyse the facial muscles used for frowning, this not only hinders their ability to pull a displeased facial expression, but also makes it more difficult for them to identify angry expressions on other people's faces. It actually reduces amygdala activations when they are presented with images of angry faces. To understand why this happens it is important to bear in mind that whenever we see others pull any kind of emotional facial expression we automatically, and without any awareness of doing it, gently flex the same muscles in our own face. This helps us to reproduce whatever emotion *they* are feeling in our own brain, enabling us to empathise with the other person's state of mind, so we can interact with them in a manner congruent with their emotional state. Feeling some of the anger another person is feeling can also serve the purpose of getting us into the right mindset for dealing with any threats that they have detected, but we have not.

The reduction in amygdala activity induced by Botox injections to the frown muscles is promising because it means, theoretically at least, it should make the wrath-prone less likely to misidentify neutral faces as aggressive ones. Whether or not an approach like this will be worth exploring could become clear sooner rather than later. One of the few positive side effects of the spread of celebrity norms into the general public is that, as so many people are already opting to willingly inject botulinum toxin into their face in the service of vanity, it should be pretty easy to find people willing to participate in a study to test this hypothesis. You can just picture the adverts now 'Do you have anger issues? Volunteer for this study and you'll earn £100, feel less angry AND end up looking 10 years younger!'

If you don't fancy permanently paralysing your frown muscles with bacterial toxins, you might consider some neurofeedback training. Neurofeedback involves using one form of non-invasive brain imaging technique or another to provide real-time feedback on the moment-to-moment activity levels in one of several brain areas. The goal is to give the person the opportunity to develop, through trial and error, the ability to exert conscious control over activity levels in specific brain areas in an effort to achieve a therapeutic benefit.

Neurofeedback usually works by attaching electrodes to the scalp to provide instantaneous feedback on a person's ability to control brain waves known as Slow Cortical Potentials. Several studies have proven that this can be an effective way of helping people to contol their aggression. This training can not only reduce aggression, but also impulsivity, in one of the most difficult groups of people to treat: those with severe psychopathy who have been incarcerated for their crimes. Imagine what training to gain control over specific aspects of brain function with this kind of technology could do for somebody *not* dealing with a serious mental illness, and who simply wants to improve control over their temper.

Recent research has demonstrated that a form of neuro-feedback that uses MRI, rather than scalp electrodes, can enable ordinary people to exert conscious control over the levels of activation in their amygdala. While the Slow Cortial Potential technology described above has the advantage of being relatively inexpensive and highly portable, it can only take measurements across large portions of the brain surface simultaneously. MRI, while being much more expensive and less portable, has the advantage of allowing activity in areas deep inside the brain, like the amygdala for example, to be monitored specifically. Whether training a person to become able to control their amygdala activity actually translates into improved anger management remains to be seen. But given how often the amygdala has been implicated in various psychiatric conditions in which aggression problems are a key symptom, the MRI approach to neurofeedback seems very promising.

Of the many harms associated with those on the receiving end of acts of wrath, post-traumatic stress disorder (PTSD) is perhaps the most disruptive. Symptoms include repeated, regular intrusion of deeply perturbing memories into daily experience, persistent avoidance of anything associated with the traumatising experience, mood changes and hypervigilance. These typically endure for many months, or even years, after the original event. Several changes that occur in the brains of people suffering with PTSD can account for why these painful memories recur with such frequency.

The amygdala becomes hyper-responsive in people with PTSD through a process of physical structural changes that occur in response to the highly stressful event. Brain imaging studies have found that the amygdalae of people with PTSD are over-responsive and parts of the prefrontal cortex usually associated with regulation of emotional responses are less active than usual. This suggests that exposure to a potentially life-threatening event induces biological changes that ramp up the responsiveness of the amygdalae to threats *and* interfere with the brain circuitry of fear suppression that usually regulate this activity. Brain areas that would usually intervene to reduce amygdala activation when there is no genuine threat in the environment become incapable of exerting any influence. As a consequence, a person with PTSD finds themselves in a perpetually hyper-anxious state, feeling threatened when there is no real danger, and plagued by intrusive vivid memories of the traumatising experience that repeatedly interfere with their daily activities.

Looking at this from the perspective of the brain as a device working hard to minimise surprise in order to be able to accurately predict what will happen in the future, this scenario makes biological sense. If a bomb has gone off in a soldier's face while on patrol, then the threat was clearly *not* anticipated. In this regard, a biological mechanism that cranks up vigilance levels to compensate seems logical. Although a perpetual state of hypervigilance is deeply unpleasant for the individual, it *does* help to avoid a repeat of the dreadful experience, albeit to the detriment the person's day-to-day quality of life.

Various forms of psychological therapy have been proven successful in gradually reducing the amygdala's over-responsiveness to potentially threatening stimuli, helping to reduce the severity of the chronic state of anxiety. But this only succeeds if the patient is able to properly engage with the process. Sadly, when PTSD victims are asked to think back to the event as a part of their therapy, the flood of negative emotions is often so overwhelming that they can really struggle to participate.

If the deeply unpleasant experience is recalled in the company of specially trained counsellors while the victim is under the influence of MDMA (aka 'ecstasy'), they are often better able to engage with the therapy. This particular drug has a unique capacity of making people feel both intensely euphoric and deeply socially connected to others. It seems to have the capacity to prevent the emergence of the overwhelmingly unpleasant feelings that are usually triggered whenever they think back to the dreadful event that caused the PTSD in the first place. This enables the therapist to take the patient through the process of banishing the PTSD symptoms from intruding in their daily life more completely and successfully. The illegal status of so-called 'drugs of abuse' has severely hampered progress in this area of research, but of late there has been progress through clinical trials. One phase II clinical trial of 107 people who had suffered PTSD for an average of 17.8 years found that of the 90 people available for re-evaluation 12 months later, 61 no longer had PTSD. Compared to previous treatments, this therapy is the closest thing we have to a miracle cure for those whose lives have been turned upside down by PTSD.

Finally, we'll conclude this chapter by returning to the intervention we mentioned right at the start. Mindfulness meditation, as you'll recall, is an effective way of remodelling various parts of the brain, including frontopolar cortex areas involved in meta-awareness and the parts of the ACC that we know to be important for generating feelings of anger, psychological pain from social exclusion and the desire to exact revenge. Mindfulness interventions have been found to be of considerable practical use in improving self-regulation of aggressive tendencies, even in those with intellectual disabilities. These meditational practices, despite being old news to Buddhism, are the closest phenomena we have to a genuine panacea, providing a wide range of temptation-resisting benefits that start to pay dividends throughout the journey, not just when you reach the final destination. In the appendices (p. 281) you'll find a number of free, online, guided meditations to help you start developing your mindfulness skills right away.

CHAPTER TEN

Beyond Temptation

In this, the concluding chapter, various strands of the science of sin will be brought together in an effort to illuminate a logical, pragmatic and evidence-based approach to resisting the anti-social temptations mankind has (probably) been wrestling with ever since we first started roaming the Earth. The revelations brought about by scientific investigation into the origins of the universe, our planet and the biology of life have gradually made a literal interpretation of religious texts increasingly implausible for many people. As this has a tendency to render the traditional system of carrot and stick provided by the lure of heaven and the deterrent of hell ineffective in steering our behaviour towards pro-social and away from anti-social urges, this project seems timely.

We will consider how the scientific evidence attesting to the benefits of a pro-social approach to life, over and above a self-centred attitude, might help nudge our choices in a direction that should yield benefits for everyone. We will ponder how a neuro-centric perspective on the causes of anti-social behaviours deserving of the label sin or vice might help us to reinterpret other people's conduct in a way that helps us deal with them better and reduce the suffering they cause to other people. We will also indulge in a little future-gazing on the topic of new technologies that might step in to lend us a helping hand wherever alternative approaches fail to deliver the goods.

Sin bundles

St Gregory the Great's conviction was that pride is the queen of all the capital vices and in the context of the examples we've considered so far, this perspective certainly seems to have some merit. Damage to professional pride surely played a part in Amy Bishop and Hengjun Chao's carefully premeditated

acts of wrath. Add envy into the mix and the three together
could explain the motivation for Mary Konye's acid attack and
Jonathon Griffin's farmyard vandalism. In fact, there seems to
be considerable overlap between all the seven deadly sins. It
may even be the case that there is no such thing as a purebred
deadly sin. Pride may be just the most obvious source of
leakage from one into the others. The deeper we probe into
any individual act of sin, the more we find evidence of the
influence of others.

The primary motive for one nation to wage war against
another may often be more a matter of envy or greed than
wrath. As Thucydides pointed out long ago: 'The cause of all
these evils was the lust for power arising from greed and
ambition; and from these passions proceeded the violence of
parties once engaged in contention.' Speaking of war, Genghis
Khan's motivation to impregnate in excess of 500 women was
unlikely to have been driven purely by Asmodeus's libido-
provoking influence. No doubt Lucifer also played a role in
fuelling this disproportionate level of profligacy. A generous
measure of pride is surely implicated in such an eager pursuit
of sexual conquests.

When greed effects the accumulation of a great fortune, the
resultant inflated sense of self-importance often leaves people
feeling that the mundanity of day-to-day chores are beneath
them. Maids are employed to clean their houses, chefs to
prepare their meals, chauffeurs to ferry them around town,
gardeners to mow the lawns, nannies to raise their children...
Does greed lead inevitably to pride and sloth?

There seems to be much overlap between the cardinal
vices. They mingle and merge with each other readily to form
these sin bundles. Could this mean that they are driven by
the same brain circuitry? In our search for neural suspects
responsible for rendering people incapable of controlling their
narcissistic, libidinous, avaricious, invidious and/or aggressive
impulses, a certain patch of cortical real estate has cropped up
over and over again. Might the motivation to commit all seven
deadly sins emerge from a single corrupt neural network?

The pain of conflict

Any good detective hoping to catch the devils of temptation red-handed would keep a close eye on the anterior cingulate cortex (ACC). The role the ACC plays in dealing with conflict has been known for some time. Whether the conflicting signals in question are sensory, emotional, conceptual or moral, the ACC always seems to be involved in dealing with cognitive dissonance. This is the mental discomfort we feel when holding two or more contradictory beliefs or ideas in mind at the same time, for example: 'I am a good person, yet this person is treating me as if I am beneath contempt'. Both cannot be true, so something has to give. The upper or dorsal portion of the ACC, the dACC, seems as good a candidate as any other for the headquarters of Sin City. It has been implicated in such a broad spectrum of anti-social behaviours that it might even deserve a new nickname. How about the 'distressed, aggravated and conflicted cortex'?

The dACC has been implicated, across several chapters, in many circumstances in which self-centred behaviours prevail over a more pro-social attitude. In one of the few studies providing direct insight into the overlap between the deadly sins, it has been observed that narcissism (pride) impacted on the desire to take revenge (wrath), but only if the detection of a threat led to an increase in dACC activation. In other words, the more narcissistic the person in question, the more likely they were to inflict an unpleasant punishment on someone who had just spurned them, if their experience of social rejection generated a surge of activity in the dACC. This activity was interpreted by the authors of the study as the 'trigger' for anti-social behaviour, which aimed to reduce the perception of a discrepancy between the narcissist's inflated sense of self-importance and the threat to that sense of self-importance posed by social rejection. This suggests that the dACC activity does not just reflect the detection of conflict and processing of cognitive dissonance, but is the very cause of the decision to retaliate. As this behaviour is essentially an act of revenge, could we surmise that, had the activity in the

dACCs of Bishop, Chao, Griffin and Konye been somehow
dampened, their crimes might never have been committed?

This may be going too far. I'd wager that any serious
neuroscientist who happened to stumble on this book might
well find themselves fantasising about strangling me about now
(which seems apt, given the topic under discussion). The reason
that good men and women of science might want to see me
taken out is because to seriously suggest that the dACC should
be relabelled the distressed, aggravated and conflicted cortex
would be to add to the serious problem of research being
misrepresented in the press. Many science writers hungry for
headlines fall into the hyperbole trap: presenting an overly
simplistic take on the research in order to make the most
impressive and impactful headlines possible, to the exclusion of a
more balanced account of the evidence. Veracity is often deemed
less important than getting people to sit up and take notice.

The truth of the matter is that a very large body of evidence
accumulated over several decades, comprising both studies that
directly investigate the responses of individual neurons in non-
human primates *and* those that indirectly measure responses of
relatively large chunks of neurons within human brains,
suggests that the dACC is acutely sensitive to the difficulty
involved in selecting between behavioural options that are in
direct opposition to one another. In most of the studies in
non-human primates this involves them being torn between
looking to the left or looking to the right to earn the best juice
reward. The human studies often involve people trying to
figure out which of a range of options is likely to yield the
biggest cash reward balanced against the potential for some
kind of social penalty being dished out later on. The degree of
excitement exhibited by this brain area seems to revolve around
the degree of conflict between the different available choices.

What is safe to say is that the dACC probably plays a critical
role in all sorts of everyday choice conflicts. Should I stay for
one more drink, or head home before it gets too late for
public transport? Should I flirt back with this gorgeous human
being or, as I already have a partner, would it be better to avoid
temptation? Will I take a look at the dessert menu like

everyone else, or stick to my guns and risking having to endure the frustration of food envy, as I continue my vain efforts to achieve that beach-ready body? The dACC is not so much the lair in which the various Princes of Hell reside, more the battlefield where the angels and demons fight it out.

That said, the dACC may have evolved to serve a different purpose in the human brain to that of our various mammalian cousins. The human brain's reward pathway now responds to financial incentives, even though money had yet to be invented in the era during which the ventral striatum and orbitofrontal cortex first evolved their capacity to govern decisions. But once humans learn that money helps us to get our mitts on other desirable commodities, specific patches of this evolutionarily ancient brain pathway can be retrained in our species to the specific task of maximising financial gain. In a similar way, the role that the ACC plays in dealing with simple cognitive conflicts evolved long before we developed the relatively complex concept of behaviours that are culturally acceptable versus socially taboo. But once these emerged, a specific subdivision of the ACC – the dACC – may have been re-purposed in our species to deal with that particularly sophisticated and quintessentially human form of conflict too. This brain area seems to have become critically involved in humans deciding what to do in situations where pro-self and pro-social considerations come into direct conflict, in a way that causes deep social pain.

We considered how one capital vice may be at the root of all the others: pride, if you subscribe to the Gregorian system and greed if you favour the view of St Paul. But if pride and greed both stemmed from a common neural root – a hyper-responsive dACC, for example – to push decisions towards the antisocial abyss, then they could both be right. When a narcissistic person finds their sense of self-importance threatened by events that cause feelings of social pain, their insatiable desire for more may be a strategy they are drawn to so that they can accumulate an excess of resources, which serves as reassuring evidence of their superiority over others. Similarly, a greedy person's successes in their perpetual attempts to gain more wealth may inevitably serve to increase their sense of self-importance, entitlement and vanity.

Why we must go beyond temptation

Conventional wisdom tells us that the economy requires constant growth to thrive. The trouble is, as we all know deep down, this approach is unsustainable in the long run. Driving the global economy as hard as possible, focusing entirely on short-term wealth creation, not only encourages behaviours that tend to drive us apart rather than pull us together but also leads to consequences that are destroying the planet. One of the best hopes for motivating people to rein in their selfish urges is to get them to place greater value on life after death. Not in the sense of an afterlife – most modern, educated, scientifically minded people struggle to believe in that any more – but in the sense of caring about the prospect of life on Earth after we are gone, and seriously considering what we are leaving behind for future generations.

Two thousand years ago, when the entire human population of the planet numbered a few hundred million, the worst imaginable scenario was that more humans would mean making each other's lives more miserable through war, slavery and famine. Now that we number in our billions, we face the genuine threat of disrupting ecosystems and weather patterns so thoroughly and permanently, leaving so much toxic, plastic and nuclear waste in our wake, that the planet is rendered unfit not just for humans, but for most animal and plant life. Already our collective influence has led to mass extinctions on a scale only previously seen in the context of catastrophic 'acts of God' like the eruption of supervolcanoes or immense asteroids colliding with great force against the Earth's crust.

Whether we harness new technologies to help rein in our worse tendencies (discussed shortly) or rely on old-fashioned grit and determination, the future of life on Earth depends on us all taking action to improve our capacity to resist our selfish urges and give more serious consideration to the negative long term consequences of our daily choices in the grand scheme of things. Otherwise, we will find ourselves leaving to our descendants a world incapable of supporting any reasonable quality of life. In recent decades, rather than taking steps to restrain our self-centred urges, we have instead seen them ruthlessly exploited. Each of the seven deadly sins has been systematically taken advantage of by the nefarious forces of global commerce.

Our narcissistic tendencies are positively encouraged by the mantra that 'the customer is always right'. We have been left with the impression that self-obsession is a virtue through being exposed to a never-ending barrage of adverts telling us to purchase beauty, fashion and luxury products because 'you deserve it!' Indulging our sense of self-importance and nurturing vanity as an essential aspect of modern life makes us more willing to part with our money, oiling the wheels of the economy.

Sex sells, we all know that, but the impact of the constant exposure to beautiful people in marketing materials is rarely considered on a day-to-day basis. It tends to breed a dissatisfaction with ourselves. This makes us more susceptible to the implicit suggestion that, by buying certain products, we can become better people. It even warps perspectives on the qualities we should seek in our romantic partners, forging an ideal that is impossible to achieve, to further increase our vulnerability to the idea that purchasing certain goods might help us attain that elusive sense of contentment. The aim is to keep us off-balance, in a perpetual state of worrying that we should be different to however we are and discontented with whomever we happen to be.

Regular use of ubiquitous, cost-free, online pornography gradually warps attitudes to what constitutes a satisfying sex life and fuels fantasies of illicit sexual encounters. Techniques for reinforcing the bonds of intimate long-term partnerships are studiously ignored and the most popular genres of erotic film make relationships seem as disposable as plastic cutlery. Dating services now exist that are specifically targeted at married people to make cheating on a partner more convenient than ever.

Communication strategies specifically aimed at children with the express aim of entraining life-long habits of over-consumption contribute directly to overstretched healthcare systems by damaging physical and cognitive health through the global obesity pandemic. The consumer has never had more labour-saving products available to help them pursue a lifestyle that avoids expending any effort beyond that which is absolutely necessary.

If avarice is the tipping point where a perfectly reasonable desire to maximise wealth trespasses into coveting what others have, then envy has been flagrantly harnessed by the advertising world to drive sales for decades. Manufacturing pipelines and communication campaigns are strategically organised to drip-feed a never-ending succession of new products into the marketplace to ensure that those who don't have the very latest models are quickly left feeling discontented when they realise that others have even more bleeding edge versions. This ensures that high streets, online stores and shopping centres teem with consumers perpetually in search of more.

As for wrath, the arms trade is a hugely lucrative business taking advantage of the global appetite for violence, in which the UK plays a major role. The computing industry generates huge profits from creating the illusion of putting the gamer in the driving seat when it comes to committing violent crimes. Whether massacring everything that moves or carjacking vehicles to drive around a virtual-reality city committing random acts of violence, it capitalises on mankind's intrinsic appetite for destruction to the tune of billions of dollars per annum. It could even be argued that sales of merchandise to sports fans all across the globe is another example of commercial forces leveraging the thrill of inter-Group warfare for material gain. Although nobody is harmed by buying a football strip, it is still a good example of a primal urge that fits the bill of a capital vice – wrath – being expoited to boost profits.

No matter how much clutter already clogs our houses, regardless of how full our wardrobes already are, if our levels of dissatisfaction can be perpetually topped up then we will always find ourselves seeking more. The latest trick is to stimulate envy, pride *and* greed all at the same time. This triumvirate of sinful urges are well activated by promoting direct comparison with the attractive, vain and often idiotic reality TV stars that parade their antics on an hourly basis through social media updates. By normalising narcissism, by displaying the advantages they have gained through their newfound wealth and fame, the influence they wield in promoting the concept more is better has become one of the most powerful tools in marketing. No wonder the big brands are falling over themselves to sign them up.

With our pre-existing weakness towards these temptations being exploited so ruthlessly, and with the influence of multimedia campaigns being so difficult to avoid in this day and age, the outlook may seem bleak. But there is hope. While the latest marketing and advertising strategies do their best to harness the latest technology to eliminate the last vestiges of our self-restraint, other technologies may soon step in to pull us back from the brink.

Science to the rescue?

Thomas Insel is one of the neuroscientists whose studies of prairie voles established the role of the neurohormones oxytocin and vasopressin in sexual bonding. Rising swiftly up the academic ranks he ended up being director of the world's largest scientific organisation, the National Institute for Mental Health (NIMH), for over a decade. He went on to do a short stint at the helm of Verily – a Google-owned medical science company – before joining the San Francisco-based start up Headstrong. Both companies aim to harness data from the world's five billion-plus smartphone users to improve interventions for a whole host of mental illnesses.

The approach taken by Verily, Headstrong and several other twenty-first century healthcare initiatives is pretty straightforward: track digital behaviour across huge groups of individuals in conjunction with other relevant data like their medical records, then keep a vigilant, artificial intelligence-enhanced eye peeled for tell-tale predictors of symptoms of common psychiatric problems such as depression, mania and psychosis. The aim: to better predict the onset of mental illnesses and intervene to treat them before it is too late to make a difference. If these new multi-million dollar digital 'big data' research initiatives succeed where the $20 billion spent on biology-based studies during Insel's time at the NIMH failed (by his own admission), there's no reason why the same approach couldn't be applied to help us deal with antisocial behaviours, like those traditionally labelled the seven deadly sins. As promising as the potential for such an approach is, it will remain firmly on the horizon until the fight against vice is viewed as a matter of science rather than theology.

Keeping our newfound knowledge of how social isolation invariably damages our physical and mental health at the forefront of our minds, may alone be sufficient to inspire better strategies for decision-making. If the lessons of history are anything to go by, merely being told what we should and shouldn't do is unlikely to be very helpful in steering us towards the straight and narrow. Without a specific incentive to motivate pursuit of the less enticing path over and above the powerful lure of the various temptations, the finger-wagging approach doesn't have a chance of paying dividends. A better understanding of what is going on inside our brains as we process the pros and cons of decisions that have social consequences, on the other hand, might help to nudge us in the direction of the pro-social options more often. A deeper understanding of the consequences of not doing this may also help. A full acceptance of the awful repercussions awaiting us in the long run should we regularly succumb to the lure of immediate gratification, despite the damage it might cause to our social ties and eventually our health too, could make those selfish urges easier to resist.

It might even prove possible to turn the deadly sins on each other. The trick would be to incentivise people to do right by others by convincing them that it is in their own selfish best interests to do so. The temptations of sloth can be held at bay by greed and envy. People might even harness their feelings of entitlement to the best of everything (pride) or their inordinate desire to acquire more (greed) as the source of the motivation to choose the pro-social option more often. If the physical and psychological benefits that come from feeling meaningfully connected to others is the desirable commodity they want (and deserve) more of, then to achieve it all their decisions should be taken in light of the enhanced impact it will have on their group membership.

In support of this admittedly bizarre-sounding solution, one recent study showed that, far from making people behave more aggressively, increased testosterone was observed in the victors of a neuroeconomic game where domination over rivals was achieved by making more pro-social decisions. Currently mainstream culture generally propagates the belief that whoever has the most money wins. This study suggests that, by tweaking the rules of engagement to see pro-social decisions as the ultimate yardstick of success, people's competitive nature can be harnessed to motivate them to outcompete the others by being the most generous, rather than the most selfish. Experimental virtual reality worlds are already experimenting with related concepts, such as 'gift economies' where people don't sell desired commodities, but instead give them away to encourage reciprocity in the future. This is proving to be a surprisingly successful strategy.

Technology to the rescue?

Wouldn't it be great if we could use technology to measure when our own dACC is in overdrive and so likely to activate our dark side? Or better still, what if there was a form of technology that could intervene to actually change how such brain areas respond when our social connections are threatened?

The Internet of Things is a movement that is trying to embed technology into everything. Sensors are fitted into clothing to measure physiological responses like heart rate and body temperature. This information can be fed into Bluetooth devices so that we can continuously monitor our biological vital signs. Before long an icon on our screen will remind us to drink water when we are becoming dehydrated, another to suggest a suitable snack when our blood glucose is running low, and already 'smartcaps' are being made available for overworked consumers worried about their stress levels. EEG technology, which monitors electrical activity generated by the brain using electrodes attached to the scalp, has been around for decades. For most of this time it was restricted to use in laboratories due to the bulky devices required to amplify the vanishingly weak electrical signals generated by the brain and store, de-noise and crunch the data into a form from which useful information could be extracted. As technology has improved, suitably powerful devices have become much smaller and the electrodes have been adapted so that everyday headwear like baseball caps, bike helmets and hard hats can be fitted with them, the idea of using a consumer device to continuously monitor dACC activity on the move is no longer a futuristic-sounding pipe dream.

Imagine how useful it would be to have a warning light flash in your peripheral vision to inform you that your brain is currently in a state that leaves you vulnerable to making rash decisions, driven by feelings of social pain rather than calm rational analysis. Rather than giving into the temptation to lash out in anger, verbally or otherwise, you could take steps to extract yourself from the situation, eat a piece of fruit, take a 10-minute nap, perform some mindfulness meditations and then return to the fray once your dACC activity levels have subsided. To begin with, people may well ignore the warning signal in the heat of the moment, choosing to give in to the urge to cut off their nose to spite their face. Eventually, they would probably find themselves heeding the warning of dACC overdrive more often than not, having learned through trial and error that it usually leads to more favourable outcomes. Having had multiple experiences of what an overactive dACC feels like and the benefits of stepping back from the brink in those circumstances, it may become possible to ditch the smartcap altogether. People may develop a sensitivity to the subtle sensations that flag this state of mind without the need for further technological intervention. Achieving these goals would basically involve taking the neurofeedback training described in the previous chapter out of the laboratory and into the real world. There are some major technical hurdles that would need to be overcome to achieve this goal, but they are not insurmountable.

The next logical step would be a device that can intervene to calm and excite specific brain areas according to whether they are over-stimulated or underactive compared to the optimal target level. The magnetic coils required to generate the magnetic fields for effective transcranial magnetic stimulation (TMS) are currently too heavy and bulky to achieve this on the move. Even if future advances could make TMS portable, it would still be impossible to influence brain areas deep beneath the skull surface with any accuracy. But exciting new solutions are on the horizon.

Fledgling technologies like temporal interference stimulation (TIS) may one day be honed sufficiently to precisely target an overactive patch of dACC tissue to help ease those troublesome feelings of social pain. Although the latest studies have only been conducted in experimental mice, they herald the exciting prospect of carefully timed twin bursts of electrical energy, helping us to self-soothe whenever we feel ourselves on the verge of doing something we might regret. At the touch of a button we could avoid making a hasty decision, thanks to a pair of high-frequency electrical fields beaming out across the skull from electrodes positioned at two different locations on the scalp-surface, to temporarily knock out the dACC circuitry only at the spot where the two fields intersect. The stroke of genius with TIS is that the high frequency electrical stimulation does not impact on brain function. But at the point where two fields cross there is interference, which slows the frequency of electrical stimulation down to the level where brain activity *is* affected.

At the moment this technology is still at the proof-of-concept stage. It has only been tested in laboratory animals so far. Getting it to the stage where it will be ready for use in humans will not be straightforward. First, protocols will need to be developed to figure out how far apart the electrodes should be and the best electrical waveforms for changing the activity of the target brain areas, without meddling with the function of non-target brain areas. Inevitably there will be complications and side effects that need to be dealt with. Eventually this kind of technology will be available for boosting all sorts of brain capacities, as well as diminishing undesirable ones.

The question is, if a TIS cap hit the market in 2025, would you buy one? We've already established that a modicum of pride, gluttony, lust, sloth, greed, envy and wrath is adaptive.

The last thing we would want to do is risk eliminating these behaviours in their entirety. Then there are risks associated with criminal intervention – for example, people hacking into people's TIS caps to interfere with their normal mode of function. How would we deal with computer viruses that re-programmed the TIS cap so that, each time we hit the button to activate the electric fields, rather than easing our desire to lash out, it instead stimulated it. This could potentially pose the risk of compelling someone to commit cold-blooded murder, rather than the realtively innocent outburst of verbal aggression that would have taken place under normal circumstances, all because of the malevolent influence of a hacked TIS cap. Such unlikely, but plausible, concerns must be addressed before the technology is made available in the first place, in order for safeguards to be built in.

Any miracle technology promising to help us make better life decisions would have to prove itself capable of helping our brains find the Goldilocks zone with regard to urges that fall under the remit of the deadly sins. Rather than abolishing the impulses completely, temptation would need to be brought down to more manageable levels: not too much, not too little, but just right. It would have to gently nudge us away from the extremes of behaviour where the anti-social behaviours tend to lurk, without depriving us of our quintessential humanity.

Ethical minefield
Once such technological innovations have become a reality, there will be many ethical concerns relating to the potential for misusing such technologies. One of these is, assuming it was proven to be effective in helping people to behave more pro-socially, what happens if such devices were forced on people against their will? What if someone was required to wear a TIS smartcap under circumstances where they would really rather not? On the other hand, if a career criminal in and out of jail their whole life freely chose to spend the rest of their life with a pair of electrodes physically embedded in their scalp as a condition of their release, would that be so bad? If Her Majesty's Parole Board was responsible for managing a

convict's brain activity to maximise their capacity to resist antisocial impulses, rather than leaving them to their own devices, would that be acceptable even *with* the person's consent? Or does this smack of Big Brother? Such draconian measures are, no doubt, a terrifying prospect for many people, yet such solutions to that age-old problem of how to help those who can't help themselves may be just on the horizon.

It is vital that we consider the neuroethics relevant to such interventions sooner rather than later. Less sophisticated brain stimulation kits* are already being made available to consumers for home use. Keen computer gamers all over the planet are freely experimenting with them in an effort to gain the competitive edge over their rivals. Unfortunately free experimentation invariably involves people trying to crank the dial up to 11.† There are many accounts of DIY experimentalists scorching their foreheads with electrical currents so strong that no scientist in their right mind would dream of using them. Once these fledgling technologies have been honed to the point where they start making a real difference when trying to modulate human behaviour, we need to have already created guidelines to advise people on how, when and where they should and shouldn't be used. If we wait until this technology hits the market before we think about the challenges, pitfalls and disasters waiting to happen, it may already be too late.

While we wait
In the meantime, we may be able to use the Science of Sin to help us change our perspective on certain important aspects of human nature. A quote by one of the most influential US journalists of the 1930s, Dorothy Thomas, captures the main takeaway message of this book perfectly: 'Peace is not the absence

---

* Currently these are only able to affect brain areas just beneath the skull and not deeper ones like the dACC.
† A reference to the first ever mockumentary *Spinal Tap* – a heavy metal rock band obsessed with being as loud as possible who thought it was possible to achieve this by redesigning their amps to have dials that go up to 11 instead of the usual 10.

of conflict, but the ability to cope with it.' This is as true of the
space within our skulls as it is of the human interactions that take
place outside of our bodies. Conflict is inevitable and unavoidable,
but how we respond to that conflict *is* under our control.

When people do the things they know they shouldn't, it is
usually caused by emotional suffering. The best example to
support this idea is that the intensity of social pain experienced
by narcissistic people is mirrored in the strength of their dACC
activation, which in turn is proportional to the extent of the
punishment inflicted on whoever caused them to suffer the
feelings of rejection in the first place. Those who struggle with
the consequences of dysfunctional pride are hypersensitive to
rejection, resulting in an amplification of social pain, which they
try to quash with antisocial behaviours. While the evidence to
support a similar chain of cause and effect in the other deadly sins
is admittedly sparse, given that not a single neuroscience study
has ever set out to understand the neural correlates of vice *per se*,
the consistent involvement of the dACC across studies relevant
to so many of them is striking. And reasonable grounds on which
to explain the urge to act in an anti-social way as a response to,
and effort to reduce, the experience of intense social pain.

In support of this interpretation, consider this. The extensive
effort and expense people put into to making themselves
appear more physically attractive – i.e. vanity – may be
motivated by a desire to elicit compliments from others to
eliminate the pain of feeling worthless. The endless pursuit of
more money – i.e. greed – could be viewed as a means by
which to soothe the nagging feelings of social vulnerability
with the reassuring knowledge that the account balance is
going ever upwards. The lack of motivation seen in those who
seem perpetually lazy – i.e. sloth – may be a strategy to protect
themselves from the social pain of experiencing failure. (If you
don't bother trying in the first place, nobody can accuse you
of having failed.) Acts of malicious envy aim to reduce the
pain of feeling socially inferior by bringing the rival crashing
down from their pedestal. The constant pursuit of new sexual
partners can be viewed as a tactic that tries to diminish social
pain with the illusion of emotional intimacy created by

one-night-stands. People are notoriously prone to lash out in anger – i.e. wrath – to gain temporary relief from the social pain that results from feeling socially slighted. And the power of 'comfort foods' in taking the edge off emotional strife makes it plain to see how over-reliance on this approach might lead to the habits of gluttony. All the deadly sins, when viewed through this prism, are antisocial behaviours that are ultimately motivated by a desire to reduce personal suffering.

This perspective is more helpful than the traditional approach of labelling such individuals as sinners destined to be cast down to the blazing pits of hell. A person wanting to reduce their experience of social pain is not unreasonable, even if the method selected to achieve that goal is far from ideal. If the root cause of a person's anti-social behaviour is emotional suffering, then describing their conduct as evil or the work of the devil is only going to heighten their self-loathing, possibly even exacerbating the tendency to give in to whatever temptation gives them temporary relief. But religion didn't get it all wrong.

Inner turmoil is a fact of life. Attempting to eliminate inner turmoil completely is, for most people, utterly misguided. A much more achievable goal is aiming to manage conflict better, both in our private inner world and in the public world outside it. How we choose to respond to our own feelings of inner conflict and how we decide to handle the symptoms of other people's struggles when wrestling with their own, can make a heaven or hell of life on Earth.

Everybody wants to reduce their own emotional suffering; nobody could fault that. Yet the best approaches to reducing our feelings of being confused and conflicted are not always those that our instincts guide us towards. Respite from social pain can be achieved through both prosocial and antisocial means. The trouble is that the prosocial option may not seem realistic to people who have had bad experiences with this path in the past. For those who have been on the receiving end of more than their fair share of antisocial experiences, it can be difficult to imagine how the prosocial path could possibly pay dividends. For those who already feel socially isolated, the prosocial approach may seem utterly futile. Why try to do what's best for the group when, in the past, the group never seemed to care what happened to you – whether you succeed or fail, live or die?

Those who have had the worst experiences of group cooperation are those most likely to be distrustful of the unspoken social contracts of mutual back-scratching or reciprocal helping. Once a person's trust has been betrayed several times over, they are likely to find it very hard to leave themselves vulnerable to that kind of social pain again. The antisocial habits people develop through repeatedly ending up trapped in such vicious cycles are precisely the behaviours that increase the likelihood of being rejected by groups they might potentially come to associate with in the future.

If only the most vulnerable people in society could gain access to some kind of InGroup, then they might also experience the safety and security that arises from feeling valued by fellow members of a certain community. Group membership may help to reduce the feelings of social pain that gave rise to the tendency to choose antisocial behaviours in the first place. At the very least it would enable the physical and psychological benefits of group membership to be gained.

Where in your local community could a person go in search of instant group membership, a place where they might find emotional support regardless of their past transgressions? What group of humans encourages forgiveness, even for those who have a bad reputation? Who might feel positively inclined to reach out to those people who are most in need of support? Which club or collective requires their members to actively engage in charitable activities on a regular basis?

Science may be reasonably well equipped to get to the bottom of why people do the things they know they shouldn't, but it draws a blank when it comes to offering everyday people a sense of community. Religions, on the other hand, have developed fantastic facilities for offering members of the local community a sense of belonging, instant access to emotional support, rituals of weekly interaction and the opportunity to participate in charitable voluntary work. If religion ended up being completely abolished one day, in terms of throwing the baby out with the bathwater, this is what mankind would miss the most. The secular world is a long way from being able to replicate these ancient systems of community building. There's always the weekly pub quiz, sporting match or hobby group for meeting up with likeminded others, but these relatively superficial and tepid options pale in comparison to the religious alternatives in terms of their capacity to ease social pains, remind people of the importance of taking a helicopter view on life and treating other people well.

Before we turn our backs on religion for ever, we must first build properly integrated communities in which people understand that the best way to deal with inner conflict is to reach out to others, rather than give in to the impulse to do things that end up pushing them away. Communities where people feel that they genuinely belong, and in which people experience less of the social pain that causes social discord in the first place. If we want people to find themselves positively inclined to invest their time and energy into doing things that help the whole community, they need to be sold on the scientific evidence that acts of altruism bring huge benefits to the individual. The secular world must find effective methods to incentivise all the behaviours that religion has discovered work as antidotes to the poisonous influence of social pain, but without relying on the myths of heaven and hell. The first step towards building such communities is surely to ensure that members realise that people's antisocial behaviour is a symptom of their struggle to cope with their inner turmoil, rather than a sign of them being hopelessly broken or born bad.

I believe that this project deserves the highest possible priority because, in a post-religious world, if people feel there is nowhere else to turn they will increasingly withdraw into the apparent emotional security of social isolation. In so doing they will likely find the selfish options most appealing at first glance, even though this will usually result in negative social consequences in the long run. Misguided approaches like this will ultimately rob them of the very thing that makes life on Earth worth living: the feeling of being deeply connected to other people. After all, meaningful relationships aren't just nice to have, they are vital for our very wellbeing and survival.

The first step towards putting this all into action is to examine your own impulses more carefully on a daily basis. The next time you find yourself on the verge of doing something you know you shouldn't, contemplate your state of mind. If you're feeling irritable and fractious, then the urge to give in to temptation might be driven by a physiological deficit. When was the last time you ate something? Have you been overdoing the caffeine? Are you properly hydrated? A lack of basic nutrients, or surplus of stimulants, can be perfectly adequate to make the immediate gratification of giving into your base urges preferable to the choice that delivers greatest benefits in the long run. If that can't explain it, then the next most likely explanation for why you are feeling yourself driven towards selfish and antisocial behaviours is an excess of social pain. Rather than listening to the voice in your head justifying to yourself whichever course of action amounts to giving in to temptation, look instead for the root causes. Have you been embarrassed by something you did or said recently? Have you felt let down by someone, been given the cold shoulder or made to feel like a social outcast in the recent past? If so, then your desire to elicit flattery from others, flirt outrageously with a stranger, not bother pulling your weight, take more than your fair share, bring about a rival's downfall, stuff yourself to bursting point with takeaway or lash out in response to minor provocation, may simply be attempts to soothe the suffering of your inner turmoil. The instinct to make ourselves feel better in these seven particular ways have no doubt been around since our ancestors first started walking around on two legs instead of four. But just because they are ancient, doesn't mean they are right. They might bring a fleeting sense of satisfaction, but they damage our relationships, which in turn screws up our health and quality of life. By catching ourselves on the verge of giving in to these urges and choosing alternative courses of action that reduce social pain, while simultaneously bolstering rather than threatening our social ties, we can manage our inner turmoil in a way that helps us to secure all the long term benefits that come from feeling that we truly belong.

Desiderata by Max Ehrmann
(upon which I base my own conduct)

Go placidly amid the noise and haste, and remember what peace there may be in silence.
As far as possible, without surrender, be on good terms with all persons.
Speak your truth quietly and clearly; and listen to others,
even to the dull and ignorant; they too have their story.

Avoid loud and aggressive persons, they are vexations to the spirit.
If you compare yourself with others, you may become vain and bitter,
for always there will be greater and lesser persons than yourself.
Enjoy your achievements as well as your plans.

Keep interested in your own career, however humble;
it is a real possession in the changing fortunes of time.
Exercise caution in your business affairs, for the world is full of trickery.
But let this not blind you to what virtue there is;
many persons strive for high ideals,
and everywhere life is full of heroism.

Be yourself. Especially do not feign affection. Neither be cynical about love;
for in the face of all aridity and disenchantment it is as perennial as the grass.
Take kindly the counsel of the years, gracefully surrendering the things of youth.
Nurture strength of spirit to shield you in sudden misfortune.
But do not distress yourself with dark imaginings.
Many fears are born of fatigue and loneliness.

Beyond a wholesome discipline, be gentle with yourself.
You are a child of the universe no less than the trees and the stars;
you have a right to be here. And whether or not it is clear to you,
no doubt the universe is unfolding as it should.

Therefore be at peace with God, whatever you conceive Him to be.
And whatever your labors and aspirations, in the noisy confusion of life,
keep peace with your soul. With all its sham, drudgery and broken dreams,
it is still a beautiful world. Be cheerful. Strive to be happy.

Online Resources

- Guided Meditation with Eckhart Tolle (12 mins, highly recommended)
  www.youtube.com/watch?v=KsEfKk8trcc

- Guided Meditation for Relaxation and Sleep (7 mins)
  www.youtube.com/watch?v=xydWEfDr-WQ

- Grounding Guided Meditation with Scott Mills (8 mins)
  www.youtube.com/watch?v=c6w0W22zhLI

- Ocean Meditation (9 mins)
  www.youtube.com/watch?v=c2hpGer2qvI

- Mindfulness Meditation to Relieve Anxiety and Stress (9 mins)
  www.youtube.com/watch?v=Fpiw2hH-dlc

- Mindfulness Meditation, Jon-Kabat Zinn style (15 mins)
  www.youtube.com/watch?v=8v45WSuAeYI

- Journey to Inner Peace – Morning Meditation (17 mins)
  www.youtube.com/watch?v=vCzoB1pPPQM

- Chakra Balancing (23 mins)
  www.youtube.com/watch?v=Mq7RDsm9Rkc

- Asking for Nothing (35 mins)
  www.youtube.com/watch?v=NMldMnEfxX8

- Guided Meditation with Louise Hay (53 mins)
  www.youtube.com/watch?v=QpQzuOp7RI0

- Reducing the ego - strategies and tips
  www.taoism.net/theway/ego.htm

Glossary

Amygdala (plural: Amygadalae)
The brain's danger-detecting headquarters resides towards the front of the inward-facing part of the temporal lobes. When danger is detected the amygdala triggers an increase in blood pressure and oxygenation, directing blood towards the brain and muscles. The release of hormones and neuronal activation mobilises extra resources to help deal with the perceived problem. Although it is famed for its involvement in orchestrating negative emotional responses to threats, it is also involved in amplifying positive emotional responses too.

Anterior cingulate cortex (ACC)
The ACC is the front-most (anterior) part of the cingulate cortex on the inward-facing surface of each brain hemisphere, just above the corpus callosum.

Anterior insula (AI)
The anterior insula is the front half of the insular cortex, which lies at the bottom of the brain valley (formally known as sulcus) that separates the temporal lobe from the frontal lobe in both the left and right halves of the brain.

Basal ganglia
These are a group of deep brain nuclei on either side of the thalamus, responsible for initiating several vitally important functions including voluntary movements and decision making. The largest group of structures is known as the corpus striatum, comprising the putamen, caudate nucleus, globus pallidus and nucleus accumbens.

Brain stem
The brain stem, comprising the pons and the medulla, sits just above and is continuous with the spinal cord. It is responsible

for basic physiological processes, such as maintaining appropriate oxygenation, acidity and blood pressure by modulating the activity of the lungs, heart, kidneys and so on.

Cognitive dissonance
Cognitive dissonance describes the mental discomfort we typically feel when holding two or more contradictory beliefs or ideas in mind at the same time.

Corpus callosum
A bundle of about 250 million neurons, running just beneath the cingulate cortex, that connects the left and right brain hemispheres. So much moment-to-moment interaction occurs between the left and right hemispheres of the brain that the popular notion of being 'left-brained' or 'right-brained' is ridiculous. Thanks to the corpus callosum, every single human can confidently claim to be right-brained and left-brained (apart from hemispherectomy or corpus callosotomy patients).

Dorsal anterior cingulate cortex (dACC)
The upper segment of the anterior cingulate cortex, as opposed to the parts of the anterior cingulate cortex directly adjacent to the corpus callosum. The dACC is consistently implicated under circumstances where a person feels social pain.

Dorsal striatum
This is the upper part of the striatum, which consists of the caudate nucleus and the putamen. The heads of the dorsal striatum clamp around the left and right sides of the thalamus, and the tails wind back and round to follow the inner contours of the temporal lobe. This structure performs various computations essential to selecting and executing actions to achieve a specific goal.

Dorsolateral prefrontal cortex (dlPFC)
This is the upper part of the outward-facing surface of the left and right frontal lobes. Discrete patches of this chunk of

prefrontal cortex are often implicated in studies in which participants are required to restrict certain unwanted behaviours.

Functional Magnetic Resonance Imaging (fMRI)
This involves scanning many human brains, each performing the same set of experimental procedures, and looking for brain areas that are consistently activated or deactivated under one set of circumstances compared to another. Statistical techniques are then used to compare relative activity levels throughout the brain that are consistent across many people.

Hippocampus
Deep within the core of the left and right temporal lobes, these dense hubs of neural tissue are fundamentally involved in the creation and retrieval of new memories, as well as in our ability to navigate and to imagine the future.

Hypothalamus
This is the site at which the brain's hormones are manufactured and released into the bloodstream via the pituitary gland. It also sends and receives messages to structures throughout the brain, especially the brain stem.

Magnetic Resonance Imaging (MRI)
MRI is a medical imaging device that can be used to take measurements of brain structure and function. Superconducting electrical coils cooled with liquid helium are rapidly switched on and off to project radiofrequency pulses through thin slices of the brain, which effectively sends all the water molecules (dipoles) spinning at a perpendicular angle to the direction of the magnetic field. In functional MRI, the time it takes for these dipoles to to fall out of sync with each other is affected by the oxygenation levels of the blood in each tiny chunk of the brain, and can be used to infer different levels of brain activity. Measurements from each slice through the brain can be stacked up to get a snapshot of the activity levels throughout the entire brain once every couple of seconds. MRI can also

be used to look at the structure rather than the function of brain areas by taking advantage of the fact that the time spinning dipoles take to realign with the magnetic field is different in the grey matter, the white matter and the fluid-filled spaces. So using the same MRI scanner in different ways you can either measure brain function or brain structure (but not both simultaneously).

Medial orbitofrontal cortex (mOFC)
This is the part of the orbitofrontal cortex – the part of the brain sitting above the eye sockets (orbits) – directly adjacent to the inward-facing (medial) surface of the brain.

Neuron
Long, thin, wire-like brain cells that transfer information from one end to the other via pulses of discrete electrical messages (action potentials). When these reach the far end they trigger the release of chemical messengers (neurotransmitters) that spill into and across the gap (synapse) separating one neuron from the next in line. Each neuron is studded with specialised receptors that the neurotransmitter binds with to change the activity of that neuron.

Neuroplasticity
Changes made in the human brain by doing something regularly, intensively and persistently over a long period of time. Seminal work done by Dr Eleanor Maguire and colleagues at the Functional Imaging Laboratory in London involved scanning the brains of taxi drivers before and after they did 'The Knowledge'. This is an examination requiring them to memorise all the major routes and landmarks within a six-mile radius of central London to earn their black cab licence. On average this incredible feat of memory and navigation takes over two years to complete successfully and causes part of the brain called the hippocampus to become physically larger as a result of the vastly increased number of synapses (connections between neurons) created. Subsequent studies demonstrated that after

retirement the size of the taxi drivers' hippocampi returned to within the normal range. This indicates that the brain changes induced by neuroplasticity only last as long as the behaviour that causes them is maintained; it's a case of 'use it or lose it'.

Neurotransmitter
Electrical impulses ferrying information from one neuron to the next trigger chemical messengers called neurotransmitters to be released into the gap (synapse), enabling the first neuron to exert an effect on the second by making it fire its own electrical impulses to a greater or lesser degree.

Nucleus accumbens
The nucleus accumbens is part of the ventral striatum, a central hub of the reward pathway that receives input from the midbrain's ventral tegmental area and sends outputs to the orbitofrontal cortex. During decision-making it seems to assign a 'predicted value' to each option and updates these values according to whether or not the outcome of a decision turned out as expected.

Orbitofrontal cortex (OFC)
The orbitofrontal cortex describes the part of the left and right frontal lobes that sits just above the eye sockets (orbits).

Prefrontal cortex (PFC)
The prefrontal cortex is the outer surface of the frontal lobes, including both inward- and outward-facing surfaces.

Rostral anterior cingulate cortex (rACC)
The front most segment of the anterior cingulate cortex.

Striatum
The striatum – so called because it looks stripy to the naked eye – consists primarily of the nucleus accumbens (ventral striatum) and the caudate nucleus/putamen (dorsal striatum). The ventral striatum performs computations relevant to

assigning a 'predicted value' to each available option, forming the basis of a decision, while the dorsal striatum is involved in selecting and triggering voluntary movements to enable the decision to be acted upon.

Subgenual anterior cingulate cortex (sgACC)
The subgenual anterior cingulate cortex is the part of the cingulate cortex that resides just beneath the front-most part of the corpus callosum.

Thalamus
The brain's major junction box through which different parts of the outer cortex of the four brain lobes (frontal, temporal, parietal, occipital) are connected to each other. It acquires information from the outside world via the sensory organs (eyes, ears and so on) and shares information with both deeper brain hubs and the rest of the body via the spinal cord.

Theory of Mind (ToM)
Theory of Mind refers to the ability to understand a situation from another's perspective and infer what they are likely to be thinking and feeling.

Ventral striatum
The underside or lower portion of the striatum, which plays a vital role in assigning a 'predicted value' to a certain item, idea or choice. The nucleus accumbens and several other structures reside within this part of the striatum.

Ventral tegmental area
The midbrain is divided into an upper part (tectum) and a lower part (tegmentum). The ventral tegmental area is on the underside of the tegmentum from which all the brain's dopamine-containing neurons project to other parts of the brain, chiefly the nucleus accumbens and the medial orbitofrontal cortex.

Select References

A full reference and bibliography section can be found at my website www.sciofsin.com.

Chapter 1: In the Beginning

Eisenberger, N. I. and Cole, S. W. (2012). Social neuroscience and health: neurophysiological mechanisms linking social ties with physical health. *Nature Neuroscience* 15(5): 669–74.

Hawkley, L. C. and Cacioppo, J. T. (2010). Loneliness matters: a theoretical and empirical review of consequences and mechanisms. *Annals of Behavioral Medicine* 40(2): 218–27.

Heider, F. and Simmel, M. (1944). An experimental study of apparent behavior. *American Journal of Psychology* 57: 243–9.

Holt-Lunstad *et al.* (2010). Social relationships and mortality risk: a meta-analytic review. *PLoS Medicine* 7(7): e1000316.

House, J. S., *et al.* (1988). Social relationships and health. *Science* 241(4865): 540–5.

Miller, G. A., (1956). The Magic Number Seven Plus or Minus Two: Some Limits on our Capacity for Processing Information. *Psychological Review* 101(2): 343–52.

Chapter 2: Pride

Campbell, W. K., *et al.* (2000). Narcissism and comparative self-enhancement strategies. *Journal of Research in Personality* 34: 329–47.

Cascio, C. N., *et al.* (2015). Narcissists' social pain seen only in the brain. *Social Cognitive and Affective Neuroscience* 10(3): 335–41.

Edelstein, R. S., *et al.* (2010). Narcissism predicts heightened cortisol reactivity to a psychosocial stressor in men. *Journal of Research in Personality* 44(5): 565–72.

Eisenberger, N. I., *et al.* (2007). Neural pathways link social support to attenuated neuroendocrine stress responses. *Neuroimage* 35: 1601–12.

Foster, J. D., *et al.* (2003). Individual differences in narcissism: Inflated self-views across the lifespan and around the world. *Journal of Research in Personality* 37(6): 469–86.

Slavich, G. M., *et al.* (2010). Neural sensitivity to social rejection is associated with inflammatory responses to social stress. *Proceedings of the National Academy of Sciences USA* 107: 14817–22.

Wallace, H. M. and Baumeister, R. F. (2002). The performance of
    narcissists rises and falls with perceived opportunities for Glory.
    Journal of Personality and Social Psychology 82(5): 819–34.

Chapter 3: Gluttony

Micanti, F. *et al.* (2016). The relationship between emotional regulation
    and eating behaviour: a multidimensional analysis of obesity
    psychopathology. *Eating and Weight Disorders* 22(1): 105–15.
Nguyen, J. C., *et al.* (2014). Obesity and cognitive decline: role of
    inflammation and vascular changes. *Frontiers in Neuroscience* 8: 375.
Ronan, L., *et al.* (2016). Obesity associated with increased brain age
    from midlife. *Neurobiology of Aging* 47: 63–70.
Thomas, E. L. (2000). Preferential loss of visceral fat following aerobic
    exercise, measured by magnetic resonance imaging. *Lipids* 35(7):
    769–76.

Chapter 4: Lust

Burns, J. M. and Swerdlow, R. H. (2003). Right orbitofrontal tumor
    with pedophilia symptom and constructional apraxia sign. *Archives of
    Neurology* 60(3): 437–40.
Cantor, J. M., *et al.* (2008). Cerebral white matter deficiencies in
    pedophilic men. *Journal of Psychiatric Research* 42(3): 167–83.
Cantor, J. M., *et al.* (2016). Independent component analysis of resting-
    state functional magnetic resonance imaging in pedophiles. *Journal of
    Sexual Medicine* 13(10): 1546–54.
Chivers, M. L., *et al.* (2007). Gender and sexual orientation differences
    in sexual response to sexual activities versus gender of actors in
    sexual films. *Journal of Personality and Social Psychology* 93(6): 1108–21.
Fisher, H. E., *et al.* (2006). Romantic love: a mammalian brain system
    for mate choice. *Philosophical Transactions of the Royal Society of London
    B: Biological Sciences* 361(1476): 2173–86.
Voon, V., *et al.* (2014). Neural correlates of sexual cue reactivity in
    individuals with and without compulsive sexual behaviours. *PLoS
    One* 9(7): e102419.

Chapter 5: Sloth

Baum, A. *et al.* (1986). Unemployment stress: loss of control, reactance
    and learned helplessness. *Social Science Medicine* 22(5): 509–16.
Lee, I.-M., *et al.* (2012). Impact of physical inactivity on major non-
    communicable diseases worldwide: an analysis of burden of disease
    and life expectancy. *Lancet* 380(9838): 219–29.

Levy, R. and Dubois, B. (2006). Apathy and the functional anatomy of the prefrontal cortex-basal ganglia circuits. *Cerebral Cortex* 16(7): 916–28.

Chapter 6: Greed

Bartra, O., *et al.* (2013). The valuation system: a coordinate-based meta-analysis of BOLD fMRI experiments examining neural correlates of subjective value. *Neuroimage* 76: 412–27.

Christov-Moore, L. *et al.* (2016) Increasing generosity by disrupting prefrontal cortex. *Social Neuroscience* 12(2): 174–81.

Gabay, A. S., *et al.* (2014). The Ultimatum Game and the brain: a meta-analysis of neuroimaging studies. *Neuroscience and Biobehavioral Reviews* 47: 549–58.

Piff, P. K., *et al.* (2012). Higher social class predicts increased unethical behavior. *Proceedings of the National Academy of Sciences USA* 109(11): 4086–91.

Singer, T. *et al.* (2006). Empathic neural responses are modulated by the perceived fairness of others. *Nature* 439(7075): 466–9.

Chapter 7: Envy

Takahashi, H. *et al.* (2009). When your gain is my pain and your pain is my gain: neural correlates of envy and schadenfreude. *Science* 323(5916): 937–9.

Xiang, Y., *et al.* (2017). Examining brain structures associated with dispositional envy and the mediation role of emotional intelligence. *Scientific Reports* 7: 39947.

Chapter 8: Wrath

Beyer, F., *et al.* (2014). Emotional reactivity to threat modulates activity in mentalizing network during aggression. *Social Cognitive and Affective Neuroscience* 9(10): 1552–60.

Georgiev, A.V., *et al.* (2013). When violence pays: a cost–benefit analysis of aggressive behavior in animals and humans. *Evolutionary Psychology* 11(3): 678–99.

Chapter 9: Save Our Souls

Bryan, C. J., *et al.* (2016). Harnessing adolescent values to motivate healthier eating. *Proceedings of the National Academy of Sciences USA* 113(39): 10830–5.

Dewall, C. N., *et al.* (2010). Acetaminophen reduces social pain: behavioral and neural evidence. *Psychological Science* 21(7): 931–7.

Hennenlotter, A., *et al.* (2009). The link between facial feedback and neural activity within central circuitries of emotion – new insights from botulinum toxin-induced denervation of frown muscles. *Cerebral Cortex* 19: 537–42.

Rand, D. G., *et al.* (2012). Spontaneous giving and calculated greed. *Nature* 489(7416): 427–30.

Tang, Y. Y., *et al.* (2015). The neuroscience of mindfulness meditation. *Nature Reviews Neuroscience* 16(4): 213–25.

Tromholt, M. (2016). The Facebook Experiment: quitting Facebook leads to higher levels of well-being. *Cyberpsychology, Behavior, and Social Networking* 19(11): 661–6.

Chapter 10: Beyond Temptation

Chester, D. S. and DeWall, C. N. (2016). Sound the Alarm: The Effect of Narcissism on Retaliatory Aggression Is Moderated by dACC Reactivity to Rejection. *Journal of Personality* 84(3): 361–8.

Mansouri, F. A., *et al.* (2017). Monitoring Demands for Executive Control: Shared Functions between Human and Nonhuman Primates. *Trends in Neurosciences* 40(1): 15–27.

Acknowledgements

This book is dedicated to Alice Girle.

The first and biggest thanks must go to my parents, Phil and Virginia Lewis, for instilling in me an intrinsic sense of self-worth that nurtured my self-esteem without it spilling over into narcissism. Thanks a million for the unconditional love and support you've always provided, no matter how challenging I might have been along the way. The knowledge that, in your eyes at least, I am worthy of love has always helped shepherd me through my most formidable trials and tribulations to date (up to and including the writing of this book).

I'm also greatly indebted to Dave Amor and Melanie Craig who kindly gave me invaluable feedback on early proofs. A huge thank you, of course, to my agents Jo Wander and Sara Cameron for convincing me to convert this idea from a treatment for a television series into a book proposal, and to Jim Martin at Bloomsbury Sigma for commissioning it. Editor Anna MacDiarmid and copyeditor Catherine Best suggested numerous brilliant improvements throughout the manuscript so many thanks must go to them for sharing their expertise to help tame this beast.

I'd like to thank Ollie Tait at Lambent Productions for keeping me so busy with filming for the *Secrets of the Brain 2* that this book took two years to complete, rather than just one. I must thank my best friend George Wolstencroft (the guy I swapped punches with in our very own TAP test!) for providing me with an oasis of calm up in the highlands, where I could rest, recuperate and perform many days of hard labour (!), before the final push in getting this manuscript fit for the publisher's eyes.

Next up are all those who have offered me a very modern form of friendship. The employees of three coffee shops, two libraries and one hotel lobby scattered along the length of the Thames from Blackfriars Bridge to Tower Bridge and right the way up to my old PhD stomping ground in Bloomsbury. In particular my daily interactions with Rosie, Ellie and the fellas at Coffee Works; Maeve, Allie, Keeren, TJ and Lily at Citizen M on Bankside; the lovely staff whose names I never learned at Fuckoffee (surely the most photographed coffee shop in London?!), Wellcome Collection library and café, the British Film Institute library and the Bermondsey Square Hotel; they all made me feel a small but wholly accepted part of their respective InGroups. These interactions were invaluable to me because, having joined the growing ranks of digital nomads – professionals who work wherever they can find good wifi and a never-ending supply of coffee – could easily have felt socially isolated otherwise.

I owe a huge debt of gratitude to Adrian Webster, with whom I wrote my first book, *Sort Your Brain Out*. Every time I sent him a chapter he'd delete two-thirds of it and completely re-write whatever was left. It always returned to me utterly transformed. It was painful to see my work chopped, diced and re-blended; I didn't always respond well to the wielding of his cleaver. But he patiently put up with my tantrums and quietly wove spells over my first drafts, and the result of his magic touch was a best-seller. People often comment on how effortless it was to read, how quickly they managed to zip through it. I tried my very best to work a similar kind of magic with this, my first solo book effort. I hope I've had some measure of success.

Finally to all the hundreds of scientists, psychologists, psychiatrists, philosophers and religious thinkers whose experiments, ideas and discoveries this tome is based on – I am much obliged. The sheer volume of work that hits the academic journals every single year never ceases to amaze me. Without the brilliant minds who construct hypotheses about how brains work, develop ingenious studies to test them, painstakingly gather and analyse oceans of data, then endure the trials, tribulations and uncertainties of the peer review process, this book would have been pure guesswork. Some may feel their work has been misrepresented. I can only offer my apologies and assurances that this was not my intention.

I've tried my very best to read up on as much of the relevant literature as possible, but I couldn't read it all. I tried to ensure my descriptions were accurate, but with so much material to wade through I may well have got the wrong end of the stick from time to time. I see this as the synthesis of many people's endeavours, but the mistakes are all mine.

If you have any suggestions on how to improve the scientific rigour please do get in touch at www.sciofsin.com. This book is just the beginning of what I hope to be a very long conversation, so please do let me know what you think.

All that remains to be acknowledged is you, the reader – thanks for your time.

Index